FLORENCE NIGHTINGALE
AND HER ERA

GARLAND REFERENCE LIBRARY
OF SOCIAL SCIENCE
(VOL. 629)

FLORENCE NIGHTINGALE AND HER ERA
A Collection of New Scholarship

edited by
Vern Bullough
Bonnie Bullough
Marietta P. Stanton

GARLAND PUBLISHING, INC. • NEW YORK & LONDON
1990

Library of Congress Cataloging-in-Publication Data

Nightingale and her era: a collection of new scholarship / [edited
by] Vern Bullough, Bonnie Bullough, Marietta P. Stanton.
 p. cm. — (Garland reference library of social science; vol.
629)
 Papers from a conference held at the University of Buffalo.
 Includes bibliographical references.
 ISBN 0–8240–6998–6 (alk. paper)
 1. Nightingale, Florence, 1820–1910—Congresses. 2. Nurses—
England—Biography—Congresses. 3. Nursing—United States—
History—Congresses. I. Bullough, Vern L. II. Bullough, Bonnie.
III. Stanton, Marietta P. IV. Series: Garland reference library of
social science; v. 629.
RT37.N5N54 1990
610.73'092—dc20   89–25949
[B]   CIP

Printed on acid-free, 250-year-life paper
Manufactured in the United States of America

TABLE OF CONTENTS

SECTION I

**NEW SCHOLARSHIP ABOUT
FLORENCE NIGHTINGALE**

SECTION II

AMERCIAN NURSING AT THE
TURN OF THE CENTURY

SECTION III

NINETEENTH CENTURY NORMS: THE STATUS AND EDUCATION OF WOMEN AND NURSES

SECTION IV

NIGHTINGALISM AND REFORM IN PSYCHIATRIC CARE

viii

ACKNOWLEDGEMENTS

The Editors wish to acknowledge Patricia Brock-Eisenstein for all her clerical and technical support in preparing this manuscript for publication. We also wish to acknowledge Joan Bevill, Mary Boldt, Patricia Reese and Marguerite Hayes for all their hard work in implementing the conference that produced these works.

CONTRIBUTORS

Monica E. Baly, Ph.D.
Nurse Midwife
Fellow, Royal College of Nursing
Bath, England

Evelyn R. Benson, M.P.H, R.N.
Academic Advisor
Department of Nursing
LaSalle University
Philadelphia, PA

Marian J. Brook, M.S., R.N.
Doctoral Student, School of Nursing
State University of New York at
Buffalo
Buffalo, NY

Janet L. Bryant, M.S., M.A., R.N.
Doctoral Candidate in Women's History
State University of New York at
Binghamton
Commissioner of Health
Tioga County Health Department
Owego, NY

Vern Bullough, Ph.D., R.N., FAAN
Dean
SUNY Distinguished Professor
State University College at
Buffalo
Buffalo, NY

Bonnie Bullough, R.N., Ph.D.
Dean
School of Nursing
State University of New York at
Buffalo
Buffalo, NY

Kathleen Byrne Colling, Ph.D., R.N.
Associate Professor of Nursing
State University of New York at
Binghamton
Binghamton, NY

Olga Maranjian Church, Ph.D., FAAN
Professor and Chair
Graduate Nursing Program
University of Connecticut
Storrs, CT

Janice Cooke Feigenbaum, Ph.D., RN
Associate Professor of Nursing
D'Youville College
Buffalo, NY

Ellen Giarelli, Ed.D., R.N.
Independent Scholar
Lawrenceville, NJ

Sandra Lewenson, Ed.D., R.N.
Assistant Clinical Professor
Health Science Center
State University of New York at
Brooklyn
Brooklyn, NY

Lois Monteiro, Ph.D., R.N.
Division of Biology and Medicine
Brown University
Providence, RI

Jean Richardson, M.A., B.A.
Ph.D. Candidate in History
State University of New York at
Buffalo
Buffalo, NY

Natalie N. Riegler, M.A., M.P.H.,
R.N.
Doctoral Student in History and
Philosophy
Ontario Institute for Studies in
Education
Toronto, Canada

Joan Sayre, Ph.D., R.N.
Assistant Professor of Nursing
Hunter-Bellevue School
of Nursing
Hunter College, CUNY
New York, NY

Mary P. Tarbox, Ed.D., R.N.
Chairperson and Associate Professor
Department of Nursing
Mount Mercy College
Cedar Rapids, IA

Roberta Tierney, J.D., M.S.N., R.N.
Associate Professor of Nursing
Indiana University - Purdue
University at Fort Wayne
Fort Wayne, IN

Shirley Veith, Ph.D., M.A., R.N.
Associate Professor of Nursing
Kansas University Medical Center
Kansas City, KS

Martha Vicinus, Ph.D.
Professor
Department of English Language and
Literature
University of Michigan
Ann Arbor, Michigan

Judith Young, M.Sc.N., B.Sc.N.
Tutor
Faculty of Nursing
University of Toronto
Toronto, Canada

JoAnn G. Widerquist, M.A., R.N.
Department Chair/Associate
Professor of Nursing
Saint Mary's College
Notre Dame, IN

INTRODUCTION

This book is designed to explore the current state of research into the life of Florence Nightingale, the role of women, and the development of nursing in the period between 1850 and 1910, the last sixty years of Nightingale's life. It grew out of a multidisciplinary conference at the University of Buffalo designed to focus on current scholarship in this period. Though the planners of the conference knew that there was much ongoing research into this period, much of it by nurses themselves, the quality, caliber, and volume of information presented at the conference were so outstanding that all the participants were asked to submit their papers for publication. Not all did, since some had made commitments for publication elsewhere, but this collection represents most of the papers presented.

Presenters at the conference who looked at Nightingale presented a multidimensional view of her life and her times. She was not a sweet saintly woman but a driving woman who liked men but also liked her independence. She had to conform to the rules of society laid down for proper ladies and although intellectually she rebelled against them, practically she used them to get what she wanted.

Contrary to popular opinion, the establishment of modern nursing was not the main effort in her post Crimean life, but regardless of what she did, her image dominated nursing. She was the heroine after whom several generations of women patterned themselves although the image they had was of the "lady with the lamp" rather than the real Nightingale who was not only a self-sacrificing heroine, but a manipulative, often erratic, and dedicated woman who spent a great deal of her last sixty years in bed from where she could control the people in her life.

Nightingale had a tremendous impact on the health care providers of her time, and this impact persists to this day in nursing. The standards, ideals of behavior and performance she set for nurses continues to persist even though the conditions under which they were established have long since changed. Nightingale did not do this alone but through a network of friends and acquaintances, many of them women, in England and in America and elsewhere. Her correspondence is voluminous. Though the "Nightingale" system of nursing was established throughout the English speaking world and in many other parts of the world, it is not exactly what Nightingale had in mind, and in fact much of the success of modern nursing comes from the willingness of some of her successors to modify and change what she did without losing sight of her main objective which was better patient care.

In sum, Nightingale was a woman of her times, but she was a visionary who wanted the lot and status of women to change, and who wanted better care and treatment of patients. What emerges from these papers is a sense of accomplishment for nursing. This is how we began, and these are the barriers which existed (and many of them continue to exist), and though we have come a long way, we are no where near the end of the trail to where we want to be. It is Nightingale's vision, in a sense, reinterpreted to meet present needs, which can still drive us on.

SECTION I

NEW SCHOLARSHIP ABOUT FLORENCE
NIGHTINGALE

FLORENCE NIGHTINGALE AND THE ESTABLISHMENT OF THE FIRST SCHOOL AT ST. THOMAS'S - MYTH V REALITY

by

Monica E. Baly

Let Nightingale be and all was light! The popular myth is that before 1860 all was Stygian gloom as the Gamps plied their drunken way, and after 1860 all was sobriety, respectability and light. History is not like that. Reformers not only overstate their case, they often overstate the results.

Changes in the status of nursing in England ran *pari passu* with changes in medicine. The growth of teaching hospitals and a more scientific approach to medicine led to a need for better nurses, especially head nurses. Professor Abel-Smith has pointed out that by staying on one ward sisters learned what there was to be learned and 'were even prepared to instruct the housemen.' In history it is always earlier than you think! By 1845 the matron of the Middlesex had firm rules for recruitment. Nurses had to be able to read and write and they were subject to strict discipline and received instruction. As early as 1836 the Charity Commission was commenting on the improved standard of nursing in London.[1]

However, apart from the medical demand there was another reason for change after the third decade

3

4   *Florence Nightingale and the Establishment
of the First School at St. Thomas's -
Myth V Reality*

and that was the religious revival. First, after a change
in the law in 1828, the dissenters became more active
and people like Elizabeth Fry went off to
Kaiserswerth--that Mecca of all Protestant reformers-
-then returning to start a nursing institution in
London and sending her carefully chosen recruits for
training at Guy's Hospital.[2] Second, there was what
was known in England as the *Oxford Movement*--an
attempt to get back to pre-Reformation values--and
this led to a burgeoning of Anglican communities
interested in 'good works'. A number of sisterhoods
were established who devoted themselves to the
nursing of the poor sick. One example was a group of
sisters (run by Lydia Sellon and the Bishop of Exeter)
who did sterling work in nursing cholera patients in
Plymouth. Another interesting group was the Order of
St. John founded by the Bishop of London and
Nightingale's friend, Sir William Bowman, whose later
superintendent was Mary Jones, Nightingale's 'dearest
friend' who taught her much about nursing. The order
of St. John was divided into three divisions:
probationers who did a two year training in hospitals
and were not paid, nurses who were paid and sisters
who instructed. St. John's and similar institutions like
All Saints provided nurses to hospitals for a fixed sum
where no doubt they had an improving influence. By
1864 there were no less than 26 different sisterhoods
supplying nurses. The problem for hospitals was that
these orders created an empire within an empire and
there was often a conflict of loyalty and confusion
about accountability.[3]

It is important to mention this because when
the Nightingale Fund was collected in 1856 by a
grateful nation it was thought that Nightingale would
establish a Religious order--like Sellon--and the non-
conformists were not giving their money to what
seemed like a Romish venture. On the other hand,
high church people were very suspicious about
Nightingale's loyalty to the Church of England--was
she not a Unitarian? It caused a headache to the
organizers and much controversy, and apart from her

Florence Nightingale and the Establishment **5**
of the First School at St. Thomas's - Myth
V Reality

own eventual inclinations, establishing an 'order' with
the money from the fund was not an option open to
Nightingale.[4]

The received wisdom is that Nightingale could
only find 38 nurses to take to Scutari. However, if we
examine the records and the time scale carefully we
can see that she and the Herberts did not try very
hard--it was all done in a week. The problem was not
the *lack* of nurses but the insistence that they should
be accountable to Miss Nightingale and not their own
chaplains. However, because of Sidney Herbert's High
church learnings the Sellonites sent 8 sisters, and
Cardinal Manning, who knew Nightingale,
surprisingly allowed nuns from Bermondsey and
Norwood to join the party. Out of the 38 nurses, 24
were nuns or Anglican sisters. In the end, the problem
was not too few nurses but too many. Some 229 are
recorded, and, of course, there are others who are
unrecorded.[5] Nurses came out under various private
sponsors and were from all denominations. The result
was sectarian strife and confusion.

At this stage, Nightingale did not know who
made the best nurses, what they should do, or how
they should be trained. One thing she did know was
that she had had more than enough of 'do gooding'
ladies or proselytising religious sisters. It is no wonder
that when the Provisional Council of the Nightingale
Fund wrote to her and asked for her plan for the use
of the Fund she wrote back tersely 'I have no plan'
adding acidly, if she had asked for the Fund it might
have been reasonable to make such a request, but she
did not ask for such a Fund and went on to imply that
she really did not want it. Almost fanatical about the
high mortality rate in the army and the living
conditions of soldiers, the last thing she wanted to
bother about was starting a nursing school or a Fund.
When she did return in 1856, Nightingale had more
pressing matters; the reform of the army medical
services--and if necessary the army itself, the redesign
of hospitals, the collection of medical statistics, the
reform of barrack accommodation, and of course, the

6   *Florence Nightingale and the Establishment
of the First School at St. Thomas's -
Myth V Reality*

great sanatarian movement. Nightingale's mission was
to prevent ill health and unnecessary suffering.
Hospitals and nursing were low on the list. 'Hospitals'
she declared, time and again 'were an intermediate
stage of civilization'--they were dangerous places and
except for surgery the sufferer was better off at
home.[6]

The Nightingale Fund was quietly forgotten. In
the summer of 1857 as she toiled over her 800 pages of
statistics she had her famous collapse. There was the
usual Victorian diagnosis of a 'weak heart' (what could
women expect if they tried to do men's work?). With
typical melodrama she was said to be 'nigh to death.'
When she recovered--or partly recovered--she was of
course, too frail to be bullied about the Fund. When
the chairman of the Provisional Council, Sidney
Herbert, wrote to her saying that something must be
done about the Fund, she tried to pass the
responsibility on to the Council.[7] It could not have
escaped his notice that she was busy with other ploys
and was mixed up in a Byzantine intrigue about the
rebuilding of St. Thomas's hospital.

Contrary to Sir Edwin Cook, her biographer,
Nightingale had no particular interest in St. Thomas's--
-it was then in a perilous state. But the opportunist
Resident Medical Officer, Richard Whitfield,
approached her as a valuable ally to support his
faction at St. Thomas's which favored rebuilding in
the suburbs. Nightingale responded with enthusiasm
and wrote articles for the *Builder* using figures that
Whitfield had purloined.[8] Most of the doctors, on the
other hand, wanted to stay in London and there
followed a Machiavellian intrigue with both sides
bombarding one another with statistics in the press.
During the course of this correspondence there is a
letter from Whitfield that suggests that the governors
might be persuaded to accept a school of nursing in
her name. During the previous year the Fund had
made approaches to various hospitals but had had little
response.[9]

Florence Nightingale and the Establishment
of the First School at St. Thomas's - Myth
V Reality   7

In retrospect, it looks as if Nightingale clutched at a straw. There is correspondence to show that she envisaged the school of nursing developing on similar lines to medical schools 'with the ultimate elevation of that class to a profession'. We have no copy of Nightingale's plan to Mr. Whitfield but we know he turned it down.

> The class of women who now supply hospitals with sisters could not undertake a hundreth part of what you wish to impress on them as essential . . . it would be impossible to find women capable of undertaking the competitive examination you have drawn out.[10]

St. Thomas's countered with their own plan. They would accept 15 probationers as assistant nurses but instead of the separate superintendent proposed by Nightingale (who had been corresponding with Dr. Elisabeth Blackwell about this), St. Thomas's insisted that their matron, Mrs. Wardroper, must be the head of the training school with the power of hiring and firing.

Nightingale put this proposition to her Council saying "at least Mrs. Wardroper was a 'tired' matron" and suggesting it could be a humble way of starting.[11] Needless to say, the Council was not happy about the powers to be given to the matron. Sir John McNeill, for example, urged her to wait and find a superintendent of her own choosing. There are a number of letters pinpointing some of the problems that were all too soon to become apparent, including that of the contract St. Thomas's[12] was proposing, but Nightingale had the last word.

Nightingale did *not* go to St. Thomas's because it was a good hospital, but because she thought she could influence the design of a new hospital and she needed to do something about the Fund to satisfy the critics.

The negotiations were carried out by Sidney Herbert (then Secretary of State for War) already mortally ill and the secretary to the Fund, Nightingale's young poet cousin, Arthur Clough who

8   *Florence Nightingale and the Establishment
of the First School at St. Thomas's -
Myth V Reality*

was himself to die the next year. They were no match
for the treasurer of St. Thomas's described as "a deep
cunning fox." St. Thomas's saw them coming!

It was agreed that 15 probationers would work
on the wards under the instruction of the present
sisters. The Fund would pay board and lodging for the
probationers, a salary to Wardroper, a fee to Whitfield
and an allowance to the sisters who gave instruction.
No one asked whether the sisters were capable of
being teachers. The contract the probationers had to
sign gave them an allowance of tea and sugar and
uniform and bound them "to enter into service as
hospital nurses in such situations as may be offered
them for a further four years when they had finished
their year's training." It was a contract for a servant.
Nightingale protested but to no avail. She then drew
up her famous Character Sheet with its 14 heads and
then retired to nurse her grief over the deaths of Lord
Herbert and Arthur Clough, and to reform the sanitary
services of India.

Again, contrary to myth, the first ten years of
the so called school were pretty disastrous. Wardroper
selected working class girls as probationers and they
came and went with amazing rapidity. In fact, in spite
of the Fund's high powered publicity, there was no
rush of candidates, perhaps because the contract was
such a disincentive. Although record keeping was not
Wardroper's forte this contract enables the historian to
trace what happened to the Nightingale nurses. The
analysis shows that comparatively few of the
probationers were nursing at the end of the four years.
The *Lancet* wrote testily,

'one cannot help asking what is done with the
Nightingale Fund . . . we must confess to have
never come across a specimen of a Nightingale
nurse except on the wards of St. Thomas's.'[13]

During the first ten years, 196 nurses were
entered on the register but less than 60 were still
nursing, 64 had been dismissed, 4 had died in their
training and, with the exception of Agnes Jones, few
had made any mark on nursing. The fact that so many

Florence Nightingale and the Establishment   9
of the First School at St. Thomas's - Myth
V Reality

were dismissed for glaring defects like phthisis, syphilis, drug addiction, and insobriety suggests that either Wardroper's judgment was at fault, that the references and medical certificates were dishonest, or there was no choice of applicants. The records do not show how many applications there were or whether any were rejected.[14]

Nevertheless, the Fund Council continued to claim that the experiment was a success. The Council was prestigious and its publicity good. Members wrote letters to *The Times* and authoritative articles on 'reformed nursing' in magazines and journals, but by 1870 most London teaching hospitals had a training school, many of them with a less restricting contract. The changes in medicine demanded a different type of nurse. When a few better educated recruits were attracted by the publicity to the Nightingale School, they were critical of what they found, including having to stand to attention to Wardroper and to the lack of instruction. In 1867 Emma Rappe from Sweden wrote,

> We did not learn this and that at St. Thomas's and there was not held a single lecture in anatomy or physiology while I was there. I would not recommend anyone to go to St. Thomas's.

Another educated woman, Elizabeth Torrance, wrote to Nightingale that entries in the Red Register--the character sheet--'were as capricious as if a cat had made them.'[16] A comment with which this historian would agree.

For a variety of reasons, after 1867 Nightingale had more time to give to the school. Her health was also better. Moreover, she was furious because the governors of St. Thomas's had decided to rebuild, not in the healthy suburbs but on the old site on the banks of the dirty Thames which she declared to be "the worst site in London". The whole point of going to St. Thomas's had gone. When she, and her Council, now headed by her brother-in-law Sir Harry Verney, had to negotiate the building of a Nurses'

Home on this undesirable site, the correspondence now becomes slightly acrimonious and the relationships strained. There was even talk of taking the school elsewhere.

One problem was numbers. Out of income the Fund could only afford to support 10 probationers, but the hospital was on to a good thing and pressed for a contract to increase the numbers. Nightingale opposed this. Now a little late, she realized "Our school is not a training school, it is taking on half the hospital's work." "Capable probationers are actually doing the sister's work" and, "the work is so severe that the probationer's health is broken." But the Fund Council was in a dilemma. It was using public money but there was no hope that any other hospital would not drive an equally hard bargain and where else but a hospital could you train nurses? The only hope seemed to be to try and improve the arrangements with St. Thomas's. Miss Nightingale had now come round to the view that they should aim for a *better* class of recruits in order to supply *"training sisters"*. A view not popular with Mrs. Wardroper who had her own favorite sisters. "We shall eventually come to paying for training," Nightingale wrote, hoping to make the school supernummerary.

Thus, was born the idea of "special probationers" who unfortunately have gone down in history as "paying probationers" or "lady probationers," although in fact they did not all pay and some, alas, were not ladies. Specials were selected with the idea of grooming them for superintendents. Nightingale herself was ambivalent about "specials" and insisted that "the lady must be educated with her cook." 'My principle' she wrote

is to give the best training we could to any woman. Unquestionably the educated will be more likely to rise to the post of superintendent, but not because they are ladies, but because they are educated.[17]

The idea of 'grooming' was fine but it was never put into practice. Wardroper did not like

Florence Nightingale and the Establishment   **11**
of the First School at St. Thomas's - Myth
V Reality

'specials' and did all she could to obstruct a special training program. She also made certain that the specials labored as hard on the wards as anyone else. Nightingale was to bewail time and again to the secretary of the Fund, her cousin, Henry Bonham-Carter, an almost daily confidant,

> I have said this until you are tired of hearing me, we do not offer any special training to those we hold out hope of superintendence.[18]

and in 1873,

> If we had experienced sisters, if we had a matron with any system, if we had a head to the Home most certainly with 33-35 probationers at least two hours could be spared for each probationer for classes.[19]

But St. Thomas's had none of these things. The fact that St. Thomas's, along with other London hospitals, turned out a few leaders is not, as historians like Nutting and Dock[20] would have, because "they were trained to train," but because a few were educated intrepid Victorian women anxious to carve out a niche for themselves in a world where there were few opportunities for women.

The crisis came in 1871 with the opening of the new hospital. Thanks to the tales to Nightingale by the new "specials" it was realized that Whitfield was not giving the lectures for which he was paid, that Wardroper did not know one probationer from another, that the Fund's accounts were being muddled with those at the hospital, and that Wardroper was using some of the money designated for the probationers for the ordinary house-keeping. Now, it was discovered that Whitfield, to add to his sins of ommission, had added a heinious crime of commission. To quote Nightingale in a long letter written in 1872

> he had been in habits of intoxication for years. For years he has been in the habit of making his rounds at night . . . oftener tipsy than sober. At the same time his flirtations with Sister Butler were a current joke as she was absolutely unfit to be a sister and was only

12 *Florence Nightingale and the Establishment
of the First School at St. Thomas's -
Myth V Reality*

kept on by Mr. Whitfield. Mr. W has done
nothing for the probationers . . . except to
exploit his position to the verge (and beyond)
of impropriety.[21]

Meantime Wardroper's close relationship with
Whitfield was suspect. Even the cautious Henry
Bonham Carter, who was a lawyer, wrote "I do not
think that Mrs. Wardroper is able to form a sound
judgement."[22] And Nightingale, less cautious, and
always given to drama, feared for Wardroper's sanity
and said that she was acting "like an insane king by
semi divine right."[23] One thing that strikes the
researcher reading these piles of letters is to wonder
whether the writers had any fear of the laws of libel
since every possible scandal is implied.

The Nightingale Council--or rather the inner
circle--agonized over the situation. They took legal
advice. Should they spend capital and start again?
Could they found an independent school? In the end
they could see no alternative and they settled for a
compromise and this is important because the way in
which it worked out became our nursing legacy. What
we call the Nightingale system was a hotch potch of
what the Fund could wring out of St. Thomas's--
which was not much. St. Thomas's was interested in
keeping down its costs.

First, there was an attempt to bring in a
Superintendent of probationers and wrest the control
from Wardroper. Elizabeth Torrance was suggested but
this was firmly resisted by Wardroper and the medical
staff. Torrance, nonetheless was appointed but she had
to stay in the Nurses' Home and became the Home
Sister where she conducted classes in elementary
nursing to exhausted probationers. She also gave Bible
classes. For years to come Nurses' Homes were
presided over by a Home Sister who supervised morals
rather than education, it was not until 1913 that St.
Thomas's had a separate Sister Tutor. Theory and
practice were divorced and were to remain so for
many years to come.[24]

Florence Nightingale and the Establishment 13
of the First School at St. Thomas's - Myth
V Reality

Second, Henry Bonham Carter, still a young man, bearded Whitfield and demanded his resignation. After some bizarre scenes and threats, he managed to get it. He was replaced by John Croft who took his duties seriously and has left posterity with his printed lectures which are a mixture of lectures for medical students and elementary nursing.[25] The medical model had begun. Nightingale, perhaps alone saw the danger; she dreaded nurses becoming what she called "medical women". She was an ardent sanitarian while many physicians were not. She feared that medical lectures--especially new pathology--would deflect nurses from their true function which was taking thought for the patient, raising the sanitary standard, and, of course, the moral tone of the hospital. In this Nightingale--as in other things about nursing, was nothing if not inconsistent. On the other hand she complained that lectures will turn nurses into assistant doctors, while on the other we find her fearing that other hospitals are giving more advanced lectures and the "clever probationers will go elsewhere." But the tide was against Nightingale. Hospitals were attracting the new middle classes who appreciated the new smart and, preferably young and pretty, probationers. Although the old guard physicians were still antipathetic to the new style nurse, young and ambitious doctors saw nurses as their assistants to be trusted with new treatments, measuring, testing and observing, thus leaving doctors free for higher things.

Third, the probationers were to visit Nightingale at her home, and from her notes, their diaries and their letters we have some idea of what they were doing--mainly it seems, non-nursing tasks. Interestingly enough, Nightingale often disagreed with Wardroper's assessment, and it is now that the Red Register becomes covered with Nightingale's pungent remarks. The points stressed on the character sheet were to remain on the nurse's assessment form for the next half century or so.

Fourth, Nightingale started seeing Wardroper regularly, but without much effect. Nightingale often

14 *Florence Nightingale and the Establishment
of the First School at St. Thomas's -
Myth V Reality*

found her excitable and incoherent. However, for
Wardroper it must have been an impossible situation
since her first duty was to the Governors, who one
suspects regarded the school as an irrelevance.

Fifth, Nightingale began her annual addresses
to the probationers to be read by a member of the
Fund Council which grew more and more sentimental
as the years went by. The pen that was once dipped in
gall was now dipped in sugar. Contrary to the usual
story, Nightingale did not remain particularly attached
to St. Thomas's. After 1888 when her beloved
Angelique Pringle joined the Church of Rome and left
after a year as matron, she had little to do with
subsequent matrons. Control was wrested from the
Fund and she was less and less consulted. She wrote
that the probationers were louder and nastier and were
often sarcastic about appointments.

Now the Fund started to diversify and tried to
influence nursing elsewhere. After much diplomacy
and counter diplomacy in 1872 the Fund sent a team
of nurses to Edinburgh Royal Infirmary under a well
educated Quaker lady, Elisabeth Barclay. All
apparently seemed to be going well. Barclay wrote
excellent letters giving a blow by blow account at her
attempts at reform, but then after a series of enigmatic
letters and telegrams (now in the British library), it
eventually dawns on the reader that Barclay was
addicted to both opium and alcohol! Protesting
violently she was eventually removed and replaced by
her deputy, Angelique Pringle, Nightingale's "pearl of
great price" whom Barclay had done her best to
slander. The interesting thing about this episode is
that, like the row about Whitfield's drunkeness or
Wardroper's mental state, every biographer has
brushed it under the carpet. Though she had little
training Pringle was probably the best of the
Nightingales; she did establish a school of nursing at
Edinburgh which was more modern in its approach
and, unlike some of her colleagues, she herself was
hightly regarded by the doctors and governors.[24] Her
deputy at Edinburgh, Rachel Williams, also had a

Florence Nightingale and the Establishment **15**
of the First School at St. Thomas's - Myth
V Reality

stormy career. She was encouraged by Nightingale to
go to St. Mary's in London where she failed to
establish a training school. After a series of clashes
with the administration, and in spite of Bonham
Carter's best legal efforts, Williams was forced to
leave. Even Nightingale who called her "the goddess"
admitted she had a tongue like a knife and could upset
every man in the place.[25] Another special, Lucy Kidd
who was sent to Liverpool, with a glowing report from
Wardroper, to replace the saintly Agnes Jones who had
died, was quickly dismissed by the committee for
insobriety! The specials were not always successful or
suitable.[26]

Overseas it was much the same story. In 1866
a distant cousin of Nightingale, Lucy Osburn, a devout
high church-woman was sent by the Fund with a team
of five nurses to Sydney in Australia to start a school
of nursing. Like her colleagues she had to carve out an
empire; there were the usual clashes with the
authorities including disputes about her title and the
Australians fear that she was "Romish". For her part
she declared that the nurses she had brought with her
were useless. Several were dismissed. In 1868, there
was an assassination attempt on the Duke of
Edinburgh, Queen Victoria's son, and he was nursed
in the Sydney hospital--for which the Queen sent her
thanks. Osburn unwisely sent a gossipy letter to a
relative at home about the affair and it was repeated
in the London Clubs. Nightingale was furious and
disowned Osburn. Her name was erased from the list
of Nightingale nurses. To be fair to Osburn, other
Nightingale relatives who lived in Australia thought
well of her and she remained superintendent for 25
years and remains highly regarded in Australian
nursing history. Cook dismisses her in about two
sentences.[28]

Then in 1874 the committee of management in
Montreal approached Maria Machin who was then the
Home Sister at St. Thomas's. Nightingale called her
"the most spiritual" of the Nightingale's. Machin had
been brought up in Canada and evidently wanted to

16 *Florence Nightingale and the Establishment
of the First School at St. Thomas's -
Myth V Reality*

return. The fact that she became engaged to a
Canadian doctor soon after her arrival may be a clue
to this desire. Although she also wanted to get away
from Wardroper. At the same time Nightingale was
approached about the design for a new hospital in
Montreal where upon she turned to her cousin,
Captain Douglas Galton, to give advice. Once again
Nightingale in her desire to have a hand in designing
a hospital got led astray. Machin and four nurses went
out to Montreal with the idea of setting up a training
school.

It was the same old story. The nurses were not
suitable and not able to cope. After a terrible winter
one died of typhoid, one married and another rebelled.
Machin's fiance died of diptheria. More nurses were
sent out from England but they too caught typhoid,
perhaps because the hospital was built over a cesspool!
But the new hospital failed to materialize. Now, the
committee complained that the nurses were raising the
costs for the hospital. The result was a dispute
between the doctors and the administration with the
doctors taking up cudgels on behalf of the nurses. In
spite of the oil poured on this fire of acrimony from
a distance by Henry Bonham Carter, Machin and her
nurses were eventually forced to return to England.[29]

Although, Machin had grounds for complaint,
the faults were not all on one side. Her turnover of
staff was high and she did not attract loyalty. When
she returned to England she became matron at St.
Bartholomew's but her stay was short and marked with
dispute. Here she quarrelled with her deputy who
subsequently became one of the most successful of the
Nightingales starting a training school in a Poor Law
hospital. Machin eventually went out to Egypt with
the British expeditionary force. She married in Egypt
and settled in South Africa. There, "traitor" to the
tenets of the Nightingale Fund, she set up a private
nursing home, and, worse still, joined with Ethel
Manson (Mrs. Bedford Fenwick) at the British Nursing
Association. Machin was, I fear, another face turned
to the wall. Very few Nightingales remained in her

Florence Nightingale and the Establishment 17
of the First School at St. Thomas's - Myth
V Reality

favor until retirement day.[30]

No one can claim that all these experiments at home and abroad were successful. In the early days the Fund faced two insuperable difficulties that were interconnected. They lacked suitable *trained* superintendents. Leaders were sent forth because of their ladylike qualities and their moral earnestness. They were usually women used to handling servants not employees or colleagues. These qualities do not necessarily produce diplomacy and adaptability. Another factor was that nursing, as Nightingale complained, was becoming fashionable and the new style nurses were praised and in her words were becoming 'arrogant and conceited.' Another problem, hard to comprehend in these secular days, was that many were devoutly religious with strong sectarian biases. Osburn was "Romish," Pringle converted to Rome, Machin was "a stiff necked Presbyterian," Williams a Quaker and so on and all of them were not above proselytizing. Still another difficulty was that for about 20 years there were very few suitable probationers to send anywhere. Many were poorly educated and in the early days they, the nurses at St. Thomas's, set a poor example to follow. Few of the "leaders" had any kind of theoretical training. By the time the situation improved every other teaching hospital had a training school and many had "lady probationers." It was an "in thing" and the Nightingale School no longer had the edge. Very few Nightingales became superintendents at the large London hospitals. In spite of the efforts of the Fund Council, by the end of the century St. Thomas's training school was much like any other. The Fund paid for a smaller and smaller proportion of the training and it gradually became an irrelevance. Its officers were less and less consulted by the Court of Governors of the hospital and the correspondence at times is distinctly cool--verging on the hostile. In 1913, in a History of the Fund, Bonham Carter--now aged 86 years old--pointed out that originally the Fund had helped with a number of projects, midwifery, poor law nursing, community nursing and military nursing, but now it was left with just St. Thomas's and there was a question of what to do with its surplus income.

Miss Nightingale left no instruction to the Council with regard to any new application of surplus income in the objects mentioned by the Trust Deed, but it is right that it should be recorded that Miss Nightingale expressed a distinct wish not to be tied to St. Thomas's.[31] Nightingale always thought that St. Thomas's had exploited the Fund and relations were not cordial.

The Fund's contribution to nursing was that it enabled the concept of secular nurse training based on a general hospital to have been started earlier than otherwise would have been the case. The Fund did a splendid public relations job even if the early products were poor. Whether this was a good thing is a moot point. The so called Nightingale system tended to eliminate other systems simply because it was claimed to be successful. Some other systems had merit in that they trained nurses for the hospital and the community. For example, the principles of the religious orders could have been adapted on a more secular basis as indeed they were with the Agnes Karl Verband in Germany.

My contention is that contrary to popular myth, the time was not ready to do what Nightingale wanted to do. A few years later there would have been more women with a higher education who could have been trained as tutors with a better understanding of the health needs of the population. Also with the new possibilities made available by the advances in medicine, there might have been a chance to develop a separate philosophy for nursing--what it was and what it was not. Teaching had the sense to train the trainers first while nursing started at the lowest level and tried to work up.

For all its vaunted publicity and lauding by nurse historians and myth markers, the Nightingale system was not a break with the past. The personnel used to train the probationers were the products of the

Florence Nightingale and the Establishment   **19**
of the First School at St. Thomas's - Myth
V Reality

past, and without a new controlling hand a new probationer could not be forged. Nursing at St. Thomas's went on as before. We do nursing, and particularly nursing education, a great disservice by pretending that nursing suddenly became homogenous and educated because of the Nightingale school. In its first 40 years it only placed 982 nurses on the Register. Believing the myth we have clung to the system like a drowning man to a raft. Those who came after Nightingale, without her prescience and willingness to experiment, emphasized obedience and discipline long after the need had gone and when on the whole the probationers were a respectable lot. Obedience breeds conformity and we bred an unquestioning profession resistant to change.

If nurses themselves clung to the system that had made them fashionable, hospital administrators were also committed to a system that kept down their costs. As medicine changed and the hospitals opened their doors to the middle classes, there was a demand for more and better nurses. Hospitals wishing to fulfil this need seized the humble experiment of 1860 and turned it into the orthodoxy of the 1900's. Hospitals, both voluntary and public, were poor while probationers were cheap. As far as the hospital was concerned the longer the training the better. It was even better if some of the probationers paid for the privilege. Hospital budgets were planned accordingly. This is an important legacy of the system.

This is not what Nightingale intended. She saw what was happening but was helpless to do anything about it and she turned her attention both to the metaphysical world and to advocating the training of a separate corps of women sanitary missioners since nurses in her mind were apparently becoming doctor's assistants. Under the Nightingale system nursing and the hygiene undoubtedly improved. The reform and management of the nursing work force also secured a strong position for the matron and a career structure for nurses. Interestingly enough, however, by the 1890's Nightingale had her doubts about the wisdom of giving the matron so much power. But the arrangements for analyzing the central purpose of that work force and designing a training to fit that purpose were shamefully neglected. What the nurse was taught and who taught her and who examined her are questions which were left unanswered. Nightingale did not answer them and in England they are still partly unanswered. The root of this dilemma lies back in 1860 and the contents of this paper and those records in the British Library, the Greater London Record Office and elsewhere that historians previously have chosen to ignore.

NOTES

1. See Brian Abel-Smith, *A History of the Nursing Profession.* (London: William Heinemann, 1960), and Brian Abel-Smith, *The Hospitals 1800-1848.* (London: William Heinemann, 1964).
2. Edward Ryder published a compendium of Fry's journal under the title of *Memoirs of the Life of Elizabeth Fry: Life and Labors of the Eminent Philanthropist, Preacher and Prison Reformer* (New York: E. Walker's Sons 1884); two of her daughters, Katherine Fry and R.E. Cresswell, edited *Memoirs of the Life of Elizabeth Fry* (London: J. Hatchard, 1847). See also Janet Whitney, *Elisabeth Fry* (Boston: Little, Brown & Company, 1936.
3. For a discussion of these see Abel-Smith, *A History of the Nursing Profession*, and Vern L. and Bonnie Bullough, *The Care of the Sick: The Emergence of Modern Nursing* (New York: Prodist Books-Neale Watson, 1978), pp. 77-84.
4. For documentation of this see Monica E. Baly, *Florence Nightingale and the Nursing Legacy* (Dover, New Hampshire: Croom Helm, 1986), pp. 13-15. Much of this discussion in the rest

Florence Nightingale and the Establishment   **21**
of the First School at St. Thomas's - Myth
V Reality

of this paper is based upon the papers held at the Greater London Record Office (GLRO), namely *The Nightingale Collection* and *The Nightingale Fund Council Records* as well as *St. Thomas's Hospital Records.* Full citations are in Baly, *Florence Nightingale.*

5.   Irene Palmer, "Florence Nightingale and International Origins of Modern Nursing," *Image* 13(2) (June 1981):28-31.

6.   Baly, *Florence Nightingale*, pp. 11-18.

7.   *Ibid*, pp. 22-27, for the archival references.

8.   Sir Edward Cook, *The Life of Florence Nightingale*, 2 vols., (London: Macmillan, 1913 and 1914). See also Cecil Woodham-Smith, *Florence Nightingale 1820-1910* (New York: McGraw-Hill, 1951). For the "official" history of the St. Thomas' School, see *The Nightingale Training School: St. Thomas' Hospital 1960-1910* (Privately printed for the Nightingale Training School for Nurses, 1960).

9.   Baly, *Florence Nightingale*, pp. 28-30.

10.   Letter of R.G. Whitfield to Florence Nightingale, *The Nightingale Collection*, British Department of Manuscripts, British Library (Henceforth BL), Additional Manuscript 47742, 18 March, 1859, f. 65.

11.   Letter of Florence Nightingale to Sidney Herbert, *Herbert Papers*, Wilton House, vol. 1859, 24 May 1859. See also Woodham Smith, *Florence Nightingale*, p. 344.

12.   For a discussion see Baly, *Florence Nightingale*, pp. 34-39.

13.   *Lancet*, 31 March, 1866.

14.   For discussion see Baly, *Florence Nightingale*, pp. 58-62.

15.   E. Rappe to FN, BL, Additional MSS 47717, 29 November 1872, f. 120.

16.   Florence Nightingale to H. Bonham Carter (quoting E. Torrance), BL, Additional MSS 47116, 24 November 1871, f. 202.

17.   Baley, *Florence Nightingale*, pp. 52 ff. See also

Nightingale's correspondence with Macmillan's Magazine, BL, Additional MSS 45800, April 1867, f. 91.

18. Florence Nightingale to H. Bonham Carter, BL, ADD Mss. 47719, 21 October 1876, f. 170.
19. Florence Nightingale to H. Bonham Carter, BL, Add MSS 47717, 17 January, 1873, f. 147.
20. M. Adelaide Nutting and Lavinia L. Dock, *A History of Nursing*, 4 vol., (New York: Putnam, 1907-1912).
21. Florence Nightingale to H. Bonham Carter, GLRO, Nightingale Colletion (Nightingale Training School, HI/ST/NC, 1/72, 12a, June 1872, Part 2.
22. H. Bonham Carter to FN, GLRO, HI/ST/V3/72, 2 February, 1872.
23. Often Nightingale's pen seemed to be dipped in acid when she referred to Wardroper although she apparently also had affection for her. Baly, *Florence Nightingale*, p. 183.
24. Baly, *Florence Nightingale*, pp. 154-158.
25. *Ibid*, pp. 156-60.
24. *Ibid*, pp. 162-65.
25. *Ibid*, pp. 166-67.
26. *Ibid*, p. 90.
27. *Ibid*, pp. 138-42.
28. *Ibid*, pp. 142-146.
29. *Ibid*, p. 147.
30. *Ibid*.
31. Bonham Carter, Memorandum on the History of the Nightingale Fund, GLRO, A/NFC/O, 13 February 1913.

SOME THOUGHTS AND REFLECTIONS ON THE LIFE OF FLORENCE NIGHTINGALE FROM A TWENTIETH CENTURY PERSPECTIVE

by

Marian J. Brook

When Florence Nightingale returned from the Crimean War in August of 1856, she was the most written about, idolized and idealized woman of her day, perhaps the most written about, idolized and idealized woman in history. The study of her work and accomplishments on behalf of the British soldier is one of the foundational stories of modern nursing.

Florence Nightingale after the Crimean War has remained more of an enigma and is more difficult to identify with. We are less comfortable with a woman who carried out the remainder of her life's work from seclusion, as an invalid. Recent scholarship has revealed the fine intellect, the deeply spiritual sensibility, the articulate, passionate writer, but I, for one, have not been able to reconcile all of this with the fact of a reclusive invalid.

When I began to examine the life and contributions of Florence Nightingale, I found myself "resonating" to the period in her life when she withdrew from active society and asked "What was the nature of the illness which kept her bedridden and in seclusion for the rest of her life?"

23

Cook says that she restricted her life in order to devote all of her energies to the work she had undertaken to effect reform in the health system of the British Army along the lines of the changes made in Scutari.[1] Woodham-Smith states that there were numerous letters which Cook, under obligation to the family, had not used in his work. She describes the pressure of work on Miss Nightingale during the fall of 1856 and through the early months of 1857 until she collapsed completely in August of 1857. During this time of demanding work she was "plagued by Fanny and Parthe" who were sharing her suite in London and concludes that she then began to use her illness to protect herself from her mother and sister, having palpitations whenever they spoke of coming to be with her. Pickering saw her illness as a "creative psychoneurosis" affording her the privacy and freedom from family pressures to work but which in the end turned her into a "tyrannical invalid."[3]

I felt unsatisfied and looked for an explanation that didn't "blame the victim" and that avoided labels which can be used pejoratively. Many people today believe that diagnoses such as "neurosis" and "psychosomatic disorder" have been used against women to "prove" powerlessness, inferiority and lack of stability. In order to counter this, it is important to see behavior in its positive intent--to help the individual to survive. My own philosophy tells me that behavior has meaning for the individual and that behavior departing from the individual's usual (or in this case previous) ways of acting signals some special need or circumstance. As I read what has been written about Florence Nightingale's life, her experiences in the Crimea and the work she continued to carry out through most of her long life, I began to recognize the pattern of stress: overwhelming conditions to be corrected, existing lines of authority to be challenged, circumvented or overcome in order to reach the goal of bringing about improvements, unclear job description and role definition, high mortality rate among soldiers in her care. A picture first of "job

Some Thoughts and Reflections on the Life   25
of Florence Nightingale From a Twentieth
Century Perspective

burn-out" and then of "post-traumatic stress disorder"
came into focus.

These concepts are outgrowths of the work of
Selye on stress and of Wolpe on learned behavior.
Selye identified the endocrine responses to a traumatic
stimulus to which the individual had not adapted. This
"alarm reaction" is characterized by changes in
cardiovascular functioning, increased respirations,
increased muscle tone and are among the physiological
alterations in response to a stressor.[4] At about the same
time, Wolpe demonstrated that an anxious state can be
produced experimentally and hypothesized that
neurotic habits are learned in humans in response to
anxiety-producing experiences. "The stimulus-
response (trauma-anxiety) model offers a physiologic
as well as a behavioral explanation for the relationship
between trauma and anxiety."[5]

Menzies identified job stress particular to
nurses.[6] Jones wrote about the need for emotional
support for the nurse in facing the stress of patient
care.[7] Vreeland and Ellis identified interpersonal
relations among surgeons, anesthesiologists and nurses
as stressors in an ICU.[8] Freudenberger applied the
term "burn-out" to job-related stress and defined
"burn-out" as "To deplete oneself, to exhaust one's
physical and mental resources, to wear oneself out by
excessively striving to reach some unrealistic
expectaiton imposed by oneself or by the values of
society."[9] He identifies "dynamic, charismatic, goal-
oriented men and women . . .. determined idealists
who want . . . their community to be better" as being
particularly susceptible to "burn-out."[10] The Appendix
summarizes the physiologic, emotional and intellectual
components of stress.

Rogers and Nickolaus identified Florence
Nightingale with the Post-Traumatic Stress Disorder
(PTSD) recognized in veterans of the Vietnam War.[11]
PTSD is characterized by flashbacks to the war
experience along with the physiologic responses of
arousal that were experienced with the original events.
Other symptoms include

- startle response
- sleep disturbances
- guilt about surviving when others did not
- avoidance of activities that arouse recollection of the traumatic event
- diminished responsiveness to the external world
- inability to enjoy activities once found pleasurable[12]

Chronic PTSD has symptoms lasting 6 months or more.

"As the time passes, however, the patient's emphasis and orientation gradually change from a preoccupation with the actual trauma to an obsessive concern with physical disability attributable to the trauma . . .. Persons suffering from a Chronic PTSD are extremely vulnerable and sensitive to environmental stressors, since quantitatively fewer stimuli are required to elevate anxiety into a severe range."
". . . patients become convinced that they are incurable and chronically disabled and have reached an end-stage in their illness.[13]

Florence Nightingale's behavior and choice of lifestyle from August 1856 at least until 1861 can be seen as her attempts to cope with prolonged stress which began when she arrived at Scutari in 1854. When her biographies are examined from the point of view of stress it is possible to find evidence of the stressors, her frame of mind, her work habits and to see many of her actions as coping strategies. "Scratch many returnees from total war and you will find . . . . a new, permanent adaptive lifestyle."[14]

What the horrors of war are no one can imagine. They are not wounds, and blood, and fever, spotted and low, and dysentery, chronic and acute, and cold and heat and famine. They are intoxication, drunken brutality, demoralization and disorder on the part of the inferior; jealousies, meanness, indifference, selfish brutality on the part of the superior.[15]

Some Thoughts and Reflections on the Life 27
of Florence Nightingale From a Twentieth
Century Perspective

The Scutari experience included all of these for Florence Nightingale. She worked long hours nursing the men directly in the early weeks at Scutari when conditions were the worst. "I work in the wards all day and write all night."[16] She and another nurse were reported to have taken charge of the care of five soldiers, judged to be "hopeless cases" and restored them to "a fit condition for surgical treatment."[17] According to one retired soldier interviewed by Cook, admittedly when the Nightingale "legend" was old and very well established, "she used to attend to the worst cases herself."[18] She assisted at operations giving support to soldiers who had to face amputation of a limb without anesthetic and was often the comforting presence at a soldier's death.

As time went on she spent more time in administration while the nurses who came with her and orderlies did more of the bedside care. "The instruction of the orderlies in their business was one of the main uses of us in the War Hospitals."[19] As administrator, she was not only in charge of the nurses but responsible for bringing organization to the supply and maintenance of the hospitals which the Army's inadequate system had been unable to do. Each role was beset with difficulties.

As chief of nurses she was only too aware that female nursing was on trial and that in order for it to succeed the nurses had to be "better than the best." They had to be exemplary in their behavior so that no scandal would wreck the experiment. Thus she required strict regulation and supervision of their activities. No nurse was allowed in the wards after 8 PM. She personally made night rounds.

The prevailing climate of deep antipathy and suspicion between religious factions created problems of staffing. She needed to balance the proportion of Roman Catholic sisters, Church of England sisters and nurses from other Protestant groups. Sectarians created uproar over Roman Catholic sisters caring for Protestant soldiers--they were accused of proselytizing--and vice versa, Roman Catholic factions demanded Catholic nurses for Catholic soldiers. This caused a great many problems in staffing, delineation of authority, interpersonal relations and morale.

From the first she wrote impassioned official and private letters to Sidney Herbert, her superior at the War Office, to have a sanitary engineering consultant appointed. It is as a result of the work of this Commission that the death rate fell dramatically between November 1854 and May 1855.

The variety of demands, the unclearness of the roles, the unclear authority which she had in order to to carry out what she saw to be necessary to providing for the health of the soldiers amount to what is recognized today as contributing to job burnout.

> ". . . administrators many times experience that the hopes and dreams they brought with them to the position gradually extinguish while they are preoccupied with the concerns of numerous battle-fronts. Procuring necessary support and funds, justifying current allocations, expenditures, and policies and procedures, responding to continuous modifications of structure and operations, and living up to the expectations of numerous significant others, can be easily over-demanding."[20]

In May, 1855 Florence Nightingale travelled from Scutari to the hospitals in the Crimea where her authority, because of the wording of her original commission, was less clear and was challenged by many. Woodham-Smith summarizes.

> But as soon as things had slightly improved, official jealously re-awoke. In the second period, from spring of 1855 until her return to England in the summer of 1856, gratitude-- except the gratitude of the troops--and admiration disappeared, and she was victimized by petty jealousies, treacheries, and misrepresentations. Throughout this second period she was miserably depressed. At the end

Some Thoughts and Reflections on the Life 29
*of Florence Nightingale From a Twentieth
Century Perspective*

of it she was obsessed by a sense of failure.[21]

While she was in the Crimea, she became ill with "Crimean Fever," probably typhus or typhoid fever.[22] Either of these illnesses has a severe acute stage and a debilitating natural course, and it is likely that she was as ill as the initial dispatches indicated and that her convalescence took many weeks and that she carried after-effects--possibly anemia--for several years.

She returned to work at Scutari in the summer and faced more crises. Some of her nurses also died. A letter she wrote to St. John's House says of Mrs. Elizabeth Drake, a nurse from that order, "I cannot tell you what I felt when I heard of her death, unexpected alike by all. I have lost in her the best of all the women here . . . I feel like a criminal in having robbed you of one so truly to be loved and honored . . .."[23]

At this time her Aunt Mai came to Scutari to be with her when her friends and associates, the Bracebridges, left. Writing in letters during the winter of 1855-56 she describes her niece's work day. "She habitually writes till 1 or 2, sometimes 3 or 4 (AM)" and "I never saw a greater picture of exhaustion than Flo last night at 10" and later "She has attained a most wonderful calm and presence of mind. She is, I think, often deeply impressed and depressed, though she does not show it outwardly . . ."[24]

The war ended in April 1856 but Florence Nightingale stayed at Scutari until the last patient had been discharged. Then she and Aunt Mai travelled home incognito, separating in Paris. She arrived home on August 7, walking from the railway, unannounced.

Today, more is known about how to help others and ourselves to cope with stress in positive ways: share feelings, take time for self, manage your time, define your job limits and delegate some responsibility.[25] Directing anger generated by a tragedy toward steps to solve a problem or prevent another tragedy is often therapeutic. Florence Nightingale used some of these strategies intuitively and in so doing created the lifestyle and, to some degree, the personality, that was so different from that of her pre-Crimea life.

Writing had always been an important way for Nightingale to express herself. People had to write letters in order to keep in touch in those days and she had a large network of friends and relations with whom to correspond. Her frequent travels provided her with further opportunities to share in writing her thoughts and feelings about what she had seen. In her youth, Nightingale had kept diaries in which she poured out the frustration she felt at the lack of purposeful activity in her life. She wrote to help resolve her conflicting feelings about her family. In "Cassandra," written in 1852, she seems to identify the source of her frustration. "Why have women passion, intellect, moral activity--these three--and a place in society where none of the three can be exercised?"[26] "It is impossible to follow up anything systematically."[27] "Women have no means by which they can resist the claims of social life."[28] She also arrived at a "solution": "A married woman was heard to wish that she could break a limb that she might have a little time to herself."[29]

From another early diary entry one might conclude that Florence Nightingale did not freely share her innermost thoughts and feelings except with carefully chosen people.

"Very few people can sympathize with each other in any pursuit or thought of any importance. If people do not give you thought for thought, receive yours, digest it, and give it back with the impression of their own character upon it, then give you one for you to do likewise, it is best to know what one is about and not to attempt more than kindly, cheerful, outward intercourse."[30]

A letter from Parthe to a friend in August, 1856 says

"She is better, I think . . . . The physical hardships one does not wonder at her

Some Thoughts and Reflections on the Life 31
of Florence Nightingale From a Twentieth
Century Perspective

forgetting to speak of; but the marvel to me is
how the mental ones--the ignorance, the
cruelty, the falsehood she has had to
encounter--never seem to ruffle her for an
instant . . . she is as merry about little things as
ever, in the intervals of her great thought."[31]

She apparently was unable or unwilling to talk
with her family about her experiences. Shatan
identifies avoidance of intimacy and grief as
characteristic of PTSD.[32]

Florence Nightingale's Crimean nursing
contemporaries were scattered so there was no
opportunity for them to support each other. Two of
her most loyal friends and supporters during the rest
of their lives were Dr. John Sutherland and Sir John
McNeill both of whom had actually been at Scutari.

Her feelings of anger toward the Army and her
identification with the dead soldiers are revealed in
some of her writings from late 1856. "I stand at the
altar of the murdered men, and while I live, I fight for
their cause."[33]

No one can feel for the Army as I do . . . I
have had to see my children dressed in a dirty
blanket and an old pair of regimental trousers,
and to see them fed on raw salt meat, and nine
thousand of my children are lying, from causes
which might have been prevented, in their
forgotten graves. But I can never forget.[34]

She kept ". . . one of her most sacred possessions. It
was a bunch of grass which she 'had picked out of the
ground watered by our men's blood at Inkerman.'"[35]

She determined to seize the moment of national
awareness to push through reform in the Army
medical system so that such disasters as Scutari could
not happen again. This would have had the effect of
relieving her distress through direct action. She began
at once on her return home to write to Sidney Herbert
on the subject--letters which suggested to him an
"overwrought" frame of mind.[36]

The next phase of her work required outward

patience and tact in convincing first Queen Victoria and then Lord Panmure, Sidney Herbert's successor at the War Office, a reluctant reformer at best, of the need for a Royal Commission to investigate the health of the Army. It took six months for Lord Panmure to name the Commission and then he acted only after Nightingale had threatened to "go public" with her report which she had been writing in the meantime. At the same time she was involved in reviewing and suggesting changes in a military hospital already under construction. When the Commission was appointed, she worked long hours instructing the witnesses on what information they were to give.

Her frustration must have been great to have had to always work through others, but she felt that her open participation, because she was a woman and a popular heroine, would have been sensationalized and would have detracted from the message she wanted the Commission to hear. She knew of the frustration derived from inactivity when she wrote, "They (women) are all exhausted, like those who live on opium or on novels, all their lives--exhausted with feelings which lead to no action."[37]

Another source of frustration during this time was the presence of Fanny and Parthe in London with her "to enjoy being mother and sister to Florence Nightingale."[38] They kept their social round and interrupted her work frequently. "No one has enjoyed my reputation more than my own people . . ."[39] This statement may have been true or it may have reflected the irritability characteristic of an individual who is burning-out.

> The whole occupation of Parthe and Mama was to lie on two sofas and tell one another not to get tired by putting flowers into water . . .. It is a scene worthy of Moliere where two people in tolerable and even perfect health, lie on the sofa all day, doing absolutely nothing and persuade themselves and others that they are the victims of their self-devotion for another who is dying of overwork.[40]

Some Thoughts and Reflections on the Life   33
of Florence Nightingale From a Twentieth
Century Perspective

In August, 1857, after the Commission had
finished hearing evidence, she collapsed and went to
Malvern a "spa" near London. A long rambling,
disconnected letter to Dr. Sutherland, her friend and
physician, reveals some of the physiological and
emotional manifestations of PTSD or of "burn-out"
detailed in the Appendix. To quote part of the letter:

> Now in what one respect could I have done
> other than I have done? . . .. Yes but, you say,
> you might have walked or driven or eaten meat
> . . . let me tell you, O Doctor, that after any
> walk or drive I sat up all night with
> palpitation. And the sight of animal food
> increased the sickness. The man here put me,
> as soon as I arrived, on a sofa and told me not
> to move and to take no solid food at all till my
> pulse came down . . .. But shall I tell you what
> made you write to me? I have no second sight,
> I do not see visions nor dream dreams. It was
> my sister . . .. I have been greatly harassed by
> seeing my poor owl lately without her head,
> without her life . . .. Now that's me. I am lying
> without my head and you all peck at me . . ."[41]

Physiologic symptoms associated with Post-
Traumatic Stress Disorder, i.e. tachycardia, dyspnea
and tightness in the chest might well have been
experienced by her and observed by her physician
leading him to recommend that she restrict her
physical activity until her heart rate returned to
normal. At Malvern, she believed she might die very
soon. In a letter to Sidney Herbert in November, 1857
she apologizes for not staying alive "to do the 'nurses'",
commends him for his work on the Commission and
asks that he have "no chivalrous ideas about what is
'due' to my 'memory'."[42] At about the same time she
asked her uncle to help her draw up a will.

She had, however, taken some steps to allow
herself to go on working at the work she had waited
so long to find. She isolated herself from her family
and called on Aunt Mai to come and stay with her. She
knew that her health was the one weapon she could

use that would be effective in getting her mother and sister to do as she wished. Her palpitations increased whenever they threatened to come near.

Aunt Mai had been a friend and support to her in the past in her youthful struggles with her mother and then had volunteered to come to Scutari in 1855 when the Bracebridges went home. It is possible that Aunt Mai was a kindred spirit and got more than a little satisfaction at being out of the house and "at the scene of the action" herself. She probably provided necessary nurturing with her presence.

At about this time Arthur Clough, Aunt Mai's son-in-law who had, during 1857, helped with the Report while employed at the Education Office, became a permanent part of her staff, thus providing some secretarial and personal assistance.

Florence Nightingale had assessed her situation, moved to manage her time more effectively (get rid of her family and their interruptions) and conserve her energy (people came to her by appointment), arranged for some nurturing for herself (Aunt Mai) and arranged for some secretarial/personal help (Arthur Clough). In doing this she set up a way of life that worked in the short-term for her. With the huge, emotion-driven work of the Commission behind her some of her feelings left from the Crimean War may have been resolved. Some of the recommendations to the Commission were being put into effect and work on the various sub-Commissions yielded her the satisfaction of seeing some results.

Today we know that prolonged bed rest leads to further weakness and disability. Further, we know that in any chronic condition there are "illness behaviors" which start out as adaptations to pain or some other symptom but are reinforced and thus become habits. Further, according to Fordyce when conditions are present (i.e. behavior that is followed by reinforcement) learning and establishment of a habit proceeds automatically without conscious participation of the individual.[43]

The lifestyle Florence Nightingale adopted to

Some Thoughts and Reflections on the Life 35
of Florence Nightingale From a Twentieth
Century Perspective

relieve her stress was reinforced (rewarded) at many
levels. She, herself, felt relief from symptoms and the
freedom to pursue her work free from family and
other obligations. Her family rewarded the behavior
by acceding to her wishes and even offering support.
Societal expectations of an upper class woman in the
Nineteenth Century included the belief that she was
frail and delicate and gave great support to and did
not challenge the "invalid role."[44]

In the long run, Florence Nightingale's choices
may have been maladaptive, narrowing the viewpoint
of a fine intellect by restricting her interaction with
the world. I wonder what course nursing would have
taken if, for example, she had attended meetings of
the Statistical Society to which she was elected in 1858
regularly hearing new ideas arising in the rapid growth
of scientific medicine after 1860.[45]

Embracing our past is important. The "legend"
of Florence Nightingale reminds us of the essence of
nursing care: presence, compassion, concern for the
whole person, not just a medical diagnosis.
Understanding Florence Nightingale as affected by
"burn-out" addresses another issue relevant to nursing
in modern high stress environments. Viewing her
adaptation from the long perspective of history helps
us to remember to stay in tune with our own (as
individuals and as a profession) needs, feelings and
goals and not to isolate ourselves from each other,
allied professions or the society we serve.

APPENDIX

COMPONENTS OF STRESS

Physiologic

Increased heart rate
Elevated blood pressure
Tightness of chest
Breathing difficulty
Headache, fatigue
Urinary frequency
Diarrhea, nausea, vomiting
Sneezing
Insomnia, anorexia

Emotional

Irritability
Angry outbursts
Jealousy, restlessness
Lack of interest, withdrawn
Crying tendencies
Blaming others
Self-deprecating
Diminished initiative
Reduction of personal involvement with others

Intellectual

Forgetfulness, preoccupation
Blocking
Decreased fantasy life
Decreased concentration
Inattention to detail
Past, rather than present, oriented

Some Thoughts and Reflections on the Life 37
of Florence Nightingale From a Twentieth
Century Perspective

Decreased productivity
Decreased creativity
Errors in judging distance[46]

NOTES

1.   Sir Edward Cook, *The Life of Florence Nightingale*, 2 vols. New York: The Macmillan Company, 1942, p. 492.

2.   Cecil Woodham-Smith, *Florence Nightingale, 1820-1910*, New York: McGraw-Hill Book Company, Inc., 1951, "Acknowledgements."

3.   George White Pickering, *Creative Malady*, New York: Oxford University Press, 1974, p. 122.

4.   Chester B. Scrignar, *Post-traumatic Stress Disorder: Diagnosis, Treatment and Legal Issues*, New York: Praeger, 1984, p. 6.

5.   Ibid., p. 8.

6.   Isabel E.P. Menzies, "Nurses Under Stress" in Edwina A. McConnell, *Burnout in the Nursing Profession: Coping Strategies, Causes and Costs*, St. Louis: C.V. Mosby Company, 1982, pp. 239-245.

7.   Edna Mae Jones, "Who Supports the Nurse?" in McConnell, *Burnout in the Nursing Profession*, pp. 246-249.

8.   Ruth Vreeland and Geraldine L. Ellis, "Stresses in the Nurse in an Intensive Care Unit" in McConnell, *Burnout in the Nursing Profession*, pp. 250-252.

9.   Herbert J. Freudenberger, *Burn-out*, Garden City, NY: Anchor Press, 1980, p. 16.

10.   Ibid., p. 19.

11.   Barbara Rogers and Janet Nickolaus, "Vietnam Nurses," *Journal of Psychosocial Nursing and Mental Health Care*, 25 (1987), pp. 10-15.

12.   Ibid., p. 12.

13.   Scrignar, *Post-traumatic Stress Disorder: Diagnosis, Treatment and Legal Issues*, pp. 48-

50.
14. Chaim F. Shatan, "Have You Hugged a Vietnam Veteran Today?" in William F. Kelly (Ed.), *Post-Traumatic Stress Disorder and the War Veteran Patient*, New York: Brunner/Mazel Publishers, 1985, p. 15.
15. Cook, *The Life of Florence Nightingale*, p. 276.
16. Ibid., p. 234.
17. Ibid., p. 235.
18. Ibid.
19. Ibid., p. 219.
20. William Emener, Jr., "Professional Burnout: Rehabilitation's Hidden Handicap," in McConnell, *Burnout in the Nursing Profession*, p. 195.
21. Woodham-Smith, *Florence Nightingale, 1820–1910*, p. 141.
22. Pickering, *Creative Malady*, p. 115.
23. Cook, *The Life of Florence Nightingale, Volumes 1 and 2*, p. 261.
24. Ibid., pp. 295-296.
25. Carol J. Alexander, "Counteracting Burnout" in McConnell, *Burnout in the Nursing Profession*, pp. 92-87.
26. Myra Stark and C. MacDonald, *Cassandra: An Essay by Florence Nightingale*, Old Westbury, NY: The Feminist Press, 1979, p. 25.
27. Ibid., p. 31.
28. Ibid., p. 35.
29. Ibid., p. 34.
30. Cook, *The Life of Florence Nightingale*, p. 105.
31. Ibid., p. 320.
32. Shatan, "Have You Hugged a Vietnam Veteran Today?", p. 20.
33. Cook, *The Life of Florence Nightingale*, p. 318.
34. Ibid., p. 314.
35. Ibid., p. 304.
36. Ibid., p. 313.

Some Thoughts and Reflections on the Life 39
of Florence Nightingale From a Twentieth
Century Perspective

37. Stark, *Cassandra: An Essay by Florence Nightingale*, p. 41.
38. Pickering, *Creative Malady*, p. 127.
39. Ibid.
40. Ibid., p. 128.
41. Cook, *The Life of Florence Nightingale*, pp. 368-369.
42. Ibid., pp. 373-374.
43. William Fordyce, *Behavioral Methods for Chronic Pain and Illness*, St. Louis: C.V. Mosby Company, 1976, p. 32.
44. Barbara Ehrenreich and Deirdre English, *Complaints and Disorders: The Sexual Politics of Sickness*, Old Westbury, NY: The Feminist Press, 1973, pp. 17-19.
45. Zachery Cope, *Florence Nightingale and the Doctors*, Philadelphia: J.B. Lippincott Company, 1958, p. 101.
46. Marion A. Gaudinski, "Coping With Expanding Nursing Practice, Knowledge and Technology," in McConnell, *Burnout in the Nursing Profession*, p. 148.

NIGHTINGALE AND HER CORRESPONDENTS: PORTRAIT OF THE ERA

by

Lois A. Monteiro

Florence Nightingale's public persona, the myth of Nightingale, is familiar to all. The public Nightingale has been portrayed as a leader, an extraordinary woman, a selfless ministering angel, the Lady with the Lamp. Recent revisionist views have seen her as power-hungry, conniving, selfish and assertive, a woman who cared little for anyone else. Whichever view one wishes to espouse, the emphasis has been on the public person and her public deeds. In this presentation I wish to explore Nightingale the private woman, and her relationship to the other women who were her friends and confidants.

The public Nightingale would seem to have had only male friends and confidants--Sidney Herbert, the Minister of War; Arthur Clough, the poet; and Lord Palmerston quickly come to mind as those with whom she worked. Publicly, she is portrayed as the lone woman who broke with tradition to gain independence in her Victorian world. But the private Nightingale was a woman who shared women's experience of the "bonds of womanhood," and who maintained close lifetime, although sometimes rocky, friendships with a number of women. These women had little to do with her public role, except in their support and encouragement, and in the early years through their attempt to help her gain her freedom from her family.

In Great Britain, in Florence Nightingale's time, one could be a spinster, a married women, and for a lucky few a free woman of independent means. The women in Nightingale's network exemplify the kinds of roles or life patterns that Nightingale, were she a different personality, might well have experienced. Of the five women whom I will discuss, four, Mary Clarke Mohl, Hilary Bonham-Carter, Elizabeth Herbert and Selina Bacebridge, were close friends. Those were their public names--their private names were Clarkey, Hilly, Liz, and Sigma; just as Nightingale's private name was Flo. They were of different ages, the roles they played in Nightingale's life differed, their own lives were different, but they shared a common friend and were well known to one another. In some instances, and they worked to help Nightingale. The fifth woman, Harriet Martineau, was less of a friend and more of a professional peer, but she too worked to help Nightingale.

Mary Clarke Mohl was a married woman who led an independent life that was more European than English in character. Hilary Bonham-Carter, a cousin of Nightingale's, was a spinster whose life was dominated by family obligations. Selina Bracebridge was a married woman who lived in her husband's shadow. Elizabeth Herbert also lived in her husband's shadow, but after he died she began a new life as an author. Harriet Martineau was an unmarried woman with a successful career.

The relationship of Nightingale to each of the women and their relationship to each other can be seen in Nightingale's letters to them and in their letters to her and to each other.[1] Also, the Nightingale biographers and biographies of Mohl,[2] Martineau[3] and Bonham-Carter[4] add to the story. The relationships of these women suggest a shared culture of womanhood. In general, they accepted the male/female separation and lived their lives within the accepted way of behaving.

I will begin with Mary Clark Mohl as a key

figure who was close to Nightingale and was also well acquainted with all of the others. I find her the most interesting because she seems to be so "modern" and because she was probably most like Nightingale in her personality type. In my imagination she seems like a character from a Henry James novel--as if she were an American living abroad.

Mary Clarke Mohl (1793-1883) was 27 years older than Nightingale. They first met in 1838 when the 18-year-old Florence was visiting Paris for the winter with her sister and parents while alterations were being made to their home at Embly. Although Nightingale was 18 and Mary Clarke (Clarkey) was 45, she took Florence under her wing and introduced her to the Paris intellectual circle of which Clarke was a member.

Clarke, an Englishwoman by birth and heritage, was raised in France. Her Scottish grandparents had moved to France for the health of their daughter, Elizabeth (Mary's mother), who had chest problems. When Elizabeth married she lived for a time in London with her architect husband, but when Mary was eight Elizabeth moved back to Paris with her daughter, Mary, while her husband, ostensibly for financial reasons, stayed in England. Mary was brought up in a "single parent" household with her grandmother and her mother. Mary's grandmother, Mrs. Hay, knew many people, one of whom was an important Parisian woman, Madam Recamier, who had a salon and was known for her wit and charm. Mary studied painting at the Louvre and met with intellectuals and young political liberals at Madame Recamier's. At that period young Parisians were Anglophiles, particularly admiring the English writers and Mary was well read in the classics and in the newer English writers. Mary met and fell in love with Claude Fauriel, a writer and scholar on medieval Europe who was somewhat of a star in the Parisian circle and was 20 years older than Mary. Over the next 15 years, Mary gradually developed her own group, who visited daily at her home, and she maintained an intimate friendship with Fauriel, a relationship that

was accepted, without scandal, by the group in Paris.
Clarke's biography makes clear that this was a love
relationship, that Clarke and Fauriel traveled together
(with others in their company), and that Clarke
expected marriage although Fauriel continually put it
off on grounds that he had to complete his writing--
in reality he also had a woman patron to whom he was
indebted so he was not free to marry. In 1839 when
she met Nightingale, Mary was still involved with
Fauriel. After 20 years of courtship, Fauriel died, and
Mary married his friend, another scholar, Julius Mohl,
an orientalist who studied ancient Egypt and Persia
and who had been one of the regular visitors to Mary's
home. He was a distinguished scholar and, in
marriage, allowed Mary to maintain her freedom to
travel alone and to continue her many friendships. He
commented that some thought him a myth because his
wife was always "gallivanting about" alone. Nightingale
also considered Julius Mohl as a friend as well, and
wrote him letters aside from those she wrote to Mary.
Sometimes she asked him to show them to Mary. His
letters were usually about business topics--those to
Mary combined business and personal topics.

From the beginning Clarke took Nightingale
seriously. In that first winter she invited Florence to
evening discussions at Madame Recamier's salon
where Nightingale met Chateaubriand (the politician)
and listened to discussions of French and Italian
artists.[5] Back in England, Clarke suggested that
Nightingale should take up writing to express her
feelings but Nightingale responded, "You ask me why
I do not write something--I had so much rather live
than write . . . I think one's feelings waste themselves
in words, they ought to all be distilled into actions."[6]
Florence also recognized the absurdity of her daily
life. In a different letter to Clarke of July 1847, she
said,

> I am fed up to my chin in linen and
> glass, and I am very fond of housekeeping. In
> this too-highly-educated, too-little-active age
> it, at least, is a practical application of our
> theories of something--and yet, in the middle

of my lists, my green lists, brown lists, red
lists, of all my instruments of the ornamental
in culinary accomplishments which I cannot
even divine the use of, I cannot help asking in
my head, Can reasonable people want all this?
Is all this china, linen, glass necessary to make
man a Progressive animal? Is it even good
Political Economy to invent wants in order to
supply employment? "And a proper stupid
answer you'll get," says the best Versailees
(china) service; "so go and do your accounts;
there is one of us cracked."[7]

By 1848 Mary was trying to find a way for
Nightingale to come to Paris to visit the Sisters of
Charity Hospital. Florence Nightingale had stopped in
Kaiserswerth on her way home from Rome the
previous year. Mary's plan was for Florence and her
mother to visit with Mary and her husband Julius
Mohl in Frankfurt and while there Nightingale could
go to Kaiserswerth (near Frankfurt). But the plan
failed when riots broke out in Frankfurt.

Nightingale did not get back to Kaiserswerth
until 1851 while her mother and sister were at
Carlsbad. Florence's cousin, Hilary Bonham-Carter,
who was also a friend of Clarke's, wrote to Mary
about the visit to Kaiserswerth, "Please Clarkey
darling keep it a secret even though you may not
perceive why it should be one."[8] In 1852 Mary wrote
to Hilary about Florence:

Tell Flo and yourself that the thing I
like best is that she should be perfectly free to
do her own foolishness, let alone wickedness if
she likes . . . Mrs. Nightingale knows I am very
discreet, so if after a time Flo tells of a fancy
to go to some wicked place the folk in England
will fancy she is still with me, and I will keep
it snug.[9]

Florence was again trying to go to Paris to visit the
Sisters of Charity. She did get there, in February 1853,
but before she could visit the Sisters she was called
back to England because her grandmother was ill. In
May 1853, when she *again* went to Paris, she did enter

the Sisters but that time caught measles. She convalesced at Clarke's house with only Julius Mohl in attendance because Clarke was in England.

At about this time, Spring 1853, Nightingale got her first nursing position as head of the Harley Street Institution, a position that was made possible by another woman friend. When she wrote Clarkey about the Harley Street Governing Committee, and her problems with it, Clarke replied "trample on the committee and ride the Fashionable Assess roughshod round Grovesnor Square."

The Nightingale/Clarke friendship lasted until Mary's death in 1883. Nightingale stopped in Paris on her way to Crimea in 1854, but from then until about 1860, Nightingale had little time for Clarke, and at one point made her have an appointment to visit. Mary seems to have understood (or at least accepted it). In 1856 Mary commented

> Florence is a great artist. She has a strong creative individuality . . . It is only since she has burst out like a thunderbolt in her own way that she has done anything worthwhile. What folly and cruelty to have made her for years give up her individuality under pretence what she must live for other people.[10]

The Clarke-Nightingale letters of the post Crimea period from 1860 until Clarke's death in 1883 are more relaxed. In these letters Florence and Clarke discuss Mohl, many mention cats, for Clarke gave Nightingale kittens about which they exchanged minute details. Florence wrote to Clarke about more important government matters such as India, but more often wrote about mutual friends, about invitations to visit in London. The one I find most interesting is a late letter written by Florence in 1875 when Nightingale was staying with her ill mother in Upper Norwood. Nightingale at age 55 was once again trapped by family responsibility. Her mother was ill and had lost her mental facilities. Florence wrote:

> I am out of humanity's reach in a Red Villa like a Monster Lobster: a place which has

>no "raison d'etre" except the raison d'etre of
>Lobsters or Crabs: viz. to go backwards: and to
>feed and be fed on: in charge of my mother,
>by Doctor's orders.

The letter continues:

>Stranger vicissitudes than mine in life
>few men have had: vicissitudes from slavery to
>power: and from power to slavery again: it does
>not *seem* like a "vicissitude" a villa at Norwood:
>yet it is the strangest I yet have had. It is the
>only time for 22 years that my work has not
>been the first reason for deciding where I
>should live: and how I should live. Here it is
>the last. It is the caricature of a life.[11]

Florence ended the letter by telling Mary that when
Mary is in London she should feel free to stay at
Florence's house at 35 South Street if she likes even
though the house is empty because Florence is with
her mother.

To sum up this relationship, the two women
remained friends, with Mary helping Florence in the
early days and with the two sharing common friends
and interests throughout life. One of these common
friends was Hilary Bonham-Carter.

Hilary was Florence's cousin. Florence's
mother, Frances Smith, and Hilary's mother, Joanna,
were sisters. Hilary who was Florence's childhood
friend was one year younger than Florence (1821-
1865), and was the oldest girl in her family. Her father
died when she was seventeen and her mother came to
depend on Hilary for help with a large family of
younger siblings. Hilary, like Florence, was educated
at home, but in 1838 she spent six months at a
finishing school in Liverpool. The headmistress of the
school was Harriet Martineau's sister Rachel, and in
1841 Hilary spent some time visiting Harriet
Martineau, a woman writer who was also a friend of
Florence's.

Hilary had an interest in drawing and in her
youth took lessons in her home town from a local
artist. In 1842 the widowed Mrs. Smith, Hilary's
grandmother, decided to take her family on a grand

tour of Europe, and in June they were in Paris where Hilary visited with Mary Clarke whom she already knew through Florence and through Mary's visits to the Nightingale home in Embly. Clarke and Hilary became compatriots in finding a way for Florence to get to visit hospitals, as mentioned above, but Clarke also took on the task of getting Hilary to seriously consider doing work in art. In 1849, at Clarke's invitation, Hilary went to Paris to live and study art for a year. Unfortunately, she studied oil painting and she had little discipline for that medium. And, in fact, preferred drawing. A failure in oil painting, she returned home in a year.[12] This acceptance of failure totally frustrated Mary, and there are many letters to Flo and to Hilary encouraging Hilly to work on her art.

Nightingale, especially in her younger years, confided in Hilary, and Hilary did her best to help Florence. For example, in frustration with her life Florence wrote Hilary rather melodramatically:

> Oh that tadpole of restless activity, which swims round and round under the glassy surface of our civilized life--we talk and we dine and we dress as if the tadpoles, our hopes, were not breeding in thousands in silence and abandoned in despair; all seems unreal like a dream; "everything I do always seems to me false without being a like."[13]

In another letter she tells Hilary about a German lady who, not being Catholic, could not take the vows of a sister of charity but who nursed in a hospital. Florence in the letter wonders "if this lady extended it into anything like a Protestant sisterhood, and if she had any plans which would embrace women of an educated class; and how she disposed of the difficulties of surgeons making love to her and of living with women of indifferent character."[14] This sounds like a very inexperienced young woman writing, although by then Nightingale was 26 years old.

During these years Hilary was busy spending most of her time helping her family. She was always

"needed at home" and "could not be spared" to do what
she wanted to do. She stopped taking art lessons.
Clarkey wrote her often telling her to work, one such
letter says "is it not disgusting that you do not set to
and work instead of twaddling forever . . . to faddle
away your talent as you do. Why not reserve so much
as a day for yourself which nothing can break
through."[15] Clarke also wrote "Hilly" is

> a slave to her kind heart. It's all very well
> when it's for Flo, whom she dotes upon, but
> for a parcel of brothers, sisters, uncles, aunts,
> cousins, etc. it is very provoking. She is like
> someone that has been boned, as meat is. She
> is like a molluscous animal; she has lost all
> power of enjoyment--all the sharp and crisp
> edges of her impressions are so blunted by
> constantly giving up all for other people that
> she cares for nothing . . . All because she
> (Hilly) is single, she is to be at all their becks
> and calls. 'What can *she* have to do!--she has
> neither husband nor child!' So her soul is not
> her own; it's only married folk who have a
> right to such a possession.[16]

In the period of Nightingale's heavy activity
after her 1854 return from the Crimea, when
Nightingale's illness confined her to bed, her Aunt
Mai was the person who stayed to take care of her.
But Aunt Mai finally left, and in 1860 Hilary moved
in to manage the household and act as a social
secretary. During this period Nightingale begrudgingly
accepted Hilary's help, yet she also felt ambivalence
that Hilary should be doing her own work. At this
time Nightingale commissioned Hilary to do woodcuts
for her book on India. She directed Hilary's work, the
"less picturesque, the fewer lines, the less laborious
therefore the better. The more barely executed the
better" (letter 1862). Hilary's woodcuts were used as
illustrations for "Observations on the Sanitary State of
the Army in India."[17] In fall of 1862 and spring of
1863 Florence tried to get Hilary to go to Paris with
the Mohls. Finally, in irritation Nightingale told
Hilary to leave--"it would not be right for me any

more to absorb your life in letter writing and
housekeeping."

Nightingale in a letter to Mary Clarke wrote
that cutting off Hilary was like cutting off a limb.
Clarky responded:

> . . . You say you were obliged to
> "amputate your own limb by sending her
> away," but my dearest, if she is as useful to
> you as a limb, why should you amputate her?
> Keep her as she is--you keep your limb with
> all its sores . . . I'm sure of this: she loves you
> better than anyone else does, and it would be
> balm to her poor worn-out spirit if she thought
> she was useful to you . . . question whether the
> thing she likes best in the world is not being
> with you and being useful to you. When she is
> with me I want nothing from her except to be
> exact at the dinner hour and not to talk all the
> evening--oh, that I cannot endure! I only want
> her to work for herself,--and the first years
> she did so; but the last she spent much time in
> faddling at Aunt Mai's and Uncle Nicholson's
> and Mrs. Martin's--and now I am not sure this
> is not necessary for her happiness, this
> faddling after other people. I'm a selfish body
> and can't abide it--but we aren't all alike,
> luckily. . . . Now, if she is a limb to you, you
> are the very person for her, for she dotes on
> you--it is a pleasure to her, and an honour. I
> agree with you: she *ought* to do for herself. But
> I am not sure her nature can now bear it. I give
> it to you as a problem--think about it.[18]

Florence did not take Mary's advice to have
Hilary return as secretary-housekeeper, although there
are letters inviting Hilary for visits. Soon after this
break Hilary became ill and sadly was diagnosed as
having cancer. After an illness of about a year Hilary
died. Florence wrote to Mary Clarke:

> London, on September 8, 1865
> . . . There is *not a single person*, except
> yourself, who does not think that Hilary's
> family were quite right in the most monstrous

of slow murders--and that Hilary was worth
nothing better than to be sacrificed--and all
for what? . . . The fetichism of Family is a
worse fetichism than that of Sunday. Because
that only rolls its Juggernaut car one day of the
week--the other, every day in the week. I shall
never cease to think, as long as I live, of you
and Mr. Mohl as Hilly's *only* friends . . .[19]

Hilary died the next day on September 9, 1865.
Hers is perhaps the saddest of our stories. As a selfless
spinster she was taken advantage of by all. As Clarkey
once said, Hilary was like wool, kind, warm and
comfortable and lain on by everybody.[20] But her life
was a common one for the unmarried eldest daughter.

Elizabeth Herbert's life pattern was also
common. She was the well bred young woman of good
family who married the wealthy and well positioned,
handsome man. Her life is one that Nightingale might
have expected to live had she married.

Nightingale met Elizabeth Herbert (1822-1911)
in Rome in the winter of 1847-48 when Florence was
there on an extended visit with other family friends,
Selina and Charles Bracebridge, and Elizabeth was
there on her honeymoon. Both women were about 25
years old at the time they met. Liz was married to
Sidney Herbert who is well known as a key figure in
Nightingale's life. Florence was introduced to Liz by
Selina who knew Elizabeth Herbert. They became
friends during the Rome visit, and shortly after their
return Florence visited at the Herbert's home. In her
letters Nightingale refers to Elizabeth as Liz or Lizzie,
and Liz called Florence Flo. By 1851 they were close
enough friends for Florence to stay with Liz for about
six weeks during Liz's confinement for her second
child. In fact, when Flo was supposed to leave, Liz
asked Florence's mother "for a few more days of dear
Florence."[21] In a way, Florence of 1850, before her
release, sounds like Hilary of 1860. When Nightingale
was at Kaiserworth in 1851, the Herberts visited her,
and in 1852 she stayed with them at their home in
London. In a late letter to Clarke (1870) Nightingale
wrote of the death of one of the Herbert's children,

probably the one who was born at the time Florence
Nightingale stayed with Liz. The young man was
killed in a shipwreck. Florence wrote to Mary, "The
Captain is gone down--with 500 men--and Reginald
Herbert-Sidney Herbert's boy--(*my* boy as they
always called him)--such a noble gallant lad--the very
flower of the flock--is lost with her."[22]

Nightingale's famous professional relationship
was with Sidney Herbert, Liz's husband. Yet it was Liz
Herbert who was the key to Florence's first job when
she learned of the possible job for Florence at Harley
Street. Liz, as one of the committee members, fought
to get the position for Nightingale. She wrote to
Florence about going to one of the committee
meetings. "I thought some wicked cats might be there
who would set up their backs, and if so, I would like
to have mine up too."[23] Liz defended Nightingale
against the committee.

Furthermore, when Nightingale decided to go
to the Crimea, she wrote to *Liz* not to Sidney Herbert.
The famous letter is as follows:

My dearest I went to Belgrave Square
this morning for the chance of catching you,
or Mr. Herbert even, had he been in Town. A
small private expedition of nurses has been
organized for Scutari and I have been asked to
command it. I take myself out and one nurse .
. . I do not mean that I believe the *Times*
accounts, but I do believe we may be of use to
the poor wounded wretches.[24]

In the letter she asked Liz to negotiate her release
from her engagement with the Harley street
committee--unless the committee thoroughly approved
she could not honorably break her engagement.
Finally, she asked Liz to gauge her husband's reaction.
"What does Mr. Herbert say to the scheme itself? Does
he think it would be objected to by the authorities?
Would he give us any advice or letters of
recommendation?"

This famous letter crossed mails with Sidney
Herbert's famous letter of the same day asking her to
lead a group of nurses to Scutari. F.B. Smith has made

much of the politics of Nightingale writing to Liz
rather than directly to Sidney Herbert, and views it as
a manipulative act. Given her relationship with Liz,
and given that Liz was her "boss" as the committee
member at Harley Street, the appeal to Liz seems
logical, but as Smith suggests, it could all have been
planned in advance.

One can get a sense of Liz's private view of
Nightingale from an 1855 letter from Liz to Selina
Bracebridge when Nightingale was complaining
because Mary Stanley was being sent to the Crimea
with a second party of nurses. Lize wrote "Perhaps it
is wholesome for us to be reminded that Flo is still a
mortal, which we were beginning to doubt."[25]

After the Crimea experience, in the frenzied
period of Army Reform in which Nightingale and
Herbert were working closely on a daily basis, Liz
seems to have acted in support of Florence's ambition
for Herbert. They had occasional letters regarding
Sidney Herbert's health. In Sept. 1858, when Sidney
Herbert had an attack of pleurisy, Florence wrote Liz
to tell her not to let him go out. Also Liz acted as
Sidney's secretary--e.g. a December 1857 note
"Dearest--Sidney wishes me to send you these if you
will be so kind as to look them over." And, when
Sidney was very ill, December 1860, and Florence
urged him to stay on as Minister of War but give up
his seat in Commons Liz wrote: "A thousand thanks to
you for all you have said and done. God Bless you for
all your love and sympathy."[25] Finally, after his death
(March 1862) Liz told Florence that "If you never wish
to live for your own sake, yet bear to live, dearest, for
a time to carry out his work and to keep his memory
fresh." Further evidence of their friendship can be
found in Florence's mention of Liz in a will written
when Nightingale thought that she was dying in
1857.[26]

But lest we think that all was fondness let me
add a quote from a letter from Florence to Mary
Clarke in December of 1861 in which Nightingale was
complaining that no woman ever had sympathy for
her:

> Now Sidney Herbert's wife just did the
> Secretary's work for her husband (which I have
> had to do without) out of pure sympathy. *She
> did not understand his policy* [italics mine]. Yet
> she could write his letters for him like a
> man.[28]

Also, lest we think that Liz had no life apart
from her husband's, we should note that in the early
years of her marriage she had set up lodging houses
for farm workers and had helped families who wished
to emigrate "to the colonies" to do so. After his death
she seems to have become a very active writer. In that
period Liz and Nightingale had very little contact but
they did exchange sympathy notes on the anniversary
of Sidney Herbert's death. In 1865 Liz Herbert joined
the Roman Catholic Church and after that time she
wrote many books on religious figures mostly
published by church-related publishers, some
published in the U.S. Also, she wrote travel books
about the Holy land.

Liz is scarcely mentioned in her husband's
biography, does not have a biography of her own, and
many of her letters to Nightingale are missing.
Nevertheless, she was an important figure for the
private Nightingale, and as we learn more about her,
an important figure in her own right.

Selina Bracebridge (1799-1874), another key
woman friend who played a mother surrogate role for
Nightingale, was more dependent on her husband,
Charles Bracebridge. The Bracebridges, often referred
to as a couple in the biographies, were about twenty
years older than Florence, and were friends of the
family. Selina became Florence's ally in her fight
against her mother and sister. In fact, after Mr.
Bracebridge's death Florence wrote to Mary Clarke to
say

> He and she have been the creators of
> my life . . . when I think of all the places I
> have been with them, of the immense
> influence they had in shaping my own life--
> more than earthly father and mother to me--

I cannot doubt that they leave behind them
their mark on the century.[29]

Selina, who was 75 when her husband died, wrote
Florence to say that she would not last long without
him, and her prediction was right for she lived only
two years after his death. Florence visited Selina the
day before she died. To Clarke Nightingale wrote

She was more than a mother to me--
what should I have been without her . . .
Sunday morning I was by her bed as soon as
she spoke. She knew me at once.[30]

The places Nightingale has been with Selina
were Rome, Paris, Egypt, Kaisersworth and the
Crimea. Years later Nightingale wrote to Mary Clarke
about the time in Rome, when the Bracebridge's first
got her away from England and away from her mother
and sister:

I confess I never enjoyed any time in
my life so much as my time at Rome . . . and
yet I can scarcely tell why . . . It was too a time
pregnant to me of all my future life--for my
intimacy with Sidney Herbert began there--
under the dear Bracebridge's wing. But I could
not tell that at the time.[31]

Nightingale often referred to Selina by a
nickname, Sigma, the Greek sign used because of
Selina's love for Greece. Sometimes the sign alone is
used in place of the name. Selina in Florence's pre-
Crimea days was like a guardian angel, always
rescuing her at the right moment, and Florence for a
time idolized Selina. Florence's invitation for the
Rome trip was arranged by the Bracebridges and, in
fact, was a key point in Nightingale's career. The trip
to Egypt, which was undertaken two years later, was
also important because on the return from Egypt they
traveled through Europe and Florence and had the
chance to make contact with Kaisersworth.

Few of the letters in the Nightingale
collections were written to Selina, but many family
letters to Selina refer to her. She was also on the
Harley Street Committee along with Liz Herbert.[32]
Similarly, Liz and Selina worked together to help

Florence immediately after the decision to go to
Scutari. It was Selina and Liz who interviewed the
nurses to select those who would be sent. Selina
Bracebridge went to the Crimea with Nightingale,
although it was her husband who was needed to take
care of financial details. Selina was given
responsibility for soldiers' gifts, and for the care and
attention to Florence. She returned to England before
Nightingale did. Some of Florence's letters from
Scutari, after Selina left, were joint letters sent to Mr.
and Mrs. Nightingale and Mr. and Mrs. Bracebridge.

After the Crimea the letters to Selina are more
of the housekeeping kind--how she is feeling,
mentions of visits to London. The key role for Selina
was in the life of the young Florence, as is clear from
Nightingale's comment to Clarke, "What should I have
been without her."[33]

Before going into the final figure, Harriet
Martineau, I would like to emphasize the inter-
relationship of the five women we have been
discussing: Florence, Hillary and Liz--all the same age
within one year--and Mary and Selina, both 20 years
older. Besides their individual friendships with
Nightingale, these women knew each other and there
were friendships between them, e.g. Liz was close to
Selina, Hilary and Mary were good friends. They
should not be seen only in their individual connection
to Nightingale, but rather as a support system for each
other, as well as for Florence, a cross-linked group.
All were remarkably loyal to Florence Nightingale,
even when she treated them badly. Sometimes they
worked together behind the scenes to help her; e.g.,
Liz and Selina were both on the Harley Street
Committee, Hilary and Mary worked together to get
Florence to Paris to visit the Sisters of Charity. They
were doing this not because Florence Nightingale was
famous, but because she was a friend who needed
help. Granted they recognized her genius, but to them
she was Flo; Dearest Flo; Old Flo; Flo with the cats;
the woman who was their peer, and their friend--not
the legend who was larger than life.

I have kept Martineau for last because I think

the relationship to her was somewhat different--it was a more public, more impersonal interaction--an acquaintance rather than a friend. But Martineau too had cross-cutting connections primarily with Hilary, but also with Mary Clarke. Harriet Martineau was born in 1802 and died in 1876. Her interaction with Nightingale was most intense after the Crimea and through the years of Parliamentary reforms. Martineau was a political journalist, one of the few women writers of her time. As the daughter of a prosperous textile manufacturer, she received a good education. She traveled to the United States in the early 1830's and wrote a book, *Society in America*, about her visit. Through the 1830's and 1840's Martineau wrote newspaper articles and in 1852 she became a regular columnist for the *Daily News*. Nightingale had known of Martineau for years. For example, she mentions Martineau in an 1840 letter to her grandmother, recommends Martineau's books in an 1842 letter to a friend, and in an 1843 letter to her sister, Nightingale mentions that she had heard from Martineau. The height of the correspondence took place in the six years from 1858-1866, and focuses mainly on Nightingale's political business, the reforms of the Army, and India's sanitary problems.

Nightingale contacted Martineau when her attempts to pressure reform in the Army in 1857-58 were going too slowly; she turned to public opinion as the pressure source. Her acquaintance on the *Daily News*, Harriet Martineau, was an answer. On November 30, 1858, Nightingale wrote to Martineau, and noting that Martineau had an interest in army matters, she enclosed a copy of her confidential report "for private reading only."[34] Nightingale fed Martineau information to use in *News* articles on the need for Army Reform. These articles did appear, and eventually were republished by Martineau as a book called *England and her Soldiers*. Nightingale wrote telling Martineau how much she liked the manuscript and (that she) was "sure it will help universally," she continued to say that she "had corrected a few technical mistakes and altered two or three words only."

        Although *England and Her Soldiers* was
written by Martineau, it illustrates the way the two
women worked together. Nightingale continued to be
able to work "from offstage," anonymously supplying
political facts and information while Martineau
communicated this knowledge to the public. Martineau
could not have written the *News* articles or *England
and Her Soldiers* without the knowledge, cooperation
and writing of Nightingale, and Nightingale could not
have found a better way to pressure the government
into accepting her reforms. Thus, it is obvious that the
two needed each other to achieve their goals but were
not really intimate friends.

        Several times in the next few years Nightingale
asked Martineau point blank for her help in sparking
public opinion, including once asking for a favorable
article in the *Daily News* concerning Sidney Herbert.
After telling her of "Sidney Herbert's retirement from
the House of Commons and that he is suffering from
a disease of the kidneys and the doctors give him but
a year," she mentioned that she felt "it is so important
that the *Daily News* should help him through . . ."[35]
Note that it was also for this period that Liz thanked
Nightingale for her sympathy and support. However,
the major thrust of the friendship between Florence
Nightingale and Harriet Martineau was on the
political-business sphere which resulted in fruitful
collaboration. These two women used each other and
each other's position to accomplish their own political
goals.

        The picture of Nightingale that emerges from
a review of her personal rather than business
correspondence shows her to be different from the
totally self-sufficient, independent woman that she is
often protrayed to be. While she was, of course, self-
confident and determined to achieve her goals, she
also accepted help from other women and recognized
her indebtedness to them. Through her letters to these
women, we can see Nightingale as a woman with
personal as well as public concerns, one who
experienced the bonds of womanhood and of female

friendship. We also can see her as a woman with self-centered concerns, for whom the goal was often more important than the private individuals who might be hurt by actions taken to meet her public goal. While Nightingale may have sometimes mistreated the women in her network and while Nightingale and history may have sometimes discounted them, these women supported her and contributed to her total achievement.

The private Hilary, Harriet, Selina, Mary and Liz were essential to the public Florence.

NOTES

1.   Goldie, S. and Bishop, W.J. *A Calendar of The Letters of Florence Nightingale* Microfiche. (Oxford: Oxford Microform Publications, 1983).

2.   Lesser, Margaret. *Clarkey: A Portrait in Letters of Mary Clarke Mohl.* (Oxford: Oxford University Press, 1984).

3.   Webb, R.K. *Harriet Martineau, A Radical Victorian.* (New York: Columbia Univ. Press, 1960).

4.   Bonham-Carter, Victor. *In a Liberal Tradition, A Social Biography* (London: Constable, 1960).

5.   Cook, Edward T. *The Life of Florence Nightingale* (2 vols., London: Macmillan and Co., 1914), 1:42.

6.   Woodham-Smith, Cecil. *Florence Nightingale 1820-1910* (London: Constable, 1950), p. 52.

7.   Cook, *Life of Nightingale*, Vol. 1, p. 42.

8.   Woodham-Smith, *Florence Nightingale*, p. 91.

9.   Lesser, *Clarkey*, p. 132.

10.   Ibid., p. 146.

11.   Manuscript letters to Mary Clarke Mohl from Florence Nightingale. Florence Nightingale Collection, Woodward Library, University of British Columbia, Vancouver, Canada, Letter

A43.
12. Bonham-Carter, *In a Liberal Tradition*, p. 102.
13. Goldie, *A Calendar of the Letters*, letter of April 25, 1848, British Museum, Mss. 45794.
14. Cook, *Life of Nightingale*, vol. 1, p. 63.
15. Lesser, *Clarkey*, p. 150.
16. Ibid., p. 165.
17. Huxley, Elspeth. *Florence Nightingale*. New York: G.P. Putnam's Sons, 1975, p. 201.
18. Lesser, *Clarkey*, p. 165.
19. Woodham-Smith, *Florence Nightingale*, p. 437.
20. Ibid., p. 93.
21. Ibid., p. 87.
22. University of British Columbia, letter A25.
23. Cook, *Life of Nightingale*, vol. 1, p. 134.
24. Woodham-Smith, *Florence Nightingale*, p. 136.
25. Cook, *Life of Nightingale*, vol. 1, p. 193.
26. Ibid., vol. 1, p. 402.
27. Ibid., vol. 1, p. 374.
28. Ibid., vol. 2, p. 15.
29. University of British Columbia, letter A36.
30. University of British Columbia, letter A42.
31. University of British Columbia, letter A30.
32. Goldie, *A Calendar*, letter of February 14, 1853.
33. University of British Columbia, letter A42.
34. Goldie, *A Calendar*, letter of November 30, 1858. British Museum, Mss. 45788.
35. Ibid., letter of January 4, 1861, British Museum, Mss 45788.

LYTTON STRACHEY'S BIOGRAPHY OF FLORENCE NIGHTINGALE: A GOOD READ, A POOR REFERENCE

by

Natalie N. Riegler

INTRODUCTION

Nurse historians acknowledge that nursing has gained much popular appeal during times of war. The Crimean War in Europe and the Civil War in the United States, both occurring at relatively the same time, heralded a new era in nursing. Each war produced nursing heroines but Florence Nightingale, at the time of the Crimean War, has come to personify the nursing image. During the interlude between the Crimea and the First World War Nightingale became *the* exemplar for nurses and books were published glorifying her life and accomplishments.[1] However, as World War I progressed, writers began to reflect society's "disillusionment with patriotism"[2] and the "pragmatism and cynicism" which "grew out of the futility and mud of Vilmy and Flanders."[3] With this reaction, writers re-interpreted the lives of noted Victorians such as Nightingale. I have chosen to look at Lytton Strachey's study of Nightingale, written during the Great War and published in the Spring of 1918[4] as part of his book the *Eminent Victorians*.[5] This book has remained popular for the public, educators and nursing historians.

Though Strachey's depiction of Nightingale has become a classic and a watershed in style for scholars in biography writing, I have become concerned with its use as a reference by historians of nursing and will argue that the user of Strachey's narrative should beware. In this paper I compare his sketch with that of Sir Edward Cook's official biography of 1913,[6] upon which it is based, and place it within the context of the accepted standards for biographical writing as described by Cook in 1914[7] and later in 1981 by Leon Edel[8] a noted authority on biography.[9] It will become apparent that Strachey's writing is very much the result of his personal experiences and cynicism.

STRACHEY AND NURSE HISTORIANS

Some historians of nursing have seen Strachey's essay as a precis of Cook's two volume narrative. For example, Beatrice and Philip Kalisch in 1983 describe it as offering "a summarization of Cook's narrative."[10] They conclude that Strachey's essay has "the unmistakable advantage over Cook of brevity and a more vibrant style."[11]

Marylouise Welch, in her 1986 article, "Nineteenth-Century Philosophic Influences on Nightingale's Concept of the Person," uses a statement from Strachey[12] to support Nightingale's empirical position that learning is based on experience. Most recently, Anne Hudson Jones in her 1988 book, *Images of Nurses*, accepts without question that

> Strachey wrote a 68-page character sketch designed to expose the true Florence Nightingale and debunk the popular notion of her.[13]

She refers to another incident as being "the factual story given by Cook and Strachey."[14]

Strachey's influence on even a more disseminated media, the film, is also acknowledged. The Kalischs point out that in nine film dramatizations of Nightingale's life between 1922 and 1965, four have Strachey as their source.[15] Jones reminds us that the American Nurses' Association in 1936 endorsed *The White Angel*, a film based on Strachey's biography.[16] She ends her article about the film by pointing out that "the filmmakers used the best known and most reliable sources available to them."[17]

Given the interest of scholars in critical analysis and revisionist nursing history the question emerges as to the importance of Strachey's biography of Nightingale. One might ask, taking a query from W.H. Greenleaf's critique of Mrs. Woodham-Smith's biography of Nightingale, what does the book add to our understanding of her life and character?[18]

COOK'S/STRACHEY'S MODEL OF BIOGRAPHY WRITING

It is apparent that Strachey had a frame of reference within which he wrote his portrait and that his writing can be assessed by his manifesto for modern biography,[19] that is, brevity and freedom of the author's spirit to "lay bare the facts of the case, as he understands them."[20] As well as these two, I will address an additional five criteria: two are Cook's 1914 standards: honesty[21] and relevancy is one,[22] while the need for a villain another, and three further measures presented by Edel in 1981, the reliability of witnesses,[23] the style of telling a life[24] and the involvement of the biographer with the protagonist.[25] Without destroying the creativity of a writer such as Strachey, let us look at each one of these seven criteria in relation to examples from his study.

Brevity

Strachey meant by brevity excluding "everything that is redundant and nothing that is significant."[26] He could afford to argue for brevity in choosing Nightingale as a subject. After all he did have Cook's 944 pages upon which to base his fifty-one pages. Strachey did acknowledge that without Cook's biography he would not have been able to write his study.[27] Thus it is logical, according to Cook's criteria in which brevity is dependent upon whether or not the "person's life-story [has] been told before,"[28] that when "most of the relevant facts" are known "brevity is . . . the wise counsel."[29] However, it is only by reading Cook's biography that the reader can understand Nightingale's development of purpose and character. Cook's story depicts Nightingale's earlier years as a period of chracter building."[30] Strachey has used brevity to present a truncated version supporting his image of Nightingale as a woman possessed.

Selection and Arrangement

Selection and arrangement are criteria encompassed in Strachey's phrase "freedom of spirit."[31] As early as 1909, he enunciated his creed, that like Livy he would alter the outcome of a battle if the style of writing demanded it.[32] I would argue that Strachey did this when he chose two stories to use as examples of Nightingale's drive to be a nurse.

Both situations selected by Strachey are considered trivial by Cook; each has been manipulated by Strachey to suit his purpose. The first story is about Nightingale and the collie dog. Strachey writes, "Why was she driven now . . ., to put her dog's wounded paw into elaborate splints as if it was a human being?"[33] If a reader had not read Rosalind Nash's criticisms,[34] or Cook's biography this story would certainly support Strachey's thesis of Nightingale as a woman driven to be a nurse; but, according to Nash, a cousin of Nightingale,[35] it is only a trivial incident included by Cook to ward off recriminations from those who knew of the story protesting it had been omitted.[36] Nash points out that the collie story originally, was told by someone who was writing to Nightingale after she had become a national heroine, and secondly, that the shepherd's working dog was actually treated with "ordinary hot-water fomentations" for a "badly bruised" leg.[37]

Cook, in his inclusion of the pastor's letter regarding this incident, considers the use of such a tale as "a natural temptation of biographers to give a formal unity to their subject" by magnifying "some childish incident as prophetic of what is to come thereafter."[38] Strachey, in construing that it was actually Florence's dog, that splints were applied, and that she provided the care, falls into this trap.

The other incident concerns Nightingale's mending of dolls. In *Eminent Victorians*, Strachey writes "Why, as a child in the nursery, when her sister had shown a healthy pleasure in tearing her dolls to pieces, had *she* shown an almost morbid one in sewing them up again?"[39] This depiction was taken from Cook's statement, "It has been recorded that she used to nurse and bandage the dolls which her elder sister damaged."[40] The paradox for Strachey is that his selection of both incidents is lamentable: since each story depicts behaviours to be found in other children, emphasis in his study is out of proportion to their importance. Whereas these two vignettes, the dog and the dolls, appear in an approximately 1000 page biography by Cook, Strachey has not only selected them both for his fifty-one page sketch thus exaggerating their importance but he has distorted their content to promote his image of Nightingale as driven, since childhood, to be a nurse.

Honesty and Relevancy

The third criteria combines honesty and relevancy. I would argue that Strachey was true to writing as an art but that he was not honest to his subject. The instance chosen is short but discloses Strachey's unfairness to the emotional side of Nightingale. He describes Sidney Herbert as being taught by, shaped by, absorbed by, and dominated through and through by Nightingale.[41] As for Arthur

Clough, he "immediately fell under the influence of Miss Nightingale."[42] In order to support his contention that Herbert and Clough were controlled by Nightingale, Strachey takes a letter out of context and changes the meaning of the original to suit his purpose. He writes

> As for the spirit of self-sacrifice, well--Sidney Herbert and Arthur Clough were men, and they indeed had shown their devotion; but women
> . . .! She would mount three widow's caps 'for a sign'.[43]

The original, as written by Nightingale to Madame Mohl, is

> But I would mount three widows' caps on my head, "for a sign." And I would cry, This is for Sidney Herbert, This is for Arthur Clough, and This, the biggest widow's cap of all, is for the loss of all sympathy on the part of my dearest and nearest [Aunt Mai].[44]

The key words at issue are "devotion," used by Strachey, and "sympathy" used by Nightingale. The Oxford Dictionary defines the former as meaning the quality of being devoted i.e., dedicated to a person; the latter is defined as an affinity between certain things by which they are affected by the same influence.[45] Here I would stress the differentiation between being dedicated to and having an affinity with someone. In the letter, Nightingale is responding to Madame Mohl's book, *Madame Recamier*, and to a conclusion that 'women are more sympathetic than men'.[46] Two examples, which Nightingale uses are Herbert and Clough. The former: "a statesman . . ., out of sympathy with me, remodels his whole life and policy"; and the latter, "a poet born if ever there was one, takes to nursing-administration in the same way, for me."[47] And what is this sympathy, it is not devotion but affinity. Nightingale continues,

> I cannot understand how Mme Recamier could give "advice and sympathy" to such opposite people . . .. I am sure I never could have given "advice and sympathy" to Gladstone

and S. Herbert--men pursuing opposite lines of policy. Also I am sure I never could have been the friend and adviser of Sidney Herbert, . . ., by simply keeping up the tone of general conversation on promiscuous matters. We debated and settled *measures* together. That is the way we did it.[48]

The substitution of "devotion" for the original "sympathy" by Strachey supports his thesis of domination, but he has altered Nightingale's meaning.

Need for a Villain

Another criteria fulfilled by Strachey, and discussed by Cook, is the need of the biographer for a villain,[49] that is, a contrasting person to act as a foil for the subject. The most dramatic villain for Strachey is Lord Panmure whose nickname of "Bison" provided Strachey with the opportunity to delight the reader. Though Strachey writes that it is Lord Panmure's friends who call him "the Bison,"[50] according to Cook, it is Nightingale and her friends who gave him the appellation.[51] How this descriptive epithet "Bison" affected Strachey's selection may be difficult to assess; nevertheless, over one-third of his study concerns Nightingale's successful fight with Lord Panmure over the re-organization of the military medical service and her unsuccessful attempts to re-organize the War Office. Events which have less evident villains received only passing notice, for example, hospital and workhouse reform, her training school for nurses and the Sanitary Commission in India.[52]

Reliability of Witnesses

Researchers may feel it is unnecessary to assess the reliability of witnesses in Strachey's study because he has used Cook's work as his source, an opus of such excellent quality that it has continued to receive the homage of writers of nursing history.[53] Nash faults

Strachey for the use of an example from Cook's biography; unfortunately it is one for which Cook has failed to provide a reference. She considers that Strachey has created an anachronism[54] when he chose to write that Nightingale said, at the time of Sidney Herbert's decision to move from the House of Commons to the House of Lords, "'One fight more, the best and the last'."[55] Nash comments that "unfortunately he [Strachey] did not remember that Miss Nightingale could not have quoted *Prospice* [a poem by Robert Browning] in 1861, as it was not published till 1864."[56] Furthermore, she adds, Cook used the quote to foreshadow "that this was to be the last fight of the two friends in another sense than they knew."[57]

I would argue that in this situation Strachey cannot be completely faulted for the error. Cook does not identify the source of the quotation and in his book it does appear to have been Nightingale who uttered it.[58] If the fault lies in a poorly identified quotation in the biography by Cook, it is only compounded by Strachey's use of it.

Style of Telling a Life

The style of telling a life is a very personal characteristic of an author. A year before Strachey wrote his study of Nightingale he read Cook's two volumes, "having turned down the offer of writing this book himself, he was particularly interested to see the kind of woman" Cook had depicted.[59]

Strachey's style of brevity and wit portrays Nightingale as living in a vacuum. For example, he writes

So she dreamed and wondered, and, taking out her diary, she poured into it the agitations of her soul . . .

As the years passed, a restlessness began to grow upon her. She was unhappy, and at last she knew it . . . She would think of nothing but how to satisfy that singular craving of hers

to be *doing* something.[60]
A reading of Cook's first volume provides the
knowledge that there was a confluence of events and
persons. Throughout her childhood and early
adulthood Nightingale met people with similar
interests: primarily male philanthropists who were
actively involved in doing good. She was meeting men
like Dr. Ward Howe, a visitor with the Nightingales in
1844, who had "formulated a scheme to make . . .
nursing available, without payment, to any American
Citizen who was aged or ill."[61] Howe supported her in
her desire to study nursing.[62]

Involvement of Biographer with Subject

The final criteria to be discussed is the degree
of involvement of the biographer with the subject,
that is, the interposition of the author between the
reader and the protagonist.[63] Few people would argue
that *Eminent Victorians* is more a vehicle for Strachey
than for Nightingale. Humphrey House in a BBC
program on July 13, 1948 spoke of Strachey as
presenting people in ludicrous situations and
surrounding them with pervasive mockery.[64]
Michael Holroyd, the biographer of Strachey,
states that this style of writing was the outcome of
Strachey's alternations in his personal life between
"submission and mortification" in his passionate
friendships. Ultimately this behaviour produced
within Strachey "a poison of accumulating resentment
which was to find its most powerful outlet in *Eminent
Victorians*."[65] The projection of such emotion was felt
by his readers; James Pope-Hennessy in a review of
Strachey's works writes that Strachey's portrait of
Nightingale taught "adolescents to snigger" at her
name.[66] Nevertheless, according to a *Times Literary
Supplement* reviewer, Strachey came closest in the
Nightingale essay to expressing admiration for a
person.[67]
It is well known that Strachey had turbulent
bi-sexual relationships.[68] These may have influenced

his need to hint at Nightingale's sexual behaviour. As
he describes it

> Hitherto, her lovers had been nothing to her
> but an added burden and a mockery; but now-
> -For a moment, she wavered. A new feeling
> swept over her--a feeling which she had never
> known before, which she was never to know
> again.[69]

It is not clear as to whether Strachey was referring to
a male-female relationship or a female-female
connection. According to Cook there was a cousin and
another man (both unnamed) to whom Nightingale was
attracted, but we learn from Cook that Nightingale
would never have considered marrying the cousin.[70]

Another possibility was Nightingale's
friendship with Marianne Nicholson. Cook describes
Marianne's relationship to Florence as a girlhood
friendship, "a great friend."[71] It is not until 1950 that
we find, according to Cecil Woodham-Smith, that the
cousin, Henry Nicholson, had formed an attachment to
Nightingale which she encouraged because it brought
her "closer to Marianne," Henry's sister. During 1846,
writes Woodham-Smith, she had "been seized by a
'passion', the most serious of all her 'passions', for her
cousin, Marianne Nicholson."[72] If Strachey was
referring to this relationship between Florence and
Marianne (commonly called a "Boston Friendship": an
acceptable love relationship between 19th century
women)[73] as a "new feeling" he might have been doing
so out of his own experiences of homosexuality.

Another example which may reflect Strachey's
own experience is his vivid picture of Nightingale and
the Crimea. I would contend that his "freedom of
spirit" to portray the event as he wished was
constrained by earlier experiences in Liverpool. First,
he follows Cook's content faithfully. Even Nash
admits that "the account of the barrack hospital at
Scutari on the whole runs spendidly in speed and
vigour."[74] But then is this the result of his student days
in Liverpool? During that time he witnessed, while on
expeditions with a Dr. Stookes, many sordid scenes.
Holroyd contends that this made a lasting impression

on Strachey which "imbued his writing on the squalor of the Crimean War . . . with an unusual simplicity and austere power."[75]

Without doubt, Strachey wrote a memorable book. In 1981, Elizabeth Longford titled her book *Eminent Victorian Women*[76] as a tribute to Strachey not for his style but because "without Strachey's brilliant and savage inventions" the idea for the book "might not have arisen."[77] Nancy Boyd also acknowledged the contribution of Strachey in her book *Josephine Butler, Octavia Hill, Florence Nightingale;*[78] she titled her chapter on Nightingale, "Eminent Victorian" because her portrait had its place in "Lytton Strachey's gallery of 'eminent Victorians'."[79]

CONCLUSION

Now we can answer Greenleaf's question posed earlier in the paper as to what Strachey's study adds to our understanding of Nightingale's life and character? In the end Strachey has contributed nothing to our knowledge except, as Nash described it, he moved Nightingale from one extreme to another: she is no longer a saint but a fiend.[80] His portrait, unlike Cook's, contains deliberate errors and fallacies.

Strachey's fame lies in his ushering in, what has become known as the era of "new" biography; and his notoriety, in the handling of information. That is, at the time of publication, his story rejected the standard two volume life history for one of brevity, wit and irreverence. But I conclude that in so doing he manipulated his selected content for a purpose other than, as he stated, to "elucidate certain fragments of the truth" about the Crimean war heroine.

NOTES

I would like to acknowledge the useful criticism given by Professor Phyllis Grosskurth to an earlier version of this paper and Lynn Kirkwood's thoughtful comments.

1.   Examples of some of the books are, Eliza F. Pollard, *Florence Nightingale: The Wounded Soldier's Friend*, London: S.W. Partridge & Co., n.d.; Sarah Tooley, *The Life of Florence Nightingale* London: Cassell and Company, Ltd., 1907; Maude E. Seymour Abbott, *Florence Nightingale: As Seen in Her Portraits*, Montreal: McGill University, n.d..

2.   Liam Lacey, "Portrait of War Poets' Friendship Poignant but Static," *Globe and Mail* (Toronto), 16 July 1988, C2.

3.   John Wilson, "The War to End All Wars," *Globe and Mail* (Toronto), 11 November 1988, A7.

4.   Ira Bruce Nadel, *Biography: Fiction, Fact and Form*, London: The Macmillan Press Ltd., 1984, 163.

5.   Lytton Strachey, *Eminent Victorians*, England: Penguin Books, 1948.

6.   Sir Edward Cook, *The Life of Florence Nightingale*, 2 vols., London: Macmillan and Co., Ltd., 1913.

7.   Sir Edward Cook, "The Art of Biography," chap. in *Literary Recreations*, London: Macmillan and Co., Ltd., 1919, 1-33.

8.   Leon Edel, "Biography and the Science of Man," in *New Directions in Biography*, ed. Anthony M. Friedson, Hawaii: University Press of Hawaii, 1981, pp. 1-11.

9.   "Notes on Contributors," *Biography* 10 (Fall 1987): 375.

10.   Beatrice J. Kalisch and Philip A. Kalisch, "Heroine Out of Focus: Media Images of Florence Nightingale. Part I: Popular Biographies and Stage Productions," *Nursing & Health Care* 4 (April 1983): 182.

11.   Kalisch and Kalisch, "Heroine Out of Focus," 184.

12.   Marylouise Welch, "Nineteenth-Century Philosophic Influences on Nightingale's

Concept of the Person," *Journal of Nursing History* 1 (April 1986): 8.

13. Anne Hudson Jones, "*The White Angel* (1936): Hollywood's Image of Florence Nightingale," in *Images of Nurses: Perspectives from History, Art, and Literature,* ed. Anne Hudson Jones Philadelphia: University of Pennsylvania Press, 1988, 223.
14. Ibid., p. 229.
15. Kalisch and Kalisch, "Heroine Out of Focus," 182.
16. Jones, ed., *Images of Nurses*, p. 176.
17 Jones, "*The White Angel*", 240.
18. W.H. Greenleaf, "Biography and the 'Amateur' Historian: Mrs. Woodham-Smith's 'Florence Nightingale'," *Victorian Studies* 3 (December 1959): 192.
19. Leon Edel, *Literary Biography,* London: Rupert Hart-Davis, 1957, 105n.
20. Strachey, *Eminent Victorians*, p. 10.
21. Cook, "The Art of Biography," 20.
22. Ibid., p. 9.
23. Edel, "Biography and the Science of Man," 11.
24. Ibid., 11.
25. Ibid., 11.
26. Strachey, *Eminent Victorians*, p. 10.
27. Strachey, Ibid., 11.
28. Cook, "The Art of Biography," p. 8.
29. Ibid., 8.
30. Cook, *The Life of Florence Nightingale*, vol. 1, xxiv.
31. Strachey, *Eminent Victorians*, p. 10.
32. Michael Holroyd, "Eminent Victorians," chap. in *Lytton Strachey: A Biography,* London: William Heinmann Ltd., 1967, 262.
33. Strachey, *Eminent Victorians*, p. 112.
34. Rosalind Nash, "Florence Nightingale According to Mr. Strachey," *Nineteenth Century* 103 (February 1928): 258-265.
35. Cook, *The Life of Florence Nightingale*, I, viii.
36. Nash, "Florence Nightingale," p. 258.
37. Ibid., 258.

38.　Cook, *The Life of Florence Nightingale*, I, 13.
39.　Strachey, *Eminent Victorians*, p. 112.
40.　Cook, *The Life of Florence Nightingale*, I, 13.
41.　Strachey, *Eminent Victorians*, p. 139.
42.　Ibid., 140.
43.　Ibid., 150.
44.　Cook, *The Life of Florence Nightingale*, II, 13, 15.
45.　*The Oxford Universal Dictionary*, 1955, 3rd rev. ed., s.v. "devotion," "sympathy."
46.　Cook, *The Life of Florence Nightingale*, vol. II, 14.
47.　Ibid., II, 14.
48.　Ibid., II, 16.
49.　Cook, "The Art of Biography," p. 29.
50.　Strachey, *Eminent Victorians*, p. 137.
51.　Cook, *The Life of Florence Nightingale*, I, 325.
52.　Strachey, *Eminent Victorians*, p. 151.
53.　Cecil Woodham-Smith, *Florence Nightingale 1820-1910*, London: Constable, 1950, p. vi; Anne Summers, review of *Florence Nightingale: Reputation and Power*, by F.B. Smith, In *History Workshop Journal* 14 (Autumn 1982): 153.
54.　Nash, "Florence Nightingale," p. 263.
55.　Strachey, *Eminent Victorians*, p. 148.
56.　Nash, "Florence Nightingale," p. 263.
57.　Ibid., 263.
58.　Cook, *The Life of Florence Nightingale*, I, 403.
59.　Michael Holroyd, *Lytton Strachey: A Biography*, Middlesex, England: Penguin Books, 1980; 1979, 583.
60.　Strachey, *Eminent Victorians*, p. 112.
61.　Woodham-Smith, "Florence Nightingale," p. 48.
62.　Cook, *The Life of Florence Nightingale*, I, 44.
63.　Cook, "The Art of Biography," p. 24.
64.　Humphrey House, "The Present Art of Biography," chap. in *All in Due Time*, Freeport, New York: Books for Libraries Press, 1955, 261.
65.　Holroyd, *Lytton Strachey*, (1980), p. 105.
66.　James Pope-Hennessy, Review of *The*

Collected Work of Lytton Strachey, by Lytton Strachey, in *Spectator* 182 (25 February 1949): 264.

67. *Times Literary Supplement*, Review of *Eminent Victorians*, by Lytton Strachey, 852 (16 May 1918): 230.
68. Holroyd, *Lytton Strachey*, (1980), pp. 645, 696-697.
69. Strachey, *Eminent Victorians*, p. 114.
70. Cook, *The Life of Florence Nightingale*, I, 98.
71. Ibid., 29.
72. Woodham-Smith, *Florence Nightingale*, p. 33.
73. Carroll Smith-Rosenberg, "The Female World of Love and Ritual: Relations Between Women in Nineteenth-Century America," in *Women's Experience in America*, ed. Esther Katz and Anita Rapone, New Brunswick, N.J.: Transaction Books, 1980, p. 259.
74. Nash, "Florence Nightingale . . ." p. 259.
75. Holroyd, *Lytton Strachey*, (1980), p. 116.
76. Elizabeth Longford, *Eminent Victorian Women* London: Papermac, 1982, Weidenfeld and Nicolson Ltd., 1981.
77. Ibid., p. 7.
78. Nancy Boyd, *Josephine Butler, Octavia Hill, Florence Nightingale: Three Victorian Women Who changed Their World*, London: Macmillan Press Ltd., 1982.
79. Ibid., 167.
80. Nash, "Florence Nightingale . . ." p. 265.

THE RECLUSE: A RETROSPECTIVE
HEALTH HISTORY OF
FLORENCE NIGHTINGALE

by

Shirley Veith

When Florence Nightingale returned from the Crimean War in 1856, she was thirty-six years of age. Although she was described at that time as being in a weak state of physical health, there is no indication that she was an invalid. Yet, after that time she made no public appearances, accepted no invitations, saw only selected visitors, and literally took to her bed. In fact, she remained in relative isolation until her death in 1910 at the age of 90. In spite of agreement in the literature that Nightingale was ill when she returned from the Crimean War, there is disagreement as to why she assumed such a bed-bound posture for so many years. Until recently, it was believed that the after effects of Crimean fever, or pressures of work forced her into retirement. More recently, however, with the advent of psycho-history Nightingale has been described as a psychoneurotic who lusted for power and fame. Smith, for example, argues that she took to her bed after the Crimean War as a way to continue the power game she had established in the Crimea.[1]

Although numerous hypotheses have been posed as explanations for Nightingale's reclusive behavior, the relationship between her self-imposed isolation and the literature on females and disease in the 19th century has not yet been explored. The problem under investigation is what role did 19th century culture play in Nightingale's invalidism. Biographies and 44 letters written by her and housed in the Clendening History of Medicine Library at the Kansas University Medical Center were examined for patterns of physical symptoms, communicable disease, signs of psychoneurosis, substance abuse, and societal deviance. Preliminary work suggested that neither physical factors nor their long-term effects should be overlooked as a possibility for Nightingale's reclusiveness. Throughout her lifetime she was diagnosed as having at least the following four illnesses: Crimean fever, sciatica, rheumatism, and dilatation of the heart. Each of the four has the potential for crippling side effects and for establishing a pattern of excessive bed rest. Therefore, the hypothesis for this study is: in the absence of medical knowledge, Nightingale's ailments became chronic and tormented her life without ending it.

Florence Nightingale was born into a society characterized by widely disparate social structures and gender expectations. The history of females and disease in the 19th century is important to an understanding of her invalidism. This relationship requires a brief look backward at females and their health care in 19th century English society. Two themes dominate the historiography of females and disease in the 19th century. The first one is woman as invalid by nature. According to this explanation, women were at the mercy of their biology and thus, a disturbance of the uterus appears to have been instrumental in females aquiring the expectation of invalidsm.[2] Since the viewpoint of woman as an invalid by nature was generally confined to the upper and middle classes, it has been linked with the idea of pure idleness as a sign that a superior lifestyle had been achieved.[3] Various reasons have been offered as explanations for women's taking to illness; first--it was an escape from boredom. Second, it was a means to get away from the pressing demands of the bedroom and kitchen. Third, it indicated an inability to cope with ambiguity of role.

The second theme which dominates the literature is that of woman as victim.[4] This theme suggests that nineteenth century physicians were hostile to their female patients and expressed their animosity in the painful and ineffective therapy they administered.[5] This situation was particularly so among health reformers who idealized the woman's place in the home concept by giving it scientific status. Most writers concede that physicians may not have been conscious of the various complications of their opinions. Nevertheless, according to such interpretations, medical treatment is seen as the mechanism by which social restraint of females was perpetrated by some doctors.

An emerging theme in the history of females and disease is that female invalidism was not due to nature or cultural forces, but rather to the absence of sufficient medical knowledge. Scholars who support this explanation argue that there were numerous women in the nineteenth century who did not expect to live through the next year, yet survived into their eighties and nineties. Supporters of this explanation admit that the evidence of longevity may be ambiguous. Nevertheless, inherent in the theme is the suggestion that without adequate medical knowledge, disease and ailments may have become chronic and made their victim's life a torment without ending it.[6] The theme of women as chronically ill served as the framework for this study.

AN ANALYSIS OF NIGHTINGALE'S HEALTH

Little information was found about Nightingale's birth, other than birthplace and parentage. From a genetic perspective, her family background suggests the potential for a long life as well as for a chronic illness. Her father, Wen, died at the age of 92 when he fell down as he went upstairs to get a newspaper. Fanny, Nightingale's mother, lived into her nineties (93) but was an invalid for many years because of rheumatism. Like Fanny, Nightingale's sister, Parthe, also was an invalid because of rheumatoid arthritis. On the paternal side, her Aunt Mai also suffered from rheumatoid disease and became an invalid. She, too, lived into her nineties.

Childhood and adolescence appear to have been relatively healthy times for Nightingale. The only indication of health problems during this time comes from Irene Palmer, a Nightingale scholar, who suggests that Nightingale's problems with sciatica and with her spine may have had their origins in some event in her youth. She supports this suggestion by the fact that Florence Nightingale wore corrective shoes, but offers no reason for such therapy. Palmer appears to be the first investigator to attempt to trace Nightingale's invalidism to physical causes. Yet her paper, "Florence Nightingale: The Myth and the Reality," only briefly discusses recurring sciatica, spinal troubles, and post menopausal osteoporosis as possible explanations for Nightingale's illness.[7] Instead, most of the space is devoted to discounting rumors about Nightingale's sexuality, morphine addiction, and a venereal disease.

If her youth was relatively healthy, young adulthood was a troublesome time for Nightingale. Throughout the decade, 1842-1852, she had several severe episodes of mental illness. She had dreams, fantasies, depression, and, in 1849 was described as "on the verge of mental collapse."[8] It is unclear whether or not medical advice was sought for Nightingale's illness at this time. What is clear is that her family prescribed the therapy. Typical of the nineteenth century upper class, Mr. and Mrs. Nightingale arranged trips to Rome and England for their daughter in the hopes that such excursions would not only change her mind about nursing but also encourage her to take her proper role in upper class English society, i.e., marriage and a family. The trips, however, had the opposite effect. After an inspection of Kaiserswerth following the Rome trip, Nightingale clearly expressed her disdain for the idle Victorian woman. She wrote a 32 page pamphlet in less than a week, incidentally, to English women who she viewed as "going mad for want of something to do."[9] Nightingale's prescription for the "busy idleness" of such women was work, happiness, and comradeship, all of which awaited them at Kaiserwerth.

Although there is general agreement in the literature that Nightingale had mental problems from 1842 to 1852, several other health related factors also need to be considered. In the summer of 1844, for example, Nightingale went to Lea Hurst, the family's summer home, and is described as ailing all through the autumn. At Christmas she was still too ill to go with her mother and sister to Waverly, but did convalesce within the next fortnight or so. Although most biographers of Nightingale link this rather lengthy illness to the fact that it preceeded her vocational revelation, Pickering is more cautious. He suggests that such a psychologically based diagnosis may be speculative.[10]

In support of Pickering's suggestion it should be noted that "during the summer of 1844 there was scarlet fever in the cottages at Lea Hurst, and she (Nightingale) was forbidden to go near them."[11] Because of Nightingale's penchant for the poor and sick, and because of her previous activity of spending the greater part of the day in the cottages, and her independent nature, it is possible that she did go to the cottages even though forbidden to do so. Since she was ailing for a lengthy time, from autumn to Christmas, the speculation of complications from a communicable disease must be considered. For whatever reason, scarlet fever was not reported for Nightingale. Nevertheless, the possibility exists that her illness at the time could have been scarlet fever or a related disease caused by streptococcus. Such a cause could account for the cardiac problems she experienced later in life.

Consideration also needs to be given to the fact that Nightingale had two episodes of an apparent communicable disease within a short period of time. In

1853 Nightingale made several trips to Paris studying and investigating various hospitals. June of this year found her staying with M. and Madame Mohl and inspecting the Maison de la Providence Hospital when she contracted measles. Nightingale herself describes this illness as a "calamity." She writes, "It really was not my fault. There were no measles at any of the posts and I had them not 18 months ago, so that, erect in the consciousness of that dignity, I should not have kept out of their way, if I had seen them. The doctor would not believe I could have had them before. I had got rid of the eruption and all that before I came." In any event convalescence was rapid and Nightingale returned to London on July 13, 1853.

     Nightingale's "calamity" as she called it demonstrates the absence of medical knowledge in 1853. She herself was confused at having measles twice in a short period of time and the physician likewise was surprised and doubtful. With hindsight, the implications of "eruptions" raise some interesting speculations. Having measles at the age of 32 itself is rather unusual, so were either of these illnesses measles? What did the "eruptions" indicate? Was it something which created health problems later in life? Is it possible that Nightingale had systemic lupus erythematosus (SLE)?

     Although there is no indication in the literature that Nightingale had SLE, it is by no means an impossibility.[13] She had, as noted earlier, several manifestations which frequently occur with SLE. These included cutaneous, arthritic, psychologic, and cardiopulmonary symptoms. Moreover, Nightingale frequently complained of weakness, which is an accompaniment to SLE, and often one of the first symptoms.[14] Nowadays physicians understand autoimmune diseases, such as SLE, and are forewarned of its implications. In Nightingale's time, the disease was not known and thus, the severity of the illness could not be appreciated.

     Moving from the speculative to the factual, biographical material clearly shows that Nightingale was seriously ill from Crimean fever in 1855. But specific symptomatology, treatment, and after effects are less clear. An 1858 book describing the medical-surgical history of the British Army which served in Turkey and the Crimea presents a fuzzy definition of Crimean fever; a low form of typhoid, or typhus, or perhaps malaria.[15] When Nightingale became ill in 1857, she herself hints that the fever at Balaclava repeated itself. Thus, numerous questions about the exact nature of her Crimean fever could be raised. Did she have malaria? Typhus? Typhoid? Were there any latent effects?

From the moment she returned to England, Nightingale began to spend more and more time in bed. As far as her health was concerned, nursing in the Crimean War had been a failure. Her old complaints of weakness, fatigue and fainting spells continued to hang on. And new complaints of sciatica, palpitations, and dysentery emerged, as did diagnoses of neurasthenia and heart problems. The winter of 1865–66 was a particularly bad time for Nightingale. In addition to her heart condition, she began to complain of severe back pain. Rheumatism of the spine was the diagnosis and massage was one of the prescribed therapies. However, this treatment gave her no relief and insomnia became an additional problem.[16] Nightingale described the situation as follows: "I have suffered so very much all the winter and spring for which nothing did me any good but a curious new fangled little operation of putting opium in under the skin, which relieves one for 24 hours, but does not improve the vivacity or serenity of one's intellect."[17] The extent to which she used this treatment is not known.

Nevertheless, there are several reasons why it is not impossible that Nightingale became a habitual taker of opium. First, she was exposed to the drug and seemed to enjoy it. Even one of her staunchest admirers admits she might have used the drug sparingly.[18] Second, Nightingale received the morphine because of undiagnosed and persistent pain; reasons which have since been proven to be one of the most common methods of initiation to the drug habit.

Third, nineteenth century treatment of neurasthenia consisted of a variety of hygenic suggestions and some medication, including opium.[19] One of Nightingale's diagnoses was neurasthenia. Fourth, in Nightingale's time the risk of addiction to opium was neither well known nor appreciated by health care professionals. Even if Nightingale herself had known or appreciated the risks of taking opium, chances are she could easily have ignored them in the belief that she was dying. In the years of her reclusiveness she was thought to be near death at least three times. In each instance she, too, believed that she was going to die and went so far as to write instructions for her funeral. Yet each time she recovered and eventually lived to be ninety years of age.

Nightingale's expectations of not living through the next year, yet surviving into her nineties, is not atypical of a number of women of this period. One example of a similar case is Ann Phillips, wife of Wendell Phillips, the abolitionist. Like Nightingale, she voluntarily shut herself off from the rest of the world in the belief that she "grew sicker every year." Ann Phillips became a chronic invalid who complained of headaches, backaches, rheumatism, etc. She also was unable to read, write, see company or make calls. Yet, she outlived not only her husband who was usually in radiant health, but also many of her contemporaries.[20]

One could argue that Ann Phillips and Florence Nightingale were worlds apart as far as geography, marital status, and productivity. Phillips lived in the United States, was married, and appeared to live in pure idleness, even though tortured by ailments. Nightingale, on the other hand, was single, lived in England, and remained an active intellectual, encouraging and engineering multiple reforms long after she retreated from society.

Despite the differences between Phillips and Nightingale, numerous similarities also existed between the two women. For example, over the years of their invalidism, both wrote melancholy letters describing their ailments. In the case of Nightingale a theme of long-suffering runs through her letters in the collection at the Clendenning History of Medicine Library. Excerpts of her letters reflect this theme.[21]

Oct 2/66

Dear Madam (Mrs. Chalmers)

.... in response to kindly asking after my health--I am an incurable invalid, entirely a prisoner of my bed (except during a periodical migration) and overwhelmed with business--

> ever your faithful and
> grateful servant
> Florence Nightingale

Jan 26/72

Dear Sir (W. Clark, C.E.)

....
....

I am sorry not to have time or strength to write more by this mail -

> Yours sincerely,
> Florence Nightingale

London March 23/78

Madam:

.... Many thanks for your kind wishes about my health: overworked as I am, it is necessarily very bad, but I thank God who still gives me work to do for him. I am indeed entirely a prisoner to my room, except when once a year I take my widowed mother to Lea Hurst, now no longer ours ..

> believe me ever your
> faithful servant
> Florence Nightingale

> 10 South St.
> Park Lane W
> March 9/86

Dear Alice Hepworth:

Please accept the (Revised) Bible which has been waiting for you for so long; not but what I sent for it for you as soon as ever I heard from you, but I have been almost unfit to do anything--and am still--but what was absolutely necessary--from illness.
....

> God bless you all--and
> your children
>
> Ever yours sincerely
> Florence Nightingale

June 19/93

My dear Miss Lukes:

....
For the last 6 months I have been very ill--often
entirely forbidden to see people, even my own and
almost unable to do the most pressing business.

ever your sincerely
Florence Nightingale

An interesting aspect of the letters in the
Clendenning collection is the difference in
Nightingale's handwriting over the years. Not only did
the letters seem to be written in pencil as time
progressed, the the style changed from a flowing
Victorian script to a rather rough, shaky form.[22]
Although both women's letters reflect
melancholy themes, they each also maintained some of
their girlish interests. For Phillips it was flowers in her
room, spring birds outside her window and organ
music drifting up from the street. For Nightingale it
was greenery and flowers in her room, a fondness for
cats, her pet owl and solace in listening to music. Such
therapies suggest that Nightingale prescribed her own
treatments. In her *Notes on Nursing*, for example, she
writes that "wind instruments, including the human
voice, and stringed instruments, capable of continuous
sound have generally a soothing effect on invalids."[23]
Another commonality between Phillips and
Nightingale was that both were diagnosed as having
neurasthenia, a common diagnosis in the 19th century,
particularly among females. Neurastheniacs would
frequently show a peevish irritability and suffered
every kind of nervous disorder ranging from hysterical
fits of crying and insomnia to constipation,
indigestion, headaches and backaches. Although in the
19th century neurasthenia was thought to be
psychosomatic in nature, there is some sketchy
evidence that a physical component may have been

involved as well. A friend of Ann Phillips, for example, described Ann's illness as "one of those mysterious complaints in which organic disease is mixed up with a good deal that is imaginary."[24] Page Smith, in her book *Daughters of the Promised Land*, suggests that the cures of delicate and ailing women were prefectly sensible since ill health was often genuine as well as psychosomatic. Examples of such cures are wearing loose clothing, taking invigorating baths, long walks, and regular exercise.[25]

Whether Nightingale's ill health was genuine or imaginary, she maintained a reclusive state for fifty-four years of her life. A comparison of her health history to the literature on females and disease in the nineteenth century suggests that such behavior was not necessarily uncommon. The comparison also suggests that nineteenth century culture supported and perhaps encouraged Nightingale's invalidism. Yet other findings point to the need for further study of the role genetics and communicable or auto-immune diseases may have played in Nightingale's invalidism.

In the absence of a full medical record it is fruitless to probe deeper into the causes of Nightingale's invalidism. I would submit, however, that the hypothesis for this study was at least partially supported. Although the evidence is scanty, it suggests the possibility that Nightingale may have had an undiagnosed chronic illness, perhaps SLE. Over the years she complained of a lack of strength, inability to do anything, and very bad health to name a few symptoms. As a result of self-diagnosis, Nightingale determined she had an incurable disease, became an invalid, and followed her own prescription which included, among other activities, listening to music. I would further submit that the fact that Nightingale thought she was dying several times, yet lived to be 90, does not support the belief that her illness was psychosomatic. Medical ignorance, poor physician training, and cultural attitudes made it difficult, if not impossible, for doctors to accurately diagnose or cure most diseases.

NOTES

1. The most recent and most outspoken critic of Nightingale is Smith, F.B., *Florence Nightingale: Reputation and Power*, London: Croom Helm, 1982.

2. Wattaley, L.A., "Male Physicians and Female Health and Sexuality in 19th Century English and American Society," *Journal of Advanced Nursing*, 1983, 8, 423-428.

3. Brancha, P. "Image and Reality: The Myth of the Idle Victorian Woman," in M. Hartman and L.W. Banner (eds.) *Clio's Consciousness Raised*, New York: Harper Colophon, 1974. pp. 179-191.

4. Identification of this theme is attributed to Morantz, R., "The Lady and Her Physician," in M. Hartman and L.W. Banner (eds.) *Clio's Consciousness Raised*, pp. 38-53.

5. Several authors have dealt extensively with the medical treatment of female diseases in the nineteenth century including Barker-Benfield, B., "The Spermatic Economy: A Nineteenth Century View of Sexuality," *Feminist Studies* (Summer, 1973) pp. 45-74; Wood, A. "The Fashionable Diseases: Women's Complaints and their Treatment in Nineteenth-Century America," *Journal of Interdisciplinary History* 4 (Summer, 1973) pp. 25-52; Smith-Rosenberg, C., "The Hysterical Woman: Sex Roles and Role Conflict in Nineteenth-Century America," *Social Research*, 39 (Winter, 1972) pp. 652-678. Although Smith-Rosenberg is more cautious than the other two authors, all detect varying degrees of animosity in the behavior of physicians toward their female patients.

6. According to Wood, "The Fashionable Disease," p. 26, there was a sizeable number of women in this period who wanted or needed to

consider themselves ill as a way to escape their female responsibilities. She also points out that there are many diseases and ailments which in the absence of medical knowledge, can become chronic and make a victim's life painful, but not cause death.

7.   Like other admirers of Nightingale, some of whom are feminist, Palmer, I., "Florence Nightingale: The Myth and the Reality," *Nursing Times*, Aug. 3, 1983, pp. 40-42 finds it difficult to acknowledge that Nightingale was not perfect.

8.   Woodham-Smith, C. *Florence Nightingale*. New York: McGraw-Hill, 1951, p. 52.

9.   Pickering, G. *Creative Malady*, New York: Oxford University Press, 1974, pp. 99-177.

10.   Pickering, G. *Creative Malady*, p. 102 is a biographer of Nightingale who has clearly labeled her as a psychoneurotic. It is unusual for him to describe this particular illness of Nightingale's as one of an "unknown nature."

11.   Woodham-Smith, C. *Florence Nightingale*, p. 35.

12.   Cook, E. *The Life of Florence Nightingale* 2 vol. London: Macmillian & Co., 1913, p. 132.

13.   Brown Bag Lunch, Feb. 6, 1989. When Nightingale's health history was presented to a group of medical-surgical nursing experts, they raised the possibility of SLE. Based on her symptoms and the medical knowledge of today, it was felt that an auto-immune disease was a distinct possibility.

14.   Torbett, M. and Erwin, J., "The Patient with Systemic Lupus Erythematosis," *American Journal of Nursing*, Aug., 1977, pp. 1299-1302.

15.   Great Britain Army Medical Department, *Medical and Surgical History of the British Army which served in Turkey and the Crimea During the War Against Russia in the years 1954-55-56*. 2 vol. London: Harrison and Sons, 1858, pp. 162-166.

16.   Huxley, E. *Florence Nightingale*, New York:

G.P. Putnam's Sons, 1975, p. 27.

17. This often quoted remark is found in Cook, E. *The Life of Florence Nightingale*, p. 106. Although the evidence is certainly scanty, it raises numerous questions such as: What does she mean by "new-fangled"? Had she been taking it by mouth before? Or is the entire idea of taking opium new?

18. Palmer, I., "Florence Nightingale: The Myth and the Reality," p. 41.

19. Haller, J., "Neurasthenia," *New York State Journal of Medicine*, Oct. 1, 1970, pp. 2489-2497.

20. Ann Phillips' letters express a growing preoccupation with her own unhappiness. She complained that all her time was spent shuttling between bed, sofa and rocking chair in her own room. Somewhat like Nightingale, in Feb. 1845 she wrote, "I have had a dreadful winter, so sick that life is a burden to me." Bartlett, I., *Wendell Phillips: Brahmin Radical* Boston: Beacon Press: 1961, p. 78.

21. From the collection of Florence Nightingale letters in the Clendenning History of Medicine Library on the Kansas University Medical Center campus.

22. Fourteen Nightingale Letters, Departments of the History of Medicine and Nursing Education, The University of Kansas Medical Center, Kansas City, Kansas, 1962. (p. 11).

23. Nightingale, F., *Notes on Nursing: What it is and What it is Not*, London: Harrison & Sons, 1974 republication, p. 33.

24. Cited in Bartlett, I. *Wendell Phillips*, p. 79.

25. There is an interesting chapter on the illness of females in relation to their longevity in Smith, P., *Daughters of the Promised Land: Women in American History*, Boston: Little, Brown & Co. 1970, pp. 131-140.

WHAT MAKES A HEROINE? GIRLS' BIOGRAPHIES OF FLORENCE NIGHTINGALE

by

Martha Vicinus

If we confine our reading to famous nineteenth-century and twentieth-century novelists, essayists and poets, we will gain a limited view of contemporary attitudes toward women. Feminist scholars have examined minor fiction and poetry, diaries, letters and personal memorabilia, but few have looked at literature written for girls. Even experts on children's literature have largely concentrated on either such famous work as Lewis Carroll's *Alice in Wonderland* or on boys' literature.[1] In this essay I will examine one strand of girls' stories, popular biographies of heroines from the 1870s to the 1950s, in order to trace the ways in which girls were encouraged and discouraged from making their mark in the public sphere.

Biographies, unlike fiction or poetry, were presumed to be factual, but they were actually constructed fictions which incorporated selected facts of an individual's life. As such, the author had ample room to stress particular traits, in order to encourage the girl reader to emulate the best and to avoid the wrong. In the biographies written between 1870 and 1900 we find a focus upon religious faith and the channeling of innate inclinations. In those written during a period of militant feminism, 1900-1920, the

90

focus was upon progress and overcoming the constraints of society. Finally, in the 1950s biographies focused upon the psychological turmoil of choosing between heretosexual love and personal ambition. Victorian women have been stereotyped as epitomizing the ideology of domesticity, but by the 1870s girls were encouraged to take women's special virtues into the wider world. I will argue that the nineteenth-century biographies gave girls more freedom, more scope for public work, than those written in the mid-twentieth century, which emphasized romantic conflict over individual action.

NINETEENTH-CENTURY GIRLS' BIOGRAPHIES

Before the seventeenth century it would be difficult to imagine biographies of women that were not about either the religious or royalty; non-domestic roles were virtually non-existent. But by the mid-nineteenth century both boys and girls faced a vastly increased variety of public roles. Formulaic biographies mediated between young readers and the increasingly complex choices they might face by providing a series of clear cut moral questions and solutions. As models for public action, they were an important alternative to the more familiar domestic girls' stories, such as Alcott's *Little Women* (1867), or the school-adventure stories, such as those written by Angela Brazil.[2] As Edward Salmon explained, "Perhaps the best reading which girls can possibly have is biography, especially female biography, of which many excellent works have been published. One cannot help as one reads the biographies of great women--whether of Miss Florence Nightingale, Mrs. Fry, or Lady Russell--being struck by the purity of purpose and God-fearing zeal which moved most of their subjects."[3]
Although gender-specific, girls' biographies often were paired with those of boys'; for every *Noble Heroes* collection there was bound to be *Noble*

Heroines. The main figures share many of the same characteristics; courage, pluck, independence, initiative and "a noble character" are admired, regardless of gender. The sturdy Protestant activism of these stories is revealed in the titles: *Heroines Every Child Should Know, Pioneer Women in Victoria's Reign, Twelve Notable Good Women of the Nineteenth Century, The World's Workers, Clever Girls of Our Time* and *Women Who Win.* Girls are expected to be more home-loving and nurturing, but both sexes must overcome the same kinds of opposition, whether against cruel Nature, or an indifferent society or institutional mismanagement.

According to these biographies, characteristics nurtured in childhood gave a woman the courage, knowledge and understanding to face adversity and opposition. The biographer, however, had to define carefully appropriate independence of thought and action. As Jennie Chappell explained, "The eagerness must be curbed, the impetuosity restrained, the energies directed into right channels, and many are the conflicts which occur between the child and the parent, the pupil and the teacher, ay, and between the higher and lower nature of the subject himself, ere the victory for right alone is won."[4] Each of the "four noble women" described by Chappell struggles with an ungovernable temper and personal religious doubts before she is ready to fight in the public world. Nevertheless, assertiveness, obstinancy and high-spiritedness are redefined as valuable characteristics, for they enable the heorine to strike out on her own.

Child heroines, like saints of old, precociously prefigure their adult life. Catherine Booth, the future wife of the founder of the Salvation Army, saw a crowd jeering at a drunken man being led to prison: "Instantly a sense of profound pity for the unfortunate culprit overmastered the horror which a gently nurtured little girl must naturally have felt, and springing to the man's side, Kate walked with him to the lock-up."[5] One biographer of Nightingale archly commented, "The truth is, Florence was born to be a nurse, and a sick doll was dearer to her than a strong and healthy one. So I fear her dolls would have been invalids most of the time if it had not been for Parthenope's little family, who often required their Aunt Florence's care."[6]

The most Victorian characteristic of heroines, like their brother heroes, is the progress they bring to some part of the wider world. They act only for the greater glory of God and English-speaking peoples, and never for personal gain--but they are commemorated in a biography specifically because they are publicly successful. The praise of independent public action makes these stories potentially radical encounters for girl readers. Indeed, Eva Hope, author of *Grace Darling: The Heroine of the Farne Islands; Her Life, and Its Lessons* forthrightly declared, "A WOMAN'S WORK IS THAT WHICH SHE SEES NEEDS DOING":

> A woman should be so far free and independent as to do that which she feels to be right, no matter though the right seem to call her to heights which she had not occupied before. And if, in her ordinary avocations, she be allowed liberty of thought and action, there is the greater probability that, when the occasion comes which demands from her strength of nerve and firm endurance, she will not be found wanting.[7]

Every biographer insisted upon the necessity of fulfilling home duties before venturing into new fields. But the disjunction between the overt message and the narrative was too great. Stories of real-life adventure, such as Grace Darling's, simply do not encourage quiescence. Even as biographies purported to teach modesty and home duties, they awakened an imaginative affinity with active, public heroines.

Womanliness, however, remained essential. Heroines proved themselves in the public world, but never lost their femininity. Grace Darling, the daughter of a Northumbrian lighthouse keeper, rows out in the storm to save nine shipwrecked people, and then nurses them back to health. Mary

Somerville is a brilliant mathematician, but she is also an excellent seamstress. Alternatively, a heroine achieved status by taking the feminine qualities of spiritual and physical nurturing into the public sphere; women could see--and help--neglected and needy people where men could not.

FLORENCE NIGHTINGALE: A CASE STUDY

By examining different biographies of Nightingale over some eighty years we can see how the same life can be told so as to include or exclude very different material. Awkward facts about her life, for example, were virtually always excluded in Victorian accounts. Unlike most heroines, Nightingale came from a wealthy family; this potential liability was overcome by describing all that she gave up in order to become a nurse. The author of *Women Who Win* commented, "There was every comfort in her home that money could provide, and no one but a genuine philanthropist could have turned away from its attractions for the briefest season. But Providence had other and larger plans for her."[8] Since self-sacrifice was a key feminine virtue, Nightingale's sacrifice of balls, London night-life and country house parties was seen as a mark in her favor; the fact that she had loathed these activities was ignored. Nightingale's calculated decision to remain sick after returning from the Crimea in order to be free from family obligations was transformed into the price she had paid for her enormous labors on behalf of the English people. Her lobbying the government to reform the army, public health and India was suppressed in favor of her efforts to turn nursing into a respectable female occupation. Such alterations, of course, were common in all popular biographies. The formula denied political manipulation, and favored stereotyped womanly characteristics and work.

Most Nightingale biographies began by describing the heroine's early signs of vocation. A

favorite anecdote was little Florence's successful
nursing of the injured sheep-dog, Cap. She and the
local minister, who had fortuitously trained in
medicine, make the rounds of the local villagers.
They find Roger, the old shepherd, unable to herd
his sheep without Cap, who has been injured by
unruly boys; Roger must now kill Cap, because he
cannot afford to feed an animal that cannot work.
Florence and the minister hasten to Roger's cottage,
where they discover that Cap only has a bad bruise:
"It was dreadfully swollen, and hurt very much to
have it examined; but the dog knew it was meant
kindly, and though he moaned and winced with pain,
he licked the hands that were hurting him."[9] Under
the eye of the minister, Florence heats water and
applies hot compresses to bring the swelling down.
Only when Cap is obviously better do they leave. A
few days later when she meets Roger, he gratefully
tells her, "Do look at the dog, miss; he be so pleased
to hear your voice . . . I be greatly obliged to you,
miss, and the vicar, for what you did. But for you I
would have hanged the best dog I ever had in my
life."[10]

The incident is obviously over-determined.
"Michievous schoolboys"--the enemies of all right-
thinking girls--have commited the thoughtless crime
of harming a working farm animal. The young lady-
bountiful prevents a sad mistake from being
committed by the ignorant peasant-shepherd. Both
the dog and the shepherd are suitably thankful. Cap,
even when under great pain, does not nip those who
do him good; when he later hears Florence's voice,
he wags his tail in gratitude, but without taking his
eyes from the sheep he is guarding. Class privilege
and class lines are maintained by everyone, including
the dog, playing the appropriate role.[11]

Even more striking, however, is the audience
for Florence. She strengthens her natural, feminine
propensity to nurse under the eye of a caring male.
In many Victorian biographies men introduced girls
to the outside world, helped them to master
necessary skills, and gave them moral approval. Often

they were ministers, teachers or relatives--desexualized, even feminized, figures whom a girl was likely to know well. A minister, like a woman, expected to care for and sympathize with the poor; an uncle could be concerned with a niece's future without worrying about discipline; even a father could bend to a child's needs in ways that a mother would not. These men, however, only guide the heroine; she herself takes the lead, following a natural, pre-existing bent--to nurse, to study or to teach.

A major strategic difficulty faced by writers of girls' biographies was how to have the heroine overcome opposition without implying that she had a contentious spirit, or that she was disobedient to authority. Obviously no daughter could disobey her parents or a clergyman. Nightingale's complicated and tempestuous relationship with her mother and sister violated expected norms for both boys and girls; biographers focused on her close relationship with her father and ignored her mother (her sister, Parthenope, appears only as a fellow playmate). Heroines could suffer from bad tempers, temporary unbelief, or wilfulness; in turn, parents could misunderstand or lack sympathy for them and their causes. But family love was inviolate.

Opposition was best characterized as an abstraction, such as unbelief, worldliness, general ignorance or prejudice, or even bureaucratic "muddle." Specific persons or actions were never to blame, though sometimes temporarily benighted figures, such as an African chieftain or a military officer, could be shown changing his mind about a missionary or a nurse. One author described Nightingale's life in the Crimea as:

> . . . a most difficult one. Everything was in disorder, and every official was extremely jealous of interference. Miss Nightingale, however, at once impressed upon her staff the duty of obeying the doctors' orders, as she did herself. . . . it would take far too much space to give all the details of that kind

but strict administration which brought comparative comfort and a low death-rate into the Scutari hospitals."[12] Another more bluntly blames the inefficiency of the "authorities" and "officials" without naming names, "From the first the indomitable will of 'the Lady-in-Chief,' as she was called, made itself felt in every department, which gradually broke down all obstacles raised by the jealousy or bad tempers of the officials . . . At the end of six months the hospital arrangements had ben brought into order."[13]

Nightingale, with the help of her nurses, is the active agent who brings order out of military chaos, but the means by which she does so must be suppressed, lest it prove to be less than admirable. In order to avoid such complications as ambition, cunning, manipulation and even dishonesty, the narrative slips over the tiresome details of Nightingale's actual daily behavior to the end result of her work. A few examples of washing patients or insisting on medication for the dying speak for the whole. Or, a specific event will mythologize the heroine. Nightingale's silent, nightly rounds through the miles of wards, when the waiting soldiers were said to kiss her passing shadow, transforms her into the "Lady with the Lamp." Metonymy serves to cover the complexities of achieving social change.

But metonymy and narrative gaps also left room for the reader to insert herself. Too many uncomfortable details left little to the imagination. If formulaic biographies were to work successfully, they had to permit the reader imaginative escape into the life of the heroine. The reader, perhaps hopeful of a different, wider life, could interweave her inchoate dreams with the narrative. The simplified actions of the heroine made identification easy, regardless of how remote they might be from the reader's life. A shadowy Nightingale could be invested with desirable characteristics more easily than one encumbered with complex motivations. The creation of vivid symbolic behavior actually counteracted the tendency of the narrative to reify women. Even though the overt message was often womanly obedience, symbolic moments, such as Nightingale's nightly vigil, permitted an imaginative identification with independent action. Fiction--created by the reader and not just the author--was an essential part of these biographies.

TWENTIETH-CENTURY BIOGRAPHIES OF NIGHTINGALE

A number of interesting alterations occur in later biographies of Nightingale, although the formula remained one of overcoming personal difficulties and social opprobrium in order to bring public improvement. In the early twentieth century the progress made since Nightingale's childhood was trumpeted. A.L. Haydon in 1909 proudly wrote, "Sixty years ago . . . [l]ocal authorities were not generally pressing in their insistence on the observation of the ordinary laws of health, and the gospel of fresh air and cold water was one that was regarded as at least dangerous."[14] Roger and Cap continued to play a central role, but descriptions of Nightingale's home life began to appear, discreetly defined as her "gilded cage," for "she longed for some useful and definite work for which she might be trained so as to take an active part in a wider sphere of life."[15]

A major change in emphasis, however, was far more detail about the attractions of a wealthy life. What had been a subtheme, Nightingale's privileged social class, became a dominant characteristic to contrast with her desire to nurse. Self-sacrifice in and of itself was no longer attractive, so that it had to be redefined as the sacrifice of material goods. Similarly, opposition was abstracted and then personified, rather than being characterized as actual unnamed but real people. For example, Society is caricatured as moralistic spinisterish women by Constance Wakeford in her 1917 biography: "[T]he dear old Mid-Victorian ladies drew their shawls over their shoulders and held up their hands in horror at the very idea of a lady becoming such a low, unlady-like person as a nurse; and as for a woman going out to the battlefield, no such outrageous thing had ever been heard of!"[16] The material world and its attractions held center stage, rather than the spiritual strivings that filled an earlier generation of biographies.

In contrast to other twentieth-century biographies, the suffragists saw Nightingale as a great leader whose true accomplishments had been obscured. Marion Holmes, in a Women's Freedom League pamphlet, redefined Nightingale as a controversial figure reminiscent of the militant suffragists:

> Florence Nightingale, the strong, capable, "brainy" woman, the woman with force, the woman who exercised a bold authority, has been obscured by the persistent presentment of the Lady with the Lamp, gentle word here, a healing touch there. Even this one-sided and inadequate conception of her great work was accepted only after her mission proved an undeniable success. The most popular heroine in history had to pay the price that is exacted of all pioneers. Bitter venomous attacks, misrepresentation, irredemably vulgar slanders, signalled her departure for the Crimea. Before her name became for all time a name to conjure with, it was the butt for coarse wit and ridicule of the day.[17]

Militant feminists, who wished to widen the leadership opportunities for women, disliked the "Lady with the Lamp," and praised instead "a great administrator and sanitarian, a strong-minded, firm-handed genius." True heroines definitely did not fit the familiar mold of gentle, caring femininity.

By the interwar years, Lytton Strachey's *Eminent Victorians* and Sir Edward Cook's definitive biography had diminished Nightingale's reputation.

Her name appeared less frequently among biographies of famous women. But in the 1950s, Nightingale reappeared, suitably psychologized. She and her sister, Parthe, were no longer described as both interested in helping the poor; rather, Parthe was "entirely different" from her in her love of frivolity and easy living. Nightingale sounds like a typical idealistic adolescent in Yvonne ffrench's description:

> She was morbid, she was self-willed, and a real problem to her parents who could not understand why she should not be as happy and contented as her sister.
>
> She became thoroughly out of sympathy with her family, her relations and their attitude to everything. Even before she was a fully grown woman she was conscious of being set apart. She felt that she had a mission to do good in the world; she felt in some way called to a dedicated life, but what that was to be she did not know. It worried her.[18]

To appeal to the modern girl reader, Nightingale's family troubles replaced Roger and Cap. The result was an attractive modernizing of an old story, but also the loss of the palpable lesson of public duty taught by nursing Cap.

The twentieth century focus upon the temptations of material wealth and family quarrels subtly undermined the arguments for individual initiative and responsibility taught by the earlier versions. Moreover, the unspoken space between initial efforts and final success that had characterized Victorian biographies now became an insurmontable gap. A girl heroine who was busy fighting with her parents and giving up balls for sick neighbors might have been more accessible than the austere heroines of the past, but she was also less capable of independent action. Indeed, ffrench credited Richard Monckton Milnes, the man Nightingale loved in her twenties, with influencing her to take an interest in the poor. Romance, rather than early childhood inclination, became the impetus for doing public good. The incorporation of sex, however muted, into the formula biography shifted the plot from a girl's negotiation between self and the public world into a triangle of self, romance and public duty.[19]

READERS' RESPONSE TO GIRLS' BIOGRAPHIES

Biographies were probably most popular among girls during latency, when they were demarcating their public world, defining their non-emotional role in it, and gaining the skills necessary to negotiate within it. The plots encouraged girls to behave instrumentally rather than relationally, rationally rather than emotionally. How well a heroine got along with her mother, sister or friends was less important than her own self-control, knowledge and determination. These traits--unlike personal relations--might all appear to be within the control of a reader, at least imaginatively. To be a nurse under Nightingale, a social worker under Agnes Weston, or a prison visitor under Elizabeth Fry could be both attractive and possible. In effect, the biographies provided vicarious practice in the unnatural role of public service at a time when most girls usually had had too much practice in family duties.

But of even greater importance, I believe, was the subtext of the biographical plot. If we define school adventure stories as a means of coming to terms with homoerotic bonding, and romance as the journey toward heterosexual bonding, then the biographies are best seen as part of the process of individuation. Biographies, like the adventure story, ignore heterosexual conflict, but like the romance, they give male approval. They describe an individual girl's journey into the public world, with the assistance of a non-threatening, non-sexual male. The father, representative of freedom and privilege, gives approval to the heroine at crucial early stages in her struggle. An active, instrumental role is rewarded with emotional support.[20]

Mother-daughter conflict is avoided in biographies by giving the mother a narrowly defined role. She teaches the young girl the proper moral behavior, and then fades from the narrative. Occasionally the mother will reappear to criticize the heroine; although loving, she does not understand the nature of her daughter. Mary Sommerville had to fight her mother's distrust of learned ladies, while Grace Darling's mother opposed her rowing to the rescue of the shipwrecked. The father is absent during the child's initial training, but present--either himself or a surrogate--when she first acts in the public domain; his support makes her action both attractive and possible. Heroines don't seem to depend upon their parents as much as other people; they obligingly recede from the narrative to await her triumphal return. All past difficulties disappear upon her happy return. What more attractive fantasy than this?

Until the 1950s girls' biographies based their plots upon the opposition between the benighted public and the far-sighted heroine. Authors avoided introducing their young readers to sexual conflict. But the post-World War II era saw the growth of the "feminine mystique," with its emphasis upon romance, the nuclear family and the subordination of women to men. This is obviously reflected in stories for girls. Since heterosexual love was considered the central emotion in all women's lives, it obviously had to be included in biographies of public heroines. But the helpful male guide cannot be romanticized without the dramatic loss of psychological independence for the girl. In her 1954 biography Yvonne ffrench describes vividly the struggle Nightingale underwent before becoming a nurse:

> Gradually, very gradually a slow change in herself was being effected. A hardening process was beginning, and dedication to a cause replaced devotion to friendship. A deliberate renunciation of her friends

gradually followed, and in her private notes she made the final act of self-denial: 'Oh, God, no more love. No more marriage. Oh God.'[21]

ffrench is truer to Nightingale's actual experience, but what young woman would want to choose public service after reading about Nightingale's painful sacrifice of the sympathetic and helpful Richard Monckton Milnes? Who wants to struggle vicariously with Nightingale's dilemma? When the biographies focused upon the heroine's struggle to choose between romance and public duty, they became stories of a failed romantic heroine, rather than a successful public figure.

The mid-twentieth century changes in the formulaic biography point to both feminist and literary contradictions. If an author added romance to the narrative, the heroine's identity became defined by her desire. Once romance was admitted, a woman could not be portrayed as a whole person if she had rejected a suitor. Literary conventions gave a man, but not a woman, heroic stature based solely upon his public life, regardless of his personal needs. The articulation of personal conflicts may have enriched the narrative of biography, but the price was a loss in the presentation of women's choices. Girls who sought affirmation outside the home learnt that they could never escape their sexual identity--a lesson many feminists have been fighting their whole adult lives. Paradoxically, the single-minded two-dimensional heroines of the past provided more imaginative scope for the reader. Since these Victorian heroines were not invested with sexual conflicts, they widened the definition of the possible. As one biographer declaimed, "There is no sex among souls; hence there is none in success. One soul with the same talents, force, and opportunities as another soul will make as many and great things happen, whether found in man or woman."[22] Asexual heroines could be admired for their intrinsic qualities, however stereotyped these may have been. Familiar feminine characteristics in unfamiliar places were a potent appeal for social change. Is it too far fetched to speculate that formulaic biographies for girls may have engendered powerful fantasies that empowered the first feminist movement?

NOTES

1. The standard survey of British children's literature is F.J. Harvey Darton, *Children's Books in England: Five Centuries of Social Life*, 2nd ed. (Cambridge: Cambridge University Press, 1958). See also Gillian Avery, *Nineteenth-Century Children: Heroes and Heroines in English Children's Stories, 1780-1900* (London: Hodder and Stoughton, 1965). Secondary works about boys' literature are legion, but see E.S. Turner, *Boys Will Be Boys*, new rev. ed. (London, 1975).

2. For a discussion of the constraining gender-roles of girls' fiction, see Elizabeth Segal, "'As the Twig is Bent ...'": Gender and Childhood Reading," *Gender and Reading: Essays on Readers, Texts and Contexts* (Baltimore: Johns Hopkins Press, 1986), pp. 165-166.

3. "What Girls Read," *Nineteenth Century*, 20 (October 1886), p. 527.

4. *Four Noble Women and Their Work* (London: S.W. Partridge, 1898), pp. 55-56.

5. Ibid., p. 126.

6. Inez N. McFee, *The Story of Florence Nightingale* (Dansville, N.Y.: F.A. Owen, n.d.), p. 7.

7. (London: Tyne Publishers, n.d.), pp. 4-5.

8. William Thayer, *Women Who Win or Making Things Happen* (London: T. Nelson and Sons, 1897), p. 44.

9. Hamilton Wright Mabie and Kate Stephens, *Heroines Every Child Should Know* (New York: Grosset and Dunlop, 1908), p. 269.

10. Lizzie Alldridge, *Florence Nightingale,*

Frances Ridley Havergal, Catherine Marsh and Mrs. Ranyard (London: Cassell, 1885), p. 14.

11. The repetition of this story for over fifty years may have been because of its similarity to the immensely popular tales of innocent waifs and dainty girls saving irreligious parents, drunken outcasts and other melodramatic figures. See Gillian Avery, *Childhood's Pattern: A Study of Heroes and Heroines of Children's Fiction, 1770-1950* (London: Hodder and Stoughton, 1975), pp. 112-120 and 150-155.

12. Alldridge, p. 25.

13. Rosa Nouchette Carey, *Twelve Notable Good Women of the Nineteenth Century* (London: Hutchinson, 1899), p. 91.

14. A.L. Haydon, *Florence Nightingale, O.M.A Heroine of Mercy* (London: Andrew Melrose, n.d. [1909]), p. 17.

15. Constance Wakeford, *The Wounded Soldiers' Friends: The Story of Florence Nightingale, Clara Barton and Others* (London: Hadley Bros., n.d. [1917]), p. 16.

16. Ibid., p. 30.

17. *Florence Nightingale: A Cameo Sketch*, 5th ed. (London: Women's Freedom League, n.d. [1913]), pp. 2-3.

18. *Florence Nightingale, 1820-1910* (London: Hamish Hamilton, 1954), p. 8.

19. My analysis here is indebted to Janice Radway's *Reading the Romance: Women, Patriarchy, and Popular Romance* (Chapel Hill: University of North Carolina Press, 1984).

20. See Michael E. Lamb, Margaret Tresch Owen and Lindsay Chase-Lansdale, "The Father-Daughter Relationship: Past, Present, and Future," *Becoming Female: Perspectives on Development*, ed. Claire B. Kopp in collab. with Martha Kirkpatrick (New York: Plenum Press, 1979), pp. 89-112, for a review of the

literature and a discussion of the importance of the father in fostering instrumental behavior in daughters. I am indebted to Susan Contratto for this reference.
21. ffrench, p. 17.
22. Thayer, p. iii.

SECTION II

AMERICAN NURSING AT THE TURN OF

THE CENTURY

NINETEENTH CENTURY WOMEN, THE NEOPHYTE NURSING PROFESSION, AND THE WORLD'S COLUMBIAN EXPOSITION OF 1893

by

Evelyn R. Benson

INTRODUCTION

"History Proving Harder to Celebrate" was the eyecatching headline of a *New York Times* article in which the reporter was describing proposals to observe the quincentennial, in 1992, of Christopher Columbus' voyage to the New World.[1] According to the article, plans to celebrate this event have been scaled down considerably. For example, Chicago has scrapped its blueprints for a 1992 World's Fair; inadequate funds and lack of political support were cited as major barriers to such an exposition.[2] To be sure, the very notion of celebrating Columbus' discovery of America has come under attack by native American Indians, who feel that "Christopher Columbus was discovered. We knew who we were."[3] Furthermore, even if the idea of discovery by outsiders were acceptable to all, there are others who claim to have been the first to have found America. The Director of the Columbus Quincentenary Commission put it this way. "Columbus probably was not the first, but he was the first to come here and go home and hold a press conference."[4]

108

Today, less than four years away from the quincentennial, we recall the quadcentennial observance of that historic event -- the World's Columbian Exposition in Chicago, 1893. Hailed as one of the most spectacular international fairs, it exhibited the latest technological achievements of that era, such as the expansion engine, Pullman cars, structural steel, the linotype, electricity; it boasted the first midway and first ferris wheel; and it was especially noted for its classical architectural theme with buildings that shone like white marble in the sunlight, so that the area on which they stood was dubbed "The White City".

More importantly, the Exposition featured the accomplishments of women and sponsored a number of international congresses and symposia, one of which included a congress on nursing. The purpose of this paper is to describe how the World's Columbian Exposition emerged as a major cultural event of the late nineteenth century, how it honored nineteenth century women and their accomplishments, and how it served as a public platform for the neophyte nursing profession.

THE WORLD'S FAIR OF 1893

The staging of a major international exposition has always been fraught with pitfalls, especially in the United States, where such events are not financially supported by the government to the extent that they are in other countries.[5] In contemporary society, the question always arises-- how wise is the expenditure of vast sums of money that such an undertaking requires when a community faces major problems of unemployment, poverty, ill health, etc.?

Perhaps the day of the large-scale world's fair has passed. Certainly, it was a popular Victorian institution, and from the mid-nineteenth century through the first part of the twentieth century hardly a year went by without at least one major international exhibition somewhere in the world. The first true world's fair, the London World's Fair, opened in the Crystal Palace in Hyde Park on May 1, 1851.[6] In its vast splendor, that Fair glorified the accomplishments of western culture in general and of mid-Victorian British culture in particular. Other notable world's fairs that followed were the Crystal Palace exhibit in New York in 1853, the Paris expositions of 1855 and 1867, the centennial celebration at Philadelphia in 1876, the great Paris exposition of 1889 that was centered around the Eiffel Tower, and the World's Columbian Exposition at Chicago in 1893.

By the late 1880s plans were being formulated for a world's fair to be held in the United States in conjunction with the celebration of the 400th anniversary of Columbus' voyage. At a time in history when older European nations still viewed America as an experiment, the staging of such a fair was regarded as a splendid opportunity to proclaim this country's greatness before the world, to debunk myths about American cultural inferiority, and to foster patriotism in a period of growing internal unrest.

In the late nineteenth century, Chicago had emerged as the major city of the midwest. With all of the social ills of a burgeoning metropolis, the city nonetheless had developed a thriving business community and a strong civic consciousness. Having been given the nod to host the Columbian Exposition, the community surmounted a variety of difficulties and produced a world's fair that surpassed its own expectations for success. That is not to say that there were no flaws; indeed, there were many shortcomings. Not the least of these was the presence of an ugly racism, the targets of which were Chinese, Blacks, and Native Americans.[7] In addition, as beautiful and spectacular as it was, the Fair was regarded by some as an illusion created to camouflage the human misery which lay all about.[8]

However, in an overall assessment of this historic event, one of its critics has pointed out that the Fair provided "a short period of peace and goodwill for Chicago in which it was felt that reasoned discussion, tradition, and idealism would have their chance to control an otherwise highly dangerous socioeconomic situation, and . . . helped to hold off the worst effects of economic panic that summer."[9]

As part of its legacy, the World's Columbian Exposition can point with pride to two features that received wide attention, although they did not appear in the original plans, namely:

(1) To emphasize the higher goals of humankind, a series of world-wide congresses on government, law, etc., were organized, and they included a nursing congress.

(2) For the first time at an international exposition, women played a conspicuous and responsible role.[10]

NINETEENTH CENTURY WOMEN: THEIR ROLE IN THE 1893 WORLD'S FAIR

In previous international expositions the representation of women did not approach that of the 1893 World's Columbian Exposition where, indeed, nineteenth century women and their accomplishments were highly visible. How this came about attests to the determination, leadership, and capability of a group of rather remarkable women.

When we speak about women of the nineteenth centry we refer to an age that in large part coincides with the Victorian period, i.e., with the era of Florence Nightingale. Nineteenth century women have been the subject of renewed interest to contemporary historians and social critics, especially to those who seek to identify and interpret the place of women in history, which, until recently, has been largely ignored. New insights have been contributed, for example, to issues such as whether or not and, if so, to what extent women of the Victorian era may have wielded power and influence on society. There are unanswered questions and differences of interpretation with regard to many issues.

Most historians do agree, however, that woman's place in nineteenth century Victorian society was severely restricted. Sex roles were solidified to an extreme. Women were subordinated to men and were relegated to the domestic sphere; at the same time they were designated the guardians of morality as loving wife and angel-mother. Furthermore, the great social forces unleashed by the Industrial Revolution, which profoundly affected every level of nineteenth century society, were especially detrimental to women. Industrialization, by separating the home from the workplace, began to force an unprecedented choice between home and children on the one hand, and the need for women to go out and earn cash wages, however meager, on the other. There was a contradiction between myth and reality--a cruel dichotomy that disrupted the lives of ordinary people. In addition, the nineteenth century saw a rise of democratic institutions from which women were excluded. Egalitarian ideas spread to both men and women, but women were left out of the political process. Although a few of the braver souls organized to work for voting rights, there was no overall solidarity among women in their efforts to correct the inequities under which they labored.[11]

These forces and events in the larger society were reflected in the organization of the World's Fair and the participation of women. From the beginning, the creators of the Fair attempted to use women in a trivial way as fund raisers and auxiliaries. It should also be noted that powerful voices within women's groups were raised against seeking a special role. Their fight was for complete equality of the sexes, and they were not in favor of a special woman's exhibit, which they saw as a form of segregation that would be demeaning.[12] However, theirs was a minority voice and other groups of women called for a pertinent and clear-cut role in the Fair.

These other groups of women included strong, intelligent, assertive leaders of society. Often they were the wealthy spouses of self-made entrepreneurs, the new class of industrial giants who had emerged in that era.[13] These women wanted the authority to organize activities that would demonstrate women's industries, art and other contributions to world society. They petitioned the U.S. Congress effectively and when President Benjamin Harrison in 1890 signed the law establishing Chicago as the site of the World's Columbian Exposition, there was a provision for a *Board of Lady Managers* which ultimately coordinated and directed local, national, and international participation and representation of women.[14] The Board was headed by Mrs. Bertha Palmer, the wife of one of Chicago's well-to-do businessmen and, in her own right, a wealthy and intelligent woman from a distinguished family.

One of the first things acted upon by the *Board* was the need to have their own building which not only would serve as their administrative center but also "would be a special exhibit, something like a museum, illustrating the progress of women through four hundred years."[15] The Woman's Building was the only one at the Fair that was decided upon through an architectural competition, the winner of which was a young woman, Sophia G. Hayden.[16] The building, itself, and what it represented emerged as one of the most distinctive features of the entire Exposition, and its popularity made it a "celebration of women".[17]

NURSING AND THE WORLD'S COLUMBIAN EXPOSITION

It was within this context of women's contribution to society that nurses and the neophyte nursing profession figured prominently at the 1893

Exhibition. Their accomplishments stood out among
other notable achievements of women that were
featured at the Exhibit. In many ways, from the
mundane to the exotic, nursing made a lasting
impression at the Columbian Exposition. Obviously
Florence Nightingale and her works were well known
and highly regarded; the possibility of having
"knowledgeable", "trained" nurses to care for the sick
in hospitals had already captured broad public
interest.

Although Nightingale had withdrawn some
years earlier from active participation in public life,
she continued to have a profound impact on nursing,
hospital, and health care reforms. She was known all
over the world; people everywhere sought her help.
Nurses who played a key role at the Columbian
Exposition looked to her for advice, counsel, and
inspiration. Her influence was noticeable throughout
the proceedings, although she was not there.

Nightingale prepared a paper, *Sick-Nursing
and Health-Nursing*, which was read at the Chicago
Exposition in 1893; it was included with those papers
presented by the Royal British Commission. In this
treatise, she discussed what "sick-nursing" ought to
be and how "sick-nurses" should be trained. She then
proclaimed the "art of Health" as being of equal
importance with the "art of sick-nursing", pointing
out that "it is the want of the art of health...of the
cultivation of health, which has only lately been
discovered." She believed that "Health-Missioners"
should go out and visit families in their homes to
teach "positive" health -- in fact, these Health-
Missioners are the prototypes of the modern British
health visitor. She also summarized briefly her views
about district nursing, which she restricted to visiting
the sick poor in their own homes.[18] One of her
disciples, Mrs. Dacre Craven, who had served as the
superintendent of the model training program for
district nurses, presented a paper at the nursing
congress that would lay the groundwork for
community nursing;[19] in this paper she pointed out

the benefits of better educational methods for district nurses.

The Expositions's Board of Lady Managers, recognizing the progress of nursing in the wake of the Nightingale reforms, were particularly impressed by the work of Ethel Bedford-Fenwick, who spearheaded the organization of the Royal British Nurses Association. At the time of the Exposition she was engaged in a fierce struggle for the establishment of a national registration system for nurses. Even though she had the sympathies of the Queen, she was encountering stiff opposition from other influential quarters, including Florence Nightingale. Thus, she welcomed the opportunity to publicize her cause when she was asked to head the British nurses' exhibit at the 1893 Columbian Exposition. At the Exposition, Mrs. Bedford-Fenwick was very warmly received and, in fact, was one of the internationally distinguished invited guests on the podium at the opening ceremonies of the Woman's Building. She was given an entire room on the second floor of the Building for her exhibit, which was singled out for an award by the Board of Lady Managers who cited it as one of the most "instructive" of all the displays.

Throughout the Exposition, Mrs. Bedford-Fenwick promoted nursing as a profession, and came out strongly for nursing registration. After she went back to England, she was instrumental in forming the Matron's Council, and, in addition, in 1899, at the meeting of the International Council of Women in London, she helped to organize the International Council of Nurses, which was the first international organization of professional women. Regarding the struggle for registration, it should be noted that the Nurse Registration Act in Britain was not passed until 1919--Bedford-Fenwick referred to it as her "Thirty Years War".[20]

One of the exhibits in the Woman's Building illustrated the astonishing feats of a young Englishwoman, Kate Marsden, who had traveled

across Siberia in 1891. Widespread interest was
aroused by the fact that she was a nurse, who at
great risk to herself, had undertaken a personal
mission to bring comfort to persons suffering from
leprosy. Her efforts and experiences are vividly
described in her book *On Sledge and Horseback to
Outcast Siberian Lepers.*

Born near London on May 13, 1859,
Marsden, at the age of 18, had gone with a group of
nurses to Bulgaria to tend the wounded in the
Russo-Turkish War (1876-77). This was where she
encountered her first cases of leprosy, and she was
deeply moved by the pain and suffering that she
witnessed. "Since then...the main subject of my
thoughts has been the wants of the lepers and how to
relieve them".[21] Of a deeply religious nature, she
prepared herself to carry out "God's work" among the
most neglected of all --the lepers in remote Siberia;
furthermore, she wanted to investigate reports of an
herb growing in that region that was believed to be
of use in healing leprosy. In 1891, Marsden set off
for Yakutsk in Eastern Siberia, trekking across
thousands of miles in primitive conditions. She
endured hardships that would have daunted the
hardiest individual--a very severe climate, the total
lack of sanitary amenities, uncomfortable and even
painful modes of transportation, drunken drivers,
lice, wolves, mosquitoes. She was often in trouble
because she did not know the language, and, finally,
she had to dispel rumors that she was a spy. Upon
reaching her destination, she found that the
conditions were even more dreadful than she had
imagined. She distributed whatever supplies she had
brought and inspired the authorities to come to the
aid of these people. In addition, when she returned
home, she continued to work in England and
America, selling her book and gathering funds for
the construction of a hospital village in 1897. At the
Columbian Exposition she reached a vast audience

and engendered support for her project. The work she did in Yakutsk was not forgotten and even under the Soviet regime as late as the 1960s she was still remembered there for her courage and humanity.[22]

In the United States, the decade of the 1890s was witnessing a rapid growth in nursing and the emergence of several outstanding nursing leaders. Some of these women were highly visible at the World's Fair, which they very effectively used as a public platform to present their views in their efforts to create a stronger foundation for the nursing profession.

The idea for holding a nursing congress had, in fact, been introduced to the World's Fair organizers by Great Britain's nursing leader, Mrs. Bedford-Fenwick. In 1892, when she came to Chicago to arrange the British nursing exhibit, she stopped in Baltimore to visit Isabel A. Hampton, Superintendent of Nurses at Johns Hopkins Hospital. Theirs was a meeting of two idealistic and enthusiastic personalities who laid the groundwork for a momentous nursing congress within the framework of the International Congress of Charities, Correction and Philanthropy. Dr. Henry M. Hurt, the Superintendent of Johns Hopkins Hospital, as Secretary of this International Congress, was responsible for a program section on Hospital, Dispensaries and Nursing.[23] Dr. John S. Billings, chairman of this section had invited Isabel Hampton to organize the subsection on Nursing.[24]
As Hampton prepared to take on this task, she asked for and received advice from Florence Nightingale, with whom she had set up a correspondence.[25]

One of the things that had been troubling Hampton and other nursing educators was the proliferation of nurses' training schools in the country. For example, Louise Darche presented a paper at the Exposition in which she warned that some hospitals were establishing schools not on the basis of sound educational principles but rather on their need for nursing service.[26] Darche, Hampton, and others were concerned about the inadequacy and lack of uniformity in the educational programs of many of these schools. Hampton presented a paper in which she pointed out these problems and urged the improvement of educational standards.

At the Nursing Congress, Hampton gathered eighteen nursing superintendents who were interested in establishing and maintaining a universal standard of training. These nurses formed a committee, which, in 1894, set up the first officially organized group of nurses, calling itself the American Society of Superintendents of Training Schools for Nurses. In 1912, the name was changed to the National League for Nursing Education, which forty years later reorganized under the present National League for Nursing.

Other seeds planted at the Exposition also bore fruit. For example, Edith A. Draper presented a paper on the "Necessity of an American Nurses' Association". This belief, that a national professional organization was needed to represent graduate nurses in all phases of nursing practice, was shared by many of the leaders of the Society of Superintendents. Thus, although their Society focused primarily on education, several of the members--notably Isabel Hampton (Robb), Adelaide Nutting, and Lavinia Dock--worked together to form a new organization in 1896, the Nurses' Associated Alumnae of the United States and Canada, utilizing the school alumnae associations as a nucleus. This organization was the forerunner of the American Nurses' Association, which was established in 1911.[27]

Further noteworthy results could be traced back to Hampton's committee at the Exposition. One of the original members, Mary E. P. Davis, in collaboration with Hampton (Robb), Dock and Nutting, was a pioneer in the work of the *American Journal of Nursing*. A devout believer in rigorous nursing education with its own theory and curriculum, Davis espoused other causes such as legal control of nursing practice. In fact, ten years after the Exposition, in 1903, four states were successful in passing licensure laws in a period of less than two months.[28]

Thus, the key issues identified by Hampton and her colleagues for presentation at the World's Fair were control over the number and type of nursing schools, the need for a national organization of nursing superintendents as well as for a national organization of nurses, and the registration of nurses. The proceedings of the conference were published as Part III, "Nursing of the Sick" from the volume "Hospitals, Dispensaries and Nursing: Papers and Discussions in the International Congress of Charities and Philanthropy, Section III, Chicago, June 12th to 17th, 1893," which has been reissued in the publication *Nursing of the Sick, 1893*.[29]

Another highlight of the Fair was the impressive array of hospital exhibits. Up through the middle of the nineteenth century, hospitals were little more than pest houses, and the only good hospital nursing was provided through various religious orders.[30] Nightingale's works in nursing and hospital care, along with the efforts of other dedicated women, e.g., Dorothea Dix, Clara Barton, Mary Ann Bickerdyke, and others, had aroused public concern over deplorable hospital conditions. By the time of the 1893 Exposition, reform was under way in many hospitals with changes in practice that were related to a rapid expansion of nurses' "training schools". At the Exposition, the Woman's Building featured several exhibits sponsored by at least a dozen New York and Philadelphia Hospitals showing their training programs for nurses, with pictures and miniature models of clean, orderly wards, beds, patients, and nurses. In addition, a group in Illinois organized its own "woman-controlled exhibit of trained nurses in actual service," and the Illinois Woman's Hospital Pavilion was built on the Fairgrounds. At this model hospital facility, emergency treatment was provided to nearly 3,000 persons during their visit to the Fair.[31]

CONCLUSIONS

The World's Columbian Exposition of 1893 emerges as a uniquely nineteenth-century institution. From an historical perspective, the World's Columbian Exposition of 1893 was the crowning cultural event of the nineteenth century in America. Looking back on the Exposition, we have noted that women played a prominent role and that nursing was represented by a group of outstanding leaders who set worthy goals and standards for the neophyte profession. They skillfully used the World's Fair as a public platform from which they proudly presented their accomplishments, clearly stated their concerns, and realistically shared their aspirations and goals. When we review what the neophyte nursing profession achieved at the end of the nineteenth and the beginning of the twentieth centuries, we find that in many instances these achievements were conceived and first publicized at the international forum provided by the 1893 Exposition.[32]

FOOTNOTES

1. Lawson, Carol. "History Proving Harder to Celebrate." *New York Times*, August 14, 1988.
2. Stanley Ziemba and John McCarron. "'I want World's Fair' Mayor Says". *Chicago Tribune*, June 21, 1985; John McCarron, "Vote Officially Kills '92 World's Fair," *Chicago Tribune*, December 5, 1987.
3. Lawson.
4. Ibid.
5. Badger, R. Reid, *The Great American Fair*. Chicago: Nelson Hall, 1979, p. 13.
6. Ibid., p. 3
7. Rydell, Robert W., *All the World's a Fair*. Chicago: The University of Chicago Press,

1984, p. 49-52, 63-67.
8. Badger, 128.
9. Ibid., 129-130.
10. Ibid., 78-79.
11. Hellerstein, Erna Olafson, Leslie Parker Hume, and Karen M. Offen (eds.), *Victorian Women*. Stanford (CA): Stanford University Press, 1981, p. 1-4.
12. Weimann, Jeanne Madeline, *The Fair Women*. Chicago: Academy Chicago, 1981, p. 33, 104.
13. Ibid., p. 5.
14. Ibid., p. 33.
15. Ibid., p. 51.
16. Applebaum, Stanley, *The Chicago World's Fair of 1893, A Photographic Record*. New York: Dover Publications, Inc., 1980, p. 69.
17. Weimann, Jeanne Madeline, "The Great 1893 Woman's Building: Can We Measure Up in 1992?" *MS.*, March, 1983, p. 65.
18. Seymer, Lucy Ridgely, *Selected Writings of Florence Nightingale*. New York: The Macmillan Company, 1954, p. 354.
19. Dolan, Josephine A., *Nursing in Society, A Historical Perspective*, 14th ed. Philadelphia: W.B. Saunders Company, 1978, p. 138.
20. Weimann (1981), p. 456-458.
21. Marsden, Kate. *On Sledge and Horseback to Outcast Siberian Lepers*. New York: Cassell Publishing Company, 1892, p. 4.
22. Benson, Evelyn, "A Nurse's Mission to Siberia: Kate Marsden 1859-1931," *American Association for the History of Nursing*. Fall, 1984, No. 6, p. 1, 4.
23. Roberts, Mary M., *American Nursing*. New York: The Macmillan Company, 1954, p. 21.
24. Dock, Lavinia L., *A History of Nursing*. New York: G.P. Putnam's, 1912, volume 3, p. 125.
25. Dolan, p. 214.
26. Ibid., p. 199.
27. Ibid., p. 267.
28. Shannon, Mary Lucille, "Nurses in American

History--Our First Four Licensure Laws," *American Journal of Nursing*, 75: 1327-1329, August 1975.

29. Hampton, Isabel A. and others, *Nursing of the Sick 1893*. New York: McGraw Hill Book Company, Inc., 1949. (Papers and discussions from the International Congress of Charities, Correction and Philanthropy, Chicago, 1893 published in 1949 under the sponsorship of the National League of Nursing Education), see esp. p. v and vi.

30. Dolan, p. 138.

31. Weimann (1981), p. 450.

32. Benson, Evelyn, "Nursing and the World's Columbian Exposition," *Nursing Outlook*, 34: 88-90, March/April 1986.

THE WOMAN'S NURSING AND SUFFRAGE MOVEMENT

Sandra B. Lewenson

The historical image of the profession of nursing has been portrayed in contemporary nursing liteature as politically conservative and nonsupportive of the women's movement,* woman suffrage, or feminism.[1] Nurse historian Ashley, for example, wrote that professional nurses "to the detriment of their own growth as professional persons" were "among the most conservative of the conservatives. With rare exception, they were non-feminist."[2] In explaining the conservatism of nurses, the historian Reverby argued that nursing's sense of duty, ethic of altruism, and social hierarchy managed to compromise the political efforts of nursing's support for equality between the sexes.[3]

Some historians represent nursing in the first two decades of this century as opposed to and disinterested in the suffrage movement. Often cited is the failure of the Nurses' Associated Alumnae of the United States and Canada to unify behind women

*"Woman" is used to refer to the woman's movement during the turn of the century and "women" is used to refer to the women's movement between 1960 and the present date.

suffrage at the 1908 national convention.[4] This image of nursing's unwillingness to support the issue of suffrage is still held today.

The purpose of this investigation is to explore the tension between the politically conservative image of nursing and the four professional nursing organizations' actual involvement in the suffrage campaign. Professional journals; proceedings of each of the four professional nursing organizations; nursing and suffrage archival collections; and historiographies of nursing, woman, and the suffrage movement were used as primary and secondary sources. The timeframe for this study, 1893 through 1920, was determined by historical events for nursing and women. The year 1983, marked the establishment of the first national professional nursing organization, The American Society of Superintendents of Training Schools, while 1920, marked the national passage of the suffrage amendment.

The four organizations studied were: (a) the American Society of Superintendents of Training Schools for Nurses (1893) renamed the National League of Nursing Education (1912) and presently known as the National League of Nursing (1952), (b) the Nurses' Associated Alumnae of the United States and Canada (1896) renamed American Nurses Association (1911), (c) the National Association of Colored Graduate Nurses (1908), and (d) the National Organization for Public Health Nursing (1912). Although the focus of each organization varied, the central thrust was the professionalization of nurses through political, social, educational, and economic change.

NURSING ORGANIZATIONS SUPPORT SUFFRAGE

The findings of this investigation indicated that the four nursing organizations repeatedly debated the issue of woman suffrage. Every nurse who was a member of one of the associations, or who read one of the nursing journals, was a participant to some extent in the suffrage debate. Additionally, nurses had voted on organizational support seven different times--five of those times in favor of supporting suffrage. While we remember the defeat of 1908 and an occasional reference to the passage in 1915, the associations' resolutions favoring women suffrage in 1912, 1915, 1918, and 1919 have been obliterated from our memory.

As early as 1899 at the Superintendents Society Sixth Annual Convention, prior to any organizational vote on suffrage, Maud Banfield expressed concern that nurses were denied positions on boards of health. The reason for that, Banfield believed, was because they lacked the vote. She explained that positions were filled as political favors and wasted on those who could not return the courtesy. As a result of this discussion, an organizational motion was passed and a committee was formed to support the placement of nurses on various boards of health.

Sophia Palmer in 1906, at the Superintendent's Society Convention Ninth convention noted that the suffragist Susan B. Anthony had contributed ". . . as much to the advancement of nurses as any other woman, improving our legal status, and all those things we enjoy."[4] Annie Damer, president of the Society, also expressed the hope that members would interest themselves in the Susan B. Anthony memorial.[5]

In 1908, the Superintendents Society had invited Dr. Margaret Bigelow, a representative of the National Suffrage Association, to address nurses on woman suffrage.[6] A newspaper clipping entitled "Nurses Approve Woman's Rights" recorded the event noting that Bigelow had been received by an enthusiastic nursing audience.[7]

Lavinia Dock often wrote and spoke about nursing and the suffrage movement. She was concerned that for too many nurses, suffrage was

> a far-off, abstract, uninteresting theme, or
> even, it may be to some, one to be avoided
> with disapproval, or with the indifference of
> the extreme specialist toward all outside of a
> specialty.[8]

However, she advised the national associations to become a " . . . great moral force on all the great social questions of the day."[9] Dock urged the Nurses' Associated Alumnae to consider the reforms of the day in place of the some of the more trivial concerns of previous times.

Helen Parker Criswell, President of the California State Nurses' Association, welcomed the Nurses' Associated Alumnae to San Francisco for their Eleventh Annual Convention in 1908. In that address, Criswell questioned the association's ability to solve professional issues without addressing itself to the issues facing women.

> How shall this, the largest organized body of professional women in existence, make for the status of the twentieth century women?[9]

However, in spite of the expressed interest in woman suffrage by some nurses, the first vote taken by the Nurses' Associated Alumnae at their 11th Annual Convention was defeated by the delegates of the state associations.[10]

While this decision seems to have remained in our historical memory bank, the pivotal notion that this decision prompted a great deal of discussion on the question of suffrage has not been remembered.

Unwilling to accept this defeat, many in nursing spent the next few years actively campaigning for professional advocacy for suffrage. The defeat prompted *The American Journal of Nursing*, the Superintendents Society, and the Nurses' Associated Alumnae to go to great lengths to give information and inform nurses on this issue. The crusade filled the nursing journals with articles, editorials, letters to the editor, and papers about suffrage. Education of the nursing membership was considered essential to dispel some of the negative ideas about this issue. Sophia Palmer, editor-in-chief of *The American Journal of Nursing*, believed that the defeat of the resolution helped to focus attention on the subject,[11] and justified the attention it was then receiving.

Nutting expressed her own support for woman suffrage. She believed that the state delegates' opposition to nursing's support of suffrage was due to ignorance rather than any deep seated feelings against woman suffrage. Nutting urged nurses, individually and collectively in the state nurses' associations, to become educated on the matter.[12]

In a similar vein, Mary Dixon stated that nurses were involved with politics even before they were born. Integral to nurses' health, wealth, and happiness was the political ability via the vote to control nursing practice, nursing directories, cleaner environments, and safer health practices.[13]

Lavinia Dock wrote of her outrage at the associations' lack of political support for suffrage. Nurses, she said, had previously responsed favorably to other reform movements such as pure food bills, almshouse reforms and social causes of tuberculosis. So different was the response to the question of suffrage that Dock argued, "how foolish to take up an almshouse propaganda and yet reject the belief that women should vote."[14]

The American Journal of Nursing's officially neutral stand on the suffrage resolution was attacked. For many, the issue of neutrality was an even greater disappointment than the associations' defeat of the resolution. Mary Dixon again wrote

> My next hope was that our magazine would present the question fairly to us, at least, but alas, I find the editorial staff is in the 'twilight zone' of neutrality and brushes this vital question carelessly aside.[15]

In defense of the journal's position, Sophia Palmer responded that she too supported the suffrage resolution. However, she reasoned that the journal was to represent the views of the professional organization it could not endorse suffrage until the professional body did so.[16]

Many nurses were concerned about the effect obtaining the ballot would have on nursing registration. In one letter the nursing registration bills were believed to be so closely linked to the vote that disbelief at nurses' apathy towards the suffrage was expressed. One nurse wrote ". . . we are going to have the suffrage, some day, and not by migrating to Colorado, either."[17]

One nurse, in favor of the American Nurses' Association's decision, Louise Croft Boyd, expressed resistance to nursing's support of suffrage out of fear of losing the battle for nursing registration. She said:

> I know men and I know legislators well enough to know that they would quickly side against a nurse registration law which was pushed forward by women who were also working in favor of equal suffrage.[18]

Woman suffrage was contested, not on grounds that women were incapable, but rather out of fear of losing the battle of other needed nursing legislation. Boyd's fear was a sentiment that certainly characterized some members of the nursing organizations.

In 1909, the American Federation of Nurses, representing both the American Society of Superintendents of Training Schools for Nurses and the Nurses' Associated Alumnae, planned to send a delegation to the International Council of Nurses Convention. However, a resolution to authorize the delegation to endorse woman suffrage again was vetoed.[19] Nonetheless, it is important to note that the vote in 1909 was the last time organizational endorsement of suffrage was defeated.

Annie Damer expressed nursing's changing attitude towards suffrage. She said:

> All through our meetings there has been an evidence of the feeling of unrest among women, and in some cases they have come out openly with a demand for the ballot.[20]

In the lobbying for organizational support of suffrage, Linna Richardson, an associate editor of the *Nurses' Journal of the Pacific Coast*, spoke of the interdependence of people. Richardson said in 1909

> ours is a woman's profession in a man's world, and we need to realize that men will take much less interest in our advancement than we take in ourselves.[21]

Annie Goodrich's comment ". . . eighteen years of this struggle has made a woman suffragist of me,"[22] at the Twelfth Annual Convention of the Nurses' Associated Alumnae, summed up many of the membership's feelings and frustrations at that time.

In 1912, the American Nurses' Association during the Fifteenth Annual Convention voted to send a delegation who would support suffrage at the next gathering of the International Congress of Nursing.[23] The discussion that preceded the vote revealed some of the views shared by the association's membership. First, Jane Delano remarked that because of her own political convictions favoring woman suffrage, she would like to support the resolution so as to avoid other delegates' future embarrassment at the International Council.[24]

Isabel McIssac voiced concern for the outcome of this resolution as well as concern for Lavinia Dock. She emphatically said ". . . we cannot let it go negatively this time. How in the world will we ever face Miss Dock if we do?"[25]

The vote was passed. The International Congress of Nursing, at their convention that year, also voted to endorse woman suffrage.[25]

The National Association of Colored Graduate Nurses was indirectly seen as supportive of the political stance on woman suffrage. This support was viewed by their participation with the 1912 convention of the International Council of Nurses when an invited delegation headed by Rosa Williams attended.[25]

Votes by the National League of Nursing Education and the Nurses' Associated Alumnae, both in 1915 and both in favor of the Susan B. Anthony Bill, resulted in professional advocacy of the bill by all four nursing organizations.[27]

The position of the National League of Nursing Education, the American Nurses' Association, and the National Association of Public Health Nursing was summarized by D. Elva Mills Stanley in the *American Journal of Nursing* that year.

> Unanimously these associations stand for the enfranchisement of women. You know this means better health, better homes and a better country to live in.[28]

The executive board meeting of the National League of Nursing Education on May 11, 1918 passed another resolution sanctioning the Federal Suffrage

Amendment, and calling for the organization to send their endorsement to the Congress of the United States.[29]

In 1918, a joint resolution of all three nursing organizations--the American Nurses' Association, the National League of Nursing Education, and the National Organization of Public Health Nursing--resolved to publicly advocate the passage of woman suffrage. The resolution also called for a message to be sent to the President of the United States, urging him to support Congress in their deliberations of political equality for woman.[30]

Neither the NOPHN or the NAGGN passed official resolutions for suffrage. Still, since their founding, the National Organization of Public Health Nurses had agreed to assist the work of the suffrage campaign.[31]

Though the National Association of Colored Graduate Nurses was not included in any of the "unanimous decisions," and never recorded an official vote of endorsement of suffrage, indirect support to suffrage is clearly evident through their professional activities. Adah Thoms, president of the association, at the Twelfth Annual Convention, argued that the ballot was an important avenue to achieve their goals.[32] The organization's concern for education, registration, health, and racial prejudice could be addressed via the vote. Thoms urged all those nurses who lived in suffrage states to exercise their right to vote.[33]

IN CONCLUSION

Among the four national nursing organizaitons, organizational endorsement of woman suffrage was announced nine different times and voted on seven. Only two of those seven votes resulted in opposition of organizational support of suffrage.

In addition, over 200 references connecting nursing and suffrage were observed during this study. The frequency of suffrage references signified the active role nursing organizations played in the early twentieth century woman movement. Autonomy of nursing practice was linked to the woman franchise. To that end, the ability to vote was directly related to the idea of "professional suffrage" or the ability to control the development of nursing. Almost always the references referred to issues that others in the woman movement were engaged with.

Thus, one might ask a new kind of question, why has nursing's involvement with the woman movement been so ignored and misrepresented in the current literature? While there may be several answers to that question, such as using the wrong criteria to judge, incomplete study of our history, and misuse of the term conservative, another answer may lie in an underlying prejudice towards nursing by society. The term "nursism" was conceived for the purpose of explaining the prejudice and omission witnessed.

Nursism, envisioned as a prejudice or bias towards nursing, is a construct that has involved an enduring value placed on the role and thus the life-work of the nurse. Furthermore, this construct, by the very nature of its bias, has had an impact on the health of the individual, the family, and the society. While the nature of this bias may not be negative, the history of nursing has suggested a subordinate and devalued view of the role of nurses and nursing.

The phenomena of nursism may explain the omission of nursing's role in the suffrage movement. The minutes of the proceedings of the nursing organizations, the journal articles, and the papers presented at times reflected an historical theme of prejudice experienced by nursing early in the century.

One example drawn from history comes from a speech delivered at a convention by Mary Riddle, president in 1911 of the American Society of Superintendents of Training Schools. Riddle questioned how to keep and attract educated women in a field that was often forgotten and remembered with dread. To attract new members into their ranks, they established committees to work on the public image of the nurse. Yet, Riddle spoke of a paradox that nurses faced. She said, they will tell us how the educated young woman may be interested in this work of ours which is paradoxical in offering so much and so little--so much of opportunity for usefulness, and so little in worldly advancement.[34]

Today this paradox seemingly remains. How do we attract people into a profession that struggles to be identified as a valued, educated, and autonomous profession? While many historians who write the history of nursing today attempt to resolve some of these issues, perhaps a closer look at some of the preconceived notions would guide us to find the solutions. Furthermore, once we jar these recollections, perhaps we will have a greater impact on sustaining the image of nursing that our pioneer leaders have intended.

NOTES

1.   See, for example, Allen, M. "Women, Nursing and Feminism: An Interview with Alice J. Baumgart," *The Canadian Nurse*, 81 (1985), 20-22. Ashley, J. Nurses in American History: Nursing and Early Feminism," *American Journal of Nursing*, 75 (1975), 1465-1467. Bullough, V.L. and Bullough, B. *History, Trends and Politics of Nursing*, Norwalk, Ct.: Appleton-Century-Crofts, 1984; Chinn, P. and Wheeler, C. "Feminism and Nursing: Can Nursing Afford to Remain Aloof from the Women's Movement?" *Nursing Outlook* 33:3 (1985), 74-77; Doona, M.E. "Nursing Revisited: Memories-Armistice and Suffrage," *The Massachusetts Nurse* 52:11 (1987), 15; Starr, D. "Poor Baby: The Nurse and Feminism," *Canadian Nurse* 70:3 (1974), 20-23; Talbott, S. and Vance, C. "Involving Nursing in a Feminist Group--NOW," *Nursing Outlook*, 29 (1981), 592-95; Vance, C., Talbott, S., McBride, A., and Mason, D. "Coming of Age: The Women's Movement and Nursing," in D.

Mason and S. Talbott, (Eds.), *Political Action Handbook for Nurses*. Menlo Park, Cal.: Addison Wesley, 1985.

2.   Ashley, "Nurses in American History," p. 1465.
3.   See Reverby, S. "A Caring Dilemma: Womanhood and Nursing in Historical Perspective," *Nursing Research*, 36:1 (1987), 5-11, and Reverby, S. *Ordered to Care: The Dilemma of American Nursing, 1850-1945*, Cambridge: Cambridge University Press, 1987.
3.   Chinn, P. "Historical Roots: Female Nurses and Political Action," *Journal of the New York State Nurses Association*, 16:2 (1985), 29-37; Doona, M.E., "Nursing Revisited," and Christy, T. "Equal Rights for Women: Voice from the Past," in *Pages from Nursing History: A Collection of Original Articles from the Pages of Nursing Outlook, The American Journal of Nursing and Nursing Research*. New York: American Journal of Nursing, 1984, pp. 63-57.
4.   Palmer, S. [Discussion of the Susan B. Anthony Memorial]. Ninth Annual Convention of the Nurses' Associated Alumnae of the United States, p. 328, Unpublished Proceedings, Boston University, Mugar Memorial Library, Nursing Archives, American Nurses Association, Board of Directors Minutes: 1897-1949 (Records of Associated Alumnae of U.S. and Canada, 1897-1912); See also Palmer, S. "Proceedings of the Ninth Annual Convention of the Nurses," N87, Box 33, Boston
5.   Damer, A. "Discussion of the Susan B. Anthony Memorial, Associated Alumnae of the United States," *The American Journal of Nursing*, 6 (1906) Ninth Annual Convention of the Nurses' Associated Alumnae of the United States, 1906, pp. 327-328. Unpublished proceedings, Boston University, Mugar Memorial Library, Nursing Archives, American Nurses Associaiton, N 87, Board of Directors Minutes, 1897-1949 (Records of Associated Alumnae of U.S. and Canada,

1897-1912), Box 33, Boston.

6. See Bigelow, M.D. "Letter from the Ohio Woman Suffrage Association," *Proceedings of the Fourteenth Annual Convention of the American Society of Superintendents of Training Schools for Nurses*, Baltimore: J.H. Furst, 1908, p. 87, and Bigelow, M.D. [Address by representative from National Woman's Suffrage Association], in those same *Proceedings*, p. 122-124.

7. Nutting, A. [Discusison of address by representative from National Woman's Suffrage Association], in *Proceedings*, pp. 124-125.

8. Dock, L.L. "Some Urgent Social Claims," *American Journal of Nursing*, 7 (1907), 895-901.

8. Ibid., p. 899.

9. Criswell, H.P. "Address of Welcome to the Nurses' Associated Alumnae of the United States, May 5, 1908," *Nurses' Journal of the Pacific Coast*, 4 (1908), 253-255.

10. Afternoon Session, 1908, [Report of the Eleventh Annual Convention of the Nurses' Associated Alumnae of the United States, Suffrage Resolution], *The American Journal of Nursing* 8 (1908), 860.

11. Palmer, S. [Editorial Policy Explained], *The American Journal of Nursing*, 9 (1908), 49-50.

12. Nutting, A., Discussion of Address by Representatives.

13. Dixon, M.B. "Votes for Women," *Nurses' Journal of the Pacific Coast*, 4 (1908), 442-447.

14. Dock, L.L. "The Suffrage Question," *American Journal of Nursing* 8 (1908), 925-926.

15. Dixon, M.B. "Letter to the Editor: A Criticism of the Editor," *American Journal of Nursing* 9 (1908), 49-49.

16. Palmer, S. [Editorial Policy Explained].

17. E.L.F., "Letters to the Editor: Extract from a Letter to Miss Dock," *American Journal of Nursing*, 9 (1908), 50-51.

18. Boyd, L.C. "Letters to the Editor: The

Suffrage--Another View," *American Journal of Nursing* 9 (1908), 135-136.

19. Secretary, [Enfranchisement proposal], *Fifteenth Annual Report of American Society of Superintendents of Training Schools for Nurses Including Report of the Second Meeting of the American Federation of Nurses, 1909*, Baltimore: J.H. Furst, 1910, p. 215.

20. Damer, A. "Address of the President During the Twelfth Annual Convention of the Nurses' Associated Alumnae of the United States," *American Journal of Nursing* 9 (1909), 901-904.

21. Richardson, L. "Reasons for Central Registries and Club Houses," Proceedings of the Twelfth Annual Convention of the American Nurses' Association. *American Journal of Nursing* 9 (1909), 983-986.

22. Goodrich, A. [Discussion of the limitation of the nursing profession in the report of the Twelfth Annual Convention of the Nurses' Associated Alumane of the United States] *American Journal of Nursing* 9 (1909), 945-47.

23. See A. Goodrich, Proceedings of the Fifteenth Annual Convention of the American Nurses' Association [Discussion of suffrage resolution]. *American Journal of Nursing* 12 (1912), 973-74, and American Nurses Association, [Suffrage Resolution Passed Fifteenth Annual Meeting of the American Nurses' Association], 1912, pp. 196-197. Unpublished proceedings, Boston University, Mugar Memorial Library, Nursing Archives, American Nurses Association, N. 87 Convention Proceedings, Box 12, Boston.

24. Delano, J. Proceedings of the Fifteenth Annual Convention of the American Nurses' Association [Discussion of suffrage resolution], *American Journal of Nursing* 12 (1912), 973-974.

25. Nutting, A. [The report of the delegate, International Council of Nurses in August, 1913] *Proceedings of the Nineteenth Annual*

Convention of the National League for Nursing Education, Baltimore: Williams and Wilkins, 1913, pp. 47-50, and also Nutting, A., "Report of the International Council of Nurses (Condensed) at the Sixteenth Annual Convention of the American Nurses' Association," *American Journal of Nursing* 13 (1913), 94-43.

26.   Williams, R. [Report of the International Congress in Cologne, Germany, Sixth Annual Convention of the National Association of Colored Graduate Nurses, September 3, 1913], pp. 57-58. Unpublished proceedings, the New York Public Library, Schomburg Center for Research in Black Culture, Rare Books, Manuscripts and Archives Section, National Association of Colored Graduate Nurse Records (1908-1951), Box 1, Volume 1, New York City.

27.   Whitney, [Susan B. Anthony Amendment], *Proceedings of the Twenty-First Annual Convention of the National League of Nursing Education*, Baltimore: Williams and Wilkins, 1915, pp. 176-178; Taylor, E.J. "Proceedings of the Eighteenth Annual Convention of the American Nurses' Association [Susan B. Anthony Amendment]," *American Journal of Nursing* 15 (1915), 1062-1063.

28.   Stanley, D.E.M. "Nursing and Citizenship," *American Journal of Nursing* 16 (1915), 15-24.

29.   National League for Nursing Education Executive Board Meeting Minutes, May 11, 1918. [Resolutions]. National League for Nursing Education Board of Directors Minutes, May 1916-June, 1922. [Machine-readable data file] Unpublished Minutes, National Library of Medicine, National League for Nursing, Bethesda, Maryland.

30.   McMillan, H.M. "Twenty-first Annual Convention of the American Nurses' Association [Report of the Committee on Resolutions]." *American Journal of Nursing*, 18 (1918), 1097.

31. National Organization of Public Health Nursing [Advertising Card, Minutes of Midyear Meeting of Executive Committee of the National Organization of Public Health, Jan. 18, 19, 20, 1915], p. 120 in Machine-Readable Data File, Unpublished Minutes, National Library of Medicine, History of Medicine Division, National League for Nursing, MS. C. 274, Box 4, Reel 11, Bethesda.

32. Thomas, A. [Opening Address, Twelfth Annual Convention of the National Association of Colored Graduate Nurses, August 19, 1919], pp. 64-65 in Unpublished proceedings, New York Public Library, Schomburg Center for Research in Black Culture, Rare Books, Manuscripts and Archives Section, National Association of Colored Graduate Nurses Records (1908-1951), Box 1, Volume 2, New York City.

33. See National Association of Colored Graduate Nursing Records, 1908-1920. Unpublished Proceedings, The New York Public Library, Schomburg Center for Research in Black Culture, Rare Books, Manuscripts and Archives Section, New York.

34. Riddle, M. "How to Obtain, Keep, and Properly Instruct the Nurse (Delivered as the President's Address at the Opening Meeting of the American Society of Superintendents of Training Schools, May 29, 1911)," *American Journal of Nursing* 12 (1911), 180-84.

THE BENEFICENT REVOLUTION:
HOSPITAL NURSING DURING
THE CIVIL WAR

by

Roberta Tierney

Although the women's rights movement in the United States dated to 1848, and while the work of Florence Nightingale in the Crimea in the mid 1850's was known and admired throughout the United States, it took the crisis created by the Civil War to unsettle traditional attitudes and propel women into the role of hospital nurses.

As the Civil War began, warfare and weaponry had reached a respectable middle age, while medical care and sanitation were still in their infancy. The Medical Department of the army was woefully outdated and unprepared for the crisis, and the lack of organization within the Department was a serious and continuing problem.[1]

At the war's onset, the largest army hospital had 40 beds.[2] Early in the war the hospitals were understaffed, unsanitary, near polluted areas, on damp ground, and sometimes near unburied bodies.[3] Naturally, the men resisted being sent to them. Moreover, the overwhelming number of sick and wounded far outstripped the capacity to care for them and created a demand for nurses that could not be met through the traditional practice of placing recuperating soldiers into that role.

138

In 1860, there was no group of trained female secular nurses in the country. Any nursing care that was needed was customarily provided by family members within the confines of the home. Considerable prejudice existed against women working outside the home.

In spite of prevailing attitude, when the first call went out in the North for female nurses in May of 1861, hundreds of women responded. This was especially surprising, since caring for soldiers was considered "unwomanly" and "unseemly"[4] and not something any respectable woman would do. These women, generally, had to struggle with their families as well as their consciences to act in such a radically unconventional way.[5]

Approximately 100 of the first volunteers were selected to attend a brief course of instruction at Bellevue Hospital provided by the Women's Central Association of Relief (later the Sanitary Commission) under the supervision of Dr. Elizabeth Blackwell.[6] Although a few nurses came with some training or some experience in civilian hospitals,[7] for the most part, the women, although well intended, entered nursing with little preparation. Kate Cumming, a southern nurse who enlisted early in the war recalled: "I had never been inside of a hospital, and was wholly ignorant of what I should be called upon to do, but I knew that what one woman (Florence Nightingale) had done another could do."[8]

Following her appointment as Superintendent of Nurses for the Federal Army in June 1861, Dorothea Dix instituted the following requirements for regular army nurses: 35-50 years of age, experience or superior education, and good character. The pay was 40 cents a day and subsistence, plus transportation. The female nurses could work in general or permanent hospitals in place of soldiers at the discretion of the medical officer in charge.[9] Volunteer nurses who enlisted with the state-recruited regiments were not subject to these regulations or restrictions.[10]

Motivations for entering the service as a nurse were as varied as the nurses themselves. Among the

early volunteers, a patriotic or Christian duty was the
major motivating force.[11] For some, it was a personal
desire to aid in work that needed to be done and to
feel useful and involved in the war effort.[12]

Some, wanting to emulate the romantic ideal of
the "ministering angel," envisioned the war as
providing that opportunity.[13] Similarly, many were
moved by the heroic example created by Florence
Nightingale in the Crimea.[14] For some, nursing service
provided an opportunity for them to become self-
sufficient, independent, and self-supporting.[15] A large
number entered into the service to accompany, and in
the event of illness or injury to care for, a husband,
father, brother, or son.[16] Or, as one mother wrote
regarding her reasons for nursing the soldiers, "I
thought perhaps if I did what I could for them, some
one would care for my sons."[17]

A few accompanied their husbands who were
physicians or ministers, and then stayed on to nurse
the sick and wounded when they saw the need.[18] Still
others were widows who entered nursing in order to
deal with their own bereavement.[19] For Clara Barton
it was a "passion for service,"[20] and for Mary Phinney
it was the "irresistible impulse TO DO, TO ACT."[21]

As the war continued, more and more nurses
were needed and women responded to the call from
the army surgeons[22] or to the solicitations of the state
sanitary agencies.[23] Emily Parsons wrote in a letter
from Benton Barracks in St. Louis on June 7, 1863
"The demand for nurses is on the increase . . . we shall
want surgical nurses . . . ."[24] A large number of women
became temporary nurses because they lived in the
area near the battlefields, and they responded to the
immediate needs of the wounded.[25] And as various
states began operating general hospitals for the
wounded, even more nurses were recruited to staff
them.[26]

The functions, expectations, and living
conditions of the nurses differed markedly depending
on the location of their assignment and the particular
time during the war when they served. Generally,

working conditions improved for the nurses as the medical, sanitary and hospital conditions improved. Those nurses assigned to the newly constructed general hospitals, such as Benton Barracks in St. Louis and Chimborazo near Richmond, Virginia, lived relatively comfortable lives with structured working conditions. Those nurses working in hospitals closer to the front lived in whatever shelter they could find, sometimes sleeping on the ground,[27] sometimes in tents or a corner of one of the hospital rooms.[28] As one nurse said ". . . when one goes nursing, all things must be expected."[29]

The treatment of female nurses by surgeons also differed considerably; some nurses reported considerate and collegial treatment,[30] while others reported a lack of "even common courtesy."[31] It must also be that some nurses expected more from the surgeons than others. Treatment from the soldiers was reported as always courteous and grateful.[32]

Regardless of where they were stationed, the work was long and arduous. As one nurse wrote in a letter to her family about the news of her work with the wounded, "Please excuse this imperfect letter, written by jerks at odd moments. My duties as nurse, leave me no leisure."[33]

Following a battle, or after receiving wounded from the front, the nurses might be kept busy for days with little opportunity for rest or personal hygiene.[34] Kate Cumming wrote, upon arriving at Corinth, Mississippi with three other women to take up nursing duties following the battle of Shiloh, "Nothing that I have ever heard or read had given me the faintest idea of the horrors witnessed here. I do not think that words are in our vocabulary expressive enough to present to the mind the realities of that sad scene."[35] There were approximately 23,000 casualties at Shiloh. At Gettysburg over 22,000 wounded were treated and many transported to permanent hospitals.[36]

Field hospitals usually were set up at the nearest point to the battle outside the range of artillery fire.[37] The hospital could be any building from a farmhouse, to a factory, barn, school, or church. After

any major battle, these hospitals would rapidly
overflow. Reed provides a vivid description of the
situation: "No available space was left unoccupied.
They lay as close as they could be packed, the
contaminated air growing worse every hour . . . The
air so close and nauseating that we often reeled with
faintness at our work . . .."[38] Usually, as soon as
possible, hospital tents were erected in an attempt to
accommodate the large number of wounded.[39]

The stated policy of the Medical Department
was to treat all wounded the same: "Humanity teaches
us that a wounded and prostrate foe is not then our
enemy."[40] The attitude among the nurses toward the
enemy wounded was expressed by Amy Bradley: ". . .
he was my enemy, but now he needs my aid."[41]

The nurses working at the field hospitals,
having the first contact with the wounded, would be
responsible for providing stimulant drinks, removing
the dirty "blood-hardened clothing,"[42] bathing and
dressing wounds, providing fresh clothing, providing
nourishment, overcoming the effects of exposure, and
assisting the surgeon.[43] These initial activities were
critical to survival in an era when natural body
defenses had to be relied upon.

Mary Phinney, describing the work in the field
hospital, wrote:

> Until you could once be in a hospital and see
> the state of the men as they come in, especially
> of those who have the blood of three weeks
> upon them and the dirt of as many months,
> you can form no idea of the undertaking. But
> the satisfaction on their faces when all is done
> and they are finally at rest is very great.
> Especially when a woman is near to nurse
> them, they seem so grateful.[44]

The nurses who worked on the transport ships
had duties similar to those nurses working in field
hospitals; and because these ships were crowded with
as many men as absolutely possible, the nurses had to
perform those duties in very cramped quarters.[45] A
surgeon describes the conditions on a transport ship at
White House, Virginia:

The condition of the (600) men was pitiable.
They were in the clothes in which they fell,
generally saturated with blood, and their
wounds were, in many cases, filled with
maggots. There were five medical officers on
board, beside dressers and female nurses. By
the time we reached Fort Monroe every man
had been washed, had his wound dressed, and
been supplied with clean under clothing.[46]

Many nurses who worked on the transports also
worked in the hospitals. Their assignments varied
according to the needs existing at any particular time.

As soon as possible, the wounded and the sick
were moved from field hospitals to regimental
hospitals or general hospitals. Some regimental
hospitals were semi-permanent, others were
temporary. As the front moved, the hospital moved.
Sometimes, the move had to be done quickly, under
fire, during retreats.[47] During one such rapid
evacuation, the hospital staff moved 700 men in 2
hours.[48]

Most female nurses worked in the general
hospitals, which were constructed in major cities
linked by rail or river to the battlefield. These
hospitals generally were orderly, comfortable, and
clean.[49] The wards were decorated with pictures and
personal objects.[50] The work was "systematized" with
each nurse assigned to a specific ward or specific
patients.[51]

The day nurses worked from 5:45 a.m. until 9
or 10:00 p.m. The general hospital staff nurse duties
included overseeing the care of assigned patients with
particularly close observation of the very sick
patients.[52] They passed medication,[53] applied splints,[54]
bathed and deloused patients, supervised the washing
and distribution of clothing,[55] and were held
responsible for the linen room, including the mending
and sewing.[56] They cleaned and prepared the men for
surgery, dressed wounds,[57] distributed meals and
assisted with feeding patients, supervised the
preparation of special diets, read to the patients, wrote
letters for patients, and labeled and mailed personal

items.[58] A small number of nurses administered
chloroform for surgery cases and assisted with
surgery.[59] On occasion the nurses accompanied the
wounded men to their home.[60] Nurses also helped with
the proper identification of those who died. A
frequently described duty was sitting with the dying
patients and then writing to the families informing
them of the soldier's death, describing the
circumstances and last words of the death bed and
usually including a lock of the person's hair.[61]

A special, personal interest in many of the
patients is apparent from the diaries and letters
written by the nurses.[62] Among the nurses best known
for their work with the soldiers are Ella King
Newsom, Kate Cumming, Mary Bickerdyke, Cordelia
Harvey, Mary Phinney, Clara Barton, Margaret
Breckinridge, Mary Husband, Helen Gilson, Anna
Etheridge, Ellen Marsh, Hattie Dada, Sarah Edson,
Caroline Burghardt, Eliza Porter, Mary Stafford,
Charlotte McKay, and Louisa May Alcott.

The number of patients assigned to a nurse
differed between hospitals. Benton Barracks, with
2,000 beds, had 1 female nurse to each 15 or 20
wards.[63] These nurses were responsible for
administrative and supervisory duties. This meant that
one nurse could have as many as 300 patients under
her immediate charge.[64] At Armory Square Hospital in
Washington, D.C., the patient to nurse ratio was
smaller with one female nurse in charge of a 50 bed
ward; approximately 40 female nurses were employed
there.[65] Sometimes the nurse received a minimum
amount of training. In at least one hospital, the nurses
received a 10 day training period before taking charge
of a ward.[66]

Supervisory duties included teaching and
supervising the new nurses,[67] assuming responsibility
for the condition of the beds, for the cleanliness and
sanitation of the unit, ventilation, and heating,[68]
assisting with morning rounds and noting orders.[69]
They also requisitioned food from the commissary,[70]
took reports on the worst cases and recording the
patient's progress,[71] directed the male nurses, (other

soldiers)[72] and generally saw that the patients' needs were met.[73]

A few nurses assumed extraordinary duties such as caring for the contagious cases, petitioning on the part of court-marshalled soldiers, or finding lodging for visiting family members.[74] Amy Bradley published the *Soldier's Journal* to inform and instruct the soldiers on procuring back pay and other benefits.[75]

The duties of the southern and northern nurses were comparable, but because of the blockade southern nurses were more often plagued by shortages of all types including medicine and hospital supplies.[76] In the South, female nurses were classified as Chief, Assistant, or Ward Matron, with salaries of $40, $35, and $30, respectively, per month. Because of high inflation, these salaries were so inadequate that some nurses had to supplement their income with a second job.[77]

One of the greatest contributions of the female nurses was their ability to organize the work of the hospital. Through their "genius for organization,"[78] they established a reputation for bringing "order" and "system" to the hospitals.[79] Obviously the pioneer hospital nurses proved their merit. As one soldier wrote: "A careful observation of over two years has taught me that nursing is fully as important as medicine. In the wards where there was the best nursing, there was always the fewest deaths."[80] Roberston Hospital at Chimborazo, for example, under the administration of Sally Thompkins, had only 73 deaths among its 1,333 patients.[81] It has been estimated that more than 184,000 lives were saved, who would otherwise have been victims of disease, as a result of the labors of female nurses.[82]

Among the many administrative nurses was Phoebe Yates Pember, who, as one of the chief matrons at Chimborazo--the largest military hospital in the world at the time--was praised for promoting the smooth operations of the hospital. Cornelia Tompkins and Emily Parsons were praised for their bringing "the system of nursing to such perfection" at

Benton Barracks.[83] The chief surgeon commented of
Louisa McCord's administrative ability in running the
hospital established at South Carolina College: "The
more she manages the better . . .."[84] Isabell Fogg was
recognized for bringing her hospital at Memphis to the
"highest point of efficiency."[85] And Maria Hall served
effectively as superintendent of the 4,000 bed Naval
Academy at Annapolis.[86]

The Civil War necessitated the construction
and development of more and better hospitals.[87] The
principles for a well run hospital, as promoted by
Florence Nightingale, including sanitation, ventilation,
regulated diets, and "careful and systematic treatment"
were all implemented by the nurses.[88] The nurses
changed the atmosphere of the hospital. As one nurse
observed, "The whole air and tone of a hospital ward
change and rise after a few days of a woman's
presence . . .."[89] The public perception of the hospital
evolved during the period of the Civil War from that
of an unhealthy institution for the sick poor to one of
care and cure, due in no small part ot the labors of the
female nurses.

The war created the stage and the essential
need for employing women in heretofore untried
ways. With the entrance into hospital nursing of
socially prominent women, possessing strong political
and humanitarian beliefs, strong education
backgrounds, and good organizational ability, nursing
began to emerge as a respectable occupation for
women in the United States.

NOTES

1.   United States War Department, Surgeon
      General's Office. *The Medical and Surgical
      History of the War of the Rebellion (1861-
      1865).* Washington, D.C.: Government Printing
      Office, 1870-1888. Holland, M.G. *Our Army
      Nurses.* Boston: B. Wilkins & Co., 1895, p. 167.
2.   Livermore, M. *My Story of the War.* Wesleyan
      University Library, Reprint 1972, p. 124.

3.   U.S. War Department, *Medical/Surgical History.*

4.   Thorp, M.F. *Female Persuasion.* New York: Archon Books, 1971, p. 1.

5.   Brockett, L.P. and Vaughn, M. *Women's Work in the Civil War: A Record of Heroism, Patriotism, and Patience.* Philadelphia: Zeigler & McCurdy, 1867. Cumming, K. *A Journal of Hospital Life in the Confederate Army of Tennessee,* 1866, Ed. Harwell, R.B. Louisiana State University Press, 1959.

6.   Brockett, L.P. *Women's Work in the Civil War*, p. 431. Holland, M.G. *Our Army Nurses*, p. 11.

7.   Woolsey, J.S. *Hospital Days.* New York: D. Van Nostrand, 1868, p. 48.

8.   Cumming, K. *Gleanings from the Southland.* Birmingham, Ala., 1895, p. 37-38.

9.   Circular No. 8, August, 1861.

10.   Logan, M. *American Women: Images and Realities.* New York: Arno Press, 1972, p. 361-365.

11.   Moore, F. *Women of the War: Their Heroism and Self-Sacrifice.* Hartford, Conn.: S.S. Scranton & Co., 1903, p. 278.

12.   Brockett, L.P. *Women's Work in the Civil War*, p. 719.

13.   Baker, N.B. *Cyclone in Calico: The Story of Mary Ann Bickerdyke.* Boston: Little, Brown, & Co., 1952, p. 51.

14.   Brockett, L.P. *Women's Work in the Civil War*, p. 71.

15.   Parsons, E. *Memoirs of Emily Elizabeth Parsons.* Boston: Little, Brown, & Co., 1880, p. 119. Nevins, A. (ed) *The Impact of the Civil War.* New York: Alfred A. Knopf, 1966, p. 44.

16.   Moore, F. *Women of the War*, p. 2.

17.   Holland, M.G. *Our Army Nurses*, p. 328.

18.   Livermore, M. *My Story of the War*, p. 168. Woolsey, J.S. *Hospital Days*, p. 41.

19.   Brockett, L.P. *Women's Work in the Civil War*, p. 514. Holland, M.G. *Our Army Nurses*, p. 328. Munroe, J. (ed.). *Adventures of an Army*

Nurse in Two Wars from Diary and Correspondence of Mary Phinney, Baroness Van Olnhausen. Boston: Little, Brown, & Co., p. 58.

20.   Ross, I. *Angel of the Battlefield: The Life of Clara Barton.* New York: Harper & Brothers Publishers, 1956.

21.   Holstein, A. Morris. *Three Years in Field Hospitals of the Army of the Potomac.* Boston: B. Wilkins & Co., 1895, p. 10.

22.   Logan, M. *American Women*, p. 361. McKay, C. *Stories of Hospital and Camp.* Philadelphia: Claxton, Remesen & Haffelfinger, 1876, p. 13.

23.   Holland, M.G. *Our Amry Nurses*, p. 197.

24.   Parsons, E. *Memoirs*, p. 97.

25.   Logan, M. *American Women*, p. 485.

26.   Holland, M.G. *Our Army Nurses*, p. 564.

27.   Brockett, L.P. *Women's Work in the Civil War*, p. 169.

28.   Munroe, J. *Adventures of an Army Nurse*, p. 34.

29.   Ibid, p. 115.

30.   Parsons, E. *Memoirs*.

31.   Woolsey, J.S. *Hospital Days*.

32.   Brockett, L.P. *Women's Work in the Civil War.* Holland, M.G. *Our Army Nurses.* Munroe, J. *Adventures of an Army Nurse.* Moore, F. *Women of the War.*

33.   Livermore, M. *My Story of the War*, p. 690.

34.   Holstein, A. *Three Years in Field Hospitals*, p. 30. Holland, M.G. *Our Army Nurses*, p. 453.

35.   Cumming, K. *A Journal of Hospital Life*, p. 15.

36.   Moore, F. *Women of the War*, p. 135. U.S. War Department, *Medical/Surgical History*, p. 142.

37.   U.S. War Department. *Medical/Surgical History.*

38.   Reed, W.H. *Hospital Life in the Army of the Potomac.* Boston: William V. Spencer, 1866. p. 26-27.

39.   U.S. War Department. *Medical/Surgical History.*

40.   U.S. War Department. *Medical/Surgical*

History, p. 99.

41.   Livermore, M. *My Story of the War*, p. 249.
Holstein, A. *Three Years in Field Hospitals*, p.
44. Moore, F. *Women of the War*, p. 397.

42.   Reed, W.H. *Hospital Life in the Army of the
Potomac*, p. 32.

43.   Moore, F. *Women of the War*, p. 280. Holland,
M.G. *Our Army Nurses*, p. 393.

44.   Munroe, J. *Adventure of an Army Nurse*, p. 87.

45.   U.S. War Department. *Medical/Surgical
History*, p. 36-37, 76. Moore, F. *Women of the
War*, p. 185. Brockett, L.P. *Women's Work in
the Civil War*, p. 194. Holland, M.G. *Our Army
Nurses*, p. 181.

46.   U.S. War Department. *Medical/Surgical
History*, p. 75.

47.   McKay, C. *Stories of Hospital and Camp*, p.
39. Munroe, J. *Adventures of an Army Nurse*,
p. 177. Nevin, A. *The Impact of the Civil War*,
p. 56. Ross, I. *Angel of the Battlefield*, p. 63.

48.   Holstein, A. *Three Years in Field Hospitals*, p.
30.

49.   Munroe, J. *Adventures of an Army Nurse*, p.
49.

50.   McKay, C. *Stories of Hospital and Camp*, p.
102-3.

51.   Moore, F. *Women of the War*, p. 375.

52.   Ibid, p. 318. Brockett, L.P. *Women's Work in
the Civil War*, p. 317.

53.   Parsons, E. *Memoirs*, p. 18. Holland, M.G. *Our
Army Nurses*, p. 181.

54.   Munroe, F. *Women of the War*, p. 77.

55.   Holstein, A. *Three Years in Field Hospitals*, p.
469.

56.   Woodward, J.J. *The Hospital Steward's
Manual*. Philadelphia, 1862. Moore, F. *Women
of the War*, p. 393.

57.   Holland, M.G. *Our Army Nurses*, p. 20.

58.   Alcott, L.M. *Hospital Sketches*. Cambridge:
The Belknap Press of Harvard University
Press, 1960 (Originally published by James
Redpath, Boston, 1863), p. 38. Moore, F.

Women of the War, 447.

59. Holland, M.G. *Our Army Nurses*, p. 181, 277, 297.

60. Brockett, L.P. *Women's Work in the Civil War*, p. 727.

61. Holland, M.G. *Our Army Nurses*, p. 233. Reed, W.H. *Hospital Life in the Army of the Potomac*, p. 121.

62. Alcott, L.M. *Hospital Sketches*. Moore, F. *Women of the War*. McKay, C. *Stories of Hospital and Camp*. Munroe, J. *Adventure of an Army Nurse*.

63. Brockett, L.P. *Women's Work in the Civil War*, 273.

64. Holland, M.G. *Our Army Nurses*, p. 150.

65. Parsons, E. *Memoirs*, p. 119.

66. Holland, M.G. *Our Army Nurses*, p. 11.

67. Thorp, M.F. *Female Persuasion*, p. 211. Parsons, E. *Memoirs*, p. 75.

68. Woodward, J.J. *Hospital Steward's Manual*.

69. Holland, M.G. *Our Army Nurses*, p. 453. Reed, W.H. *Hospital Life in the Army of the Potomac*, p. 80.

70. Woolsey, J.S. *Hospital Days*, p. 30.

71. Ibid, p. 37.

72. Holland, M.G. Our Army Nurses, p. 174. Parsons, E. *Memoirs*, p. 75.

73. Holland, M.G. *Our Army Nurses*, p. 111. *Confederate State Statutes*, 1st Congress, Session II, Ch. 17, 1862, in Cumming, K. *A Journal of Hospital Life*, p. XIV.

74. Moore, F. *Women of the War*. Brockett, L.P. *Women's Work in the Civil War*.

75. Moore, F. *Women of the War*, p. 446.

76. Logan, N. *American Women*, p. 316.

77. Nevin, A. *The Impact of the Civil War*, p. 48.

78. Moore, F. *Women of the War*, p. 246.

79. Brockett, L.P. *Women's Work in the Civil War*.

80. Moore, F. *Women's of the War*, p. 479.

81. Holland, M.G. *Our Army Nurses*, p. 108.

82. Moore, F. *Women of the War*, p. 593.

83. Brockett, L.P. *Women's Work in the Civil War*,

p. 489.
84.   Thorp, M.F. *Female Persuasion*, p. 210.
85.   Brockett, L.P. *Women's Work in the Civil War*,
       p. 508.
86.   Ibid., p. 453.
87.   At the close of the war, the Union army was
       operating 204 general hospitals with an average
       of 500 or more beds each. The Confederate
       army was operating approximately 150 general
       hospitals, 49 of which were in Richmond,
       Virginia. Davis, W. *The Civil War: First Blood*.
       Alexandria, VA: Time-Life Books, 1983, p. 95.
88.   Brockett, L.P. *Women's Work in the Civil War*.
89.   Woolsey, J.S. *Hospital Days*, p. 43.

SECTION III

NINETEENTH CENTURY NORMS: THE STATUS AND EDUCATION OF WOMEN AND NURSES

BROKEN WILLS AND TENDER HEARTS: RELIGIOUS IDEOLOGY AND THE TRAINED NURSE OF THE NINETEENTH CENTURY

by

Janet L. Bryant

Kathleen Byrne Colling

Nursing is as old as humankind, as young as a newborn babe and as inexorably tied to religion as Christ is to the church. Throughout history, the combination of women's roles as mother, nurturer and nurse has been both elevated and oppressed by religion. Twentieth century nursing originated in a nineteenth century extension of the nurturant care of the young and other family members to include care of the weak, injured, poor and elderly in the community.[1] The nurse, in caring for the infirm, epitomized the mother: constant, understanding, gentle and compassionate.[2]

Learned or trained nursing, rich with intuitive elements and housed in the hospital training schools of the late nineteenth century, was profoundly influenced by what historian Barbara Welter describes as "The Cult of True Womanood"--those attributes by which a woman judged herself and was judged by her husband, her neighbors and society. According to Welter, possession of the four cardinal virtues of domesticity, submissiveness, piety and purity,

153

154   *Broken Wills and Tender Hearts:*
Religious Ideology and the Trained
Nurse of the Nineteenth Century

guaranteed a promise of happiness and power to women in the righteous empire.[3]

Welter's framework is used as a guide in the examination of primary source materials to identify how religious ideology, as characterized in the four cardinal virtues, dominated and influenced the particular development of nursing education and practice in the Nightingale Era. Secondary source materials such as nursing histories provide background information and complement the primary source materials from Civil War nurses, nurse leaders, nurse educators and associates. Letters, poems, journal articles, administrative directives, as well as the personal and official correspondence of Florence Nightingale, Isabel Hampton, Annie Goodrich, Lavinia Dock and others reveal nursing behavior and practices that molded women and exemplified the four attributes. Welter's conceptual framework, the "Cult of True Womanhood," becomes the "Cult of True Nursinghood: The Nightingale Nurse," the ideal lady transplanted from home to hospital. Wealthy, prominent women and nursing pioneers embraced a Christian belief system which lent an aura of sanctity to the care of those in need, molded trainees into ladies and legitimized the evolution of nursing into an acceptable vocation for women.[4]

Florence Nightingale and her American disciples left nursing with the indelible stamp of their own class biases. Training emphasized character, not skills. The finished trained nurse, the "Nightingale" nurse, was simply the ideal "lady," transplanted from home to hospital and absolved of reproductive responsibilities.[5] To the patient, she brought the home to the hospital with the polished skills of domesticity. To the doctor, she brought the wifely virtue of submissiveness. To mankind, she exhibited the deep religious conviction and piety necessary to serve God through man. To the hospital community she exemplified purity.

Broken Wills and Tender Hearts: **155**
Religious Ideology and the Trained
Nurse of the Nineteenth Century

Domesticity can be defined simply as enjoyment in home life and household affairs.[6] The true dignity and beauty of the nineteenth century woman consisted in the faithful and cheerful performance of social and family duties. Sacred scripture sanctified domesticity through St. Paul's writings concerning role and reproduction.[7] Nursing was considered the natural extension of the new discipline of "domestic science." Conversely, the woman who remained at home was encouraged to see herself as a nurse practicing within the limits of the family.[8] Women's feminine drives could be sanctioned outside the home as long as these were couched in the realm of domesticity.

Nursing's ideal during the Civil War was to transform the army camp, with its masculine military code, into the home, dominated by the maternal creed.[9] An excerpt from *Aunt Becky's Civil War Diary* gives an example of domesticity during a respite from battle:

> Thanksgiving Day--In the midst of preparation a box arrived to me from home running over with just the things I needed to crown the feast--cake and butter and enough to go around withal, I felt a thankfulness which was in strict accordance with the day. Our men had an excellent dinner. The table looked homelike as we could make it by spreading sheets over it, and the new tin cups and plates, with the knives and forks were laid neatly upon it,--little hankerchiefs of cotton which the Binghamton ladies had sent for the use of our sick men became elegant dinner napkins for the day.[10]

The nurse as "mother" during the Civil War lent power to this consecrated maternal role. Wood points out that the "boys in blue" were just that--boys, and they missed their homes and sang their songs not about their sweethearts, but about their mothers. Loose military morals could be fought with hometown ethics. When duty called, nurses were fierce moral

156 *Broken Wills and Tender Hearts:*
Religious Ideology and the Trained
Nurse of the Nineteenth Century

watchdogs, chiding soldiers for playing checkers on Sunday and shooing the "Delilahs and Magdelines" away. Opening a branch of the American home at the front, enabled women to utilize domesticity as a strong focus for power in a developing profession during the war.[11]

However, this was difficult to transfer once the war was over. Women in nursing felt burdened with the "morally" uplifting tasks of housework. Popular writers extolled the virtues of bedmaking, laundry, cleaning and "tea pouring,"[12] but these duties, added to the nursing tasks, presented the nursing student with an endless array of responsibilities which exhausted and depressed her. The cap so honored and revered as a nursing symbol was worn to keep long hair clean while dusting and scurbbing. Much of this work was decidedly not nursing, but rather maid's work. Work days consisted of 14 hours, seven days a week, much of which was spent sewing, washing bandages and even cleaning windows.[13] It was no wonder that many left nursing never to return.

When the first American schools of nursing were established, the family was the institutional model for the operation of hospitals. Just as the family was the basic unit for indoctrination of evangelical beliefs, so too, the hospital family became the focal point for the lessons of nursing. All policies and procedures were designed to look out for the "household." The role of nurses was very early conceived as that of caring for the "hospital family." Like mothers in a household, nurses were responsible for the saintly tasks which met the needs of all members of the hospital family from patients to physician. All departments of the hospital from wards and operating rooms to storerooms and kitchens were staffed and kept open 24 hours a day by nurses.

In addition, women (nurses) were expected to look out for the needs of men (physicians) in the hospital family, who, for the most part, did not reside in the household, but were free to come and go. In the absence of men, women were expected to assume

Broken Wills and Tender Hearts: 157
Religious Ideology and the Trained
Nurse of the Nineteenth Century

responsibility, but this was relinquished upon the
return of the men.[14]

Nursing pioneers emphasized that to work in
the hospital the wifely virtues of absolute obedience,
the selfless devotion of mother and the kindly
discipline of a household manager were needed.
Nightingale, herself, stated the following when asked
about examinations and licensing nurses:

> nurses cannot be registered and examined any
> more than others--Woman is an instinctive
> nurse taught by mother nature.[15]

Not only was the hospital to be a home but the
nurses' residence as well. A unique factor of the
Nightingale Training School was the nurses' home, an
idea which originated with Miss Nightingale. She
believed that for nursing education to be reputable,
students had to live in a closely chaperoned home.
This was a philosophy that must have also appealed to
the parents of each pupil. A description of the
Nightingale Nurses' Home in London follows:

> Each probationer had her own bedroom there
> and shared a common living room with
> additional accommodations for classes and
> meals--the home was under the supervision of
> a home-sister, provided guided study hours,
> singing and Bible classes, and a sympathetic
> home-like atmosphere. Strict rules and
> regulations governed behavior, hours, study,
> recreation, worship and free time--no
> probationer was allowed to go out alone, she
> had to be in the company of at least one other
> probationer.[16]

In addition to domesticity, Welter's second
attribute of submissiveness was clearly operational in
the United States training schools, patterned after
Nightingale's philosophy of behavior and education.
The systematic hospital socialization of student nurses
may best be understood as a concern with authority
and control. Supervised by a trusted director of nurses,
surrounded by a tight wall of security, the school was
intended to raise a plentiful supply of women nurses-

158   *Broken Wills and Tender Hearts:*
Religious Ideology and the Trained
Nurse of the Nineteenth Century

-respectful, obedient, cheerful, submissive, hard-working, loyal, passive and religious.

Submission, according to Welter, was perhaps the most feminine virtue expected of nineteenth century women. Men were supposed to be religious, although they rarely had time for it. Women, by nature, were the passive, submissive responders, while men were the actors. This order of things was fixed by heavenly edict, i.e., man was "woman's superior by God's appointment, if not in intellectual dowry, at least by official decree."[17] Women, in all roles, especially nursing, were encouraged to accept submission without comment or criticism. To suffer in silence seemed to be the great commandment to obey. It seems no accident that the apprenticeship model was chosen as the nursing education system of the nineteenth century, for it fit the submissive female role so well.

Under this model, nursing students signed a contract with the hospital specifying the length of term of service and the small fee to be paid them. Applicants agreed to remain under the direction of the institution, to be subjected to the rules of the hospital and the discipline of the school. Officials claimed the right and had the power to discharge an apprentice at any time for reasons they judged sufficient. As in the evangelical household, obedience to authority was held sacred under all circumstances. Questioning the rules of the hospital or a physician's orders constituted "misconduct" and students were redily dismissed for doing so.[18] The wills of students, as in historian Philip Greven's evangelical code, were broken to submit to the rigors of their calling.[19] Punishment was usually withdrawal of privileges, a stern lecture by the director of nursing, or dismissal.

The apprenticeship model was devastating for nursing. In his essay on "The Subjection of Women," John Stuart Mill pointed out that systems of apprenticeship were ideal for keeping individuals subject to the will and wishes of others. Mill felt that the concept and oppressive use of apprenticeship were

Broken Wills and Tender Hearts: **159**
Religious Ideology and the Trained
Nurse of the Nineteenth Century

grossly incompatible with modern social ideas and institutions.[20]

Nursing, perhaps more than any other profession, has been influenced by social conceptions regarding the nature of women. Modern nursing originated at a time when Victorian ideals dictated that the role of women was to serve men's needs and convenience. Women were viewed as less independent, less capable of initiative and less creative than men and thus needed masculine guidance. In view of this definition of women, education was of special interest to men in the medical profession. The apprenticeship system was considered an ideal means of insuring that nurses so trained would remain "ideal" women.[21]

Hospital schools provided both a structural and functional arrangement whereby the medical profession and male officials in the hospital could claim the right to exercise control over women. These two groups cultivated the idea that they had the right (and most often the power) to determine the growth of a female profession.[22]

Physicians have been the strongest advocates of a special, isolated type of education as a means of maintaining social and intellectual control. They spent a greal deal of time emphasizing that nursing was subordinate to medicine and should remain so for public good. The "born nurse" theory supports the contention that nurses were better off without education.[23] In the following passage, analogies are made to the military and the subservient spirit of evangelical religion. Lavinia Dock, an early nursing leader, stated in 1893:

> Absolute and unquestioning obedience must be the foundation of the nurse's work and to this end complete subordination of the individual to the work as a whole is as necessary for her as for the soldier."[24]

Military discipline manifested itself early in the lives of the pupils. Essential to the system was the recognition of rank. The head of the school held the highest rank followed by assistants and then Head

160 *Broken Wills and Tender Hearts:*
Religious Ideology and the Trained
Nurse of the Nineteenth Century

Nurse. Rank extended down through the pupils. Senior pupils were of higher rank than intermediate and intermediate pupils higher than juniors. Lowest in the ladder were probationers. Rank established the head of the school as the sole source of authority; it also provided the means for transmitting authority and fixing responsibility in a straight line from the source.[25]

Inherent in the recognition of rank was a well-defined pattern of behavior. One always stood in the presence of persons of superior rank; one had no social relations with individuals of higher or lower rank. Obedience to authority and unquestioning compliance were the order of the day.[26] In addition, bands or caps signified level of nursing, just as bars and stars signified rank in the military.

Authority within nineteenth century nursing was seen in terms of sovereignty, and sovereignty, in turn, meant total power. Analogous to the evangelical notion of God's sovereignty was the sovereignty of the physician. He, together with the Matron or Director of Nursing, formed the parental team against which no nursing student (child) could fight. As Greven points out, in the evangelical family, parental power was absolute, and the crushing of the childs' will by the exertion of systematic effort on the part of parents was justified by the conviction that parental power and authority were beyond question within the confines of the household.[27] Power, authority, will and wisdom were personified in these authority figures and the nursing student had little recourse but to obey.[28]

Piety is defined as "devotion" to God. Religion, or piety, the core component of nineteenth century nursing, belonged to women of the time, as a divine right--a gift of God and nature. This "peculiar susceptibility to religion," was seen as a gift to women to throw its beams into the naughty world of men, just as the Nightingale lamp, the light of religion would harmonize, improve and enlighten the world. Women were seen as "new improved Eves," working in cooperation with the Redeemer, to bring the world

Broken Wills and Tender Hearts: **161**
Religious Ideology and the Trained
Nurse of the Nineteenth Century

back from sin.[29]

Nurses were viewed as the "new Eves" in an excerpt from an address by Annie W. Goodrich.

> For the nurse, in a very full sense, is a daughter of the religious thought of the old world and however she may, or have seemed to stray from the beaten paths, a true history must present her every new expression as a mission in response to the command, "Go and do thou likewise."[30]

In the same address, Goodrich seems to deliberately choose the word "minister" as in "minister to the sick" to emphasize the early "missionary" aspects of nursing's healing role.[31]

The heavenly mission of the nurse included healing of the soul as well as the body. Salvation of the soul to new life is exemplified in the personal experiences of Florence Nightingale. Florence felt that she was called by God and listed four such experiences in the years 1837, 1853, 1854 and 1861.[32] Florence believed that truth was discoverable through the exercise of mental powers. As she came closer to God she felt increasingly distant from any earthly church.[33]

Thus, religion was valued in nursing and viewed as complementary to piety, purity, domesticity and submissiveness. Nursing work was not perceived as leading to a rejection of religion but rather as an elevated "calling" or "vocation." The nursing collar at first was a high, stiff one, buttoned in the back and fashioned like a clerical collar. The Nightingale lamp symbolized Christ as the light of the world. The nurse, as a personal messenger of goodness, was the hand of the Lord in female piety and the willing worker in the delivery of patient care.

Hard physical labor, long hours, menial tasks and insufficient sleep characterized the lives of both student and graduate nurses. This rigorous regimen was accepted, condoned and elevated. Even the sacrifice and suffering of the nurse as she faced and met the daily demands of patient care could be reclaimed for God. Barbara Welter captures this spirit

162   'Broken Wills and Tender Hearts:
Religious Ideology and the Trained
Nurse of the Nineteenth Century

in a nineteenth century quote:

> God increased the care and sorrows of woman
> that she might be sooner constrained to accept
> the terms of salvation--her sacrifice and
> suffering could be offered up to atone for the
> sinful failings of feminine nature.[34]

In a final report, the chairman of the committee to establish a hospital school of nursing at Bellevue presents an enlightened summary of the type of nurse needed to perform and reform hospital care:

> We wish our candidates to be religious women
> but do not require that they should belong to
> any given sect. To Catholic and Protestant our
> doors are equally open: we impose no vows: we
> say to all, in the words of the founder of the
> Sisters of Charity: 'your convent must be the
> houses of the sick, your cell the chamber of
> suffering, your chapel the nearest church: your
> cloister the streets of a city or the wards of a
> hospital: the promise of your obedience your
> sole enclosure: your grate the fear of God and
> your womanly modesty your only veil.'[35]

Purity, the final attribute in Welter's quatrile was as essential as piety to a young woman. The absence of purity was viewed as unnatural and unfeminine. Without purity a woman was but a member of some lowly order. A "fallen woman" was a fallen angel unworthy of the celestial company of her sex.[36]

Until the nineteenth century, nursing care was disorganized, and though there were nuns and sisters, nursing services were also sporadically provided by women who lived by gambling, prostitution, thievery and bribery. The sick were left to fend for themselves. Death was usually at home, and only the homeless, the traveler, the very poor had to subject themselves to the filth of hospitals and the abuse of its caregivers. Women and nursing were relegated to a low, ineffectual position in society. To improve the status of nursing (which might also affect the status of women), it was necessary to establish high standards

Broken Wills and Tender Hearts: **163**
Religious Ideology and the Trained
Nurse of the Nineteenth Century

for admission to educational programs of nursing, as well as strict rules and regulations governing the character and morals of pupil nurses.[37]

According to Woodham-Smith each student selected for the Nightingale School in England had to exemplify the new image. The Nightingale nurse had to establish her character in a profession proverbial for immorality. Neat lady-like, vestal, above suspicion, she had to be the incarnate denial that a hospital nurse had to be drunken, ignorant or promiscuous. One false step by any probationer might cause scandal that would set the fledgling training school and nursing back to where many still believed it belonged, in the gutter.[38] Therefore, in theory, students were carefully evaluated and selected.

The traditional symbol of purity, the white uniform worn by a graduate nurse, was more of an early twentieth century phenomenon. Many schools did not require specific student uniforms until very late in the 1880s or 1890s. Plain attire was typical. Instead of a full white uniform, most schools agreed upon a white pinafore-like garment worn over a simple dress. At Bellevue, the underdress was of a checked gingham material.[39]

Graduate nurses and especially supervisors dressed distinctively. Isabel Hampton, the first Director of Nurses at the Johns Hopkins School of Nursing examplified the epitome of nursing leaders both in appearance and in behavior. A symbolic pureness and chastity in dress is described:

> She wore a simple black uniform cut on flowing lines. The cap, collar and cuffs were made of white fine lawn and the cap is said to have been inspired by one that she had seen worn by an ecclesiastical dignitary in Rome--when the weather was very hot, she wore a white dress.[40]

Thus, nursing education of this era was permeated with religious dogma and rigid theological discipline. Chapel attendance was mandatory and students were exposed only to what was considered

164   *Broken Wills and Tender Hearts:*
       Religious Ideology and the Trained
       Nurse of the Nineteenth Century

consistent with Christian doctrine and the feminine ideology of the day. Faculty members who introduced unorthodox ideas did not last long and students were presented with a limited body of knowledge. Indeed, in some schools, only one faculty member was present to teach all the nursing courses. Students had no freedom to express or defend their own views and the student-teacher relationship was one of authoritative repressiveness. Women were seen to be "naturally" religious and accepting of the gospel, and the dogma of nursing, so like the gospel, was to be accepted "naturally" as well.

It is our contention that the particular development of nursing practice and education in the nineteenth century was not accidental. The "cult of true womanhood" and the feminine attributes of domesticity, submissiveness, piety, and purity so dominated the American scene that nursing as a gender-linked profession could not escape them. Vestiges of this narrow, Victorian viewpoint remain with us even today.

The spirit of service, a strong sense of obedience, a symbiotic attachment to domesticity and a binding feminine image define the immutable heritage of nursing. Nowhere else is it better exemplified and deified as in the figure of the nineteenth century Nightingale nurse. The vision of the lady with the lamp represents a religious ideology that simultaneously elevates and oppresses--a double edged sword that continues to haunt and challenge nursing even today. Nursing still labors under the Christian ethos and dogma which combines the ethic of service with the traditional views of women as inferior, women as subservient to men and women's work as less valued, less important than mens' work.

Although progress has been made, nursing must remain vigilant to societal forces which threaten autonomy and professionalism in education and practice. As the twenty-first century approaches, it is time to bring a new meaning to nursing devoid of stereotypical gender-based roles and oppressive

Broken Wills and Tender Hearts: **165**
Religious Ideology and the Trained
Nurse of the Nineteenth Century

religious ideology. It is time to recognize the nurse's role as nurturer within the culture of care as a source of strength, power and economic value--a time to make the invisible relationships of care visible and as avalued as technology.

NOTES

1. Taddy, J. *A Philosophical Inquiry into Existential Phenomenology as an Approach for Nursing.* Ann Arbor, Michigan: University Microfilms, 1978, p. 54.

2. Uprichard, M. "Ferment in Nursing" in *The Challenge of Nursing*, eds. Auld, M. and Birum, L. St. Louis: C.V. Mosby, 1973, p. 24.

3. Welter, B. "The Cult of True Womanhood, 1820-1860" in *Women and Womanhood in America*, ed. Hogeland, R. Lexington, Massachusetts: D.C. Heath & Co., 1973, p. 104.

4. Ehrenreich, B. and English, D. *Witches, Midwives & Nurses - A History of Women Healers.* Old Westbury, Connecticut: The Feminist Press, 1973, pp. 34-36.

5. Ibid., p. 34.

6. *Webster's II New Riverside Dictionary.* Boston: Houghton Mifflin Co., 1984, p. 209.

7. Welter. "The Cult of True Womanhood," p. 109.

8. Ibid., p. 110.

9. Wood, A.D. "The War Within a War: Women Nurses in the Union Army," *Civil War History*, 18 (September 1972), p. 199.

10. Palmer, S. *The Story of Aunt Becky's Army Life.* New York: John F. Trow, 1867, p. 13.

11. Ibid., p. 201-202.

12. Welter, "The Cult of True Womanhood," p. 110.

13. Kalisch, P. and Kalisch, B. *The Advance of American Nursing.* Boston: Little Brown, 1978, p. 155.

14. Ashley, J.A. *Hospitals Paternalism and the*

166 *Broken Wills and Tender Hearts:*
Religious Ideology and the Trained
Nurse of the Nineteenth Century

Role of the Nurse. New York: Teachers College Press, 1967, p. 17.

15. Roberts, J. and Group, T. "The Women's Movement and Nursing," *Nursing Forum,* 12 (1973), p. 318.

16. Woodham-Smith, C. *Florence Nightingale.* New York: McGraw-Hill, 1951, pp. 234-236.

17. Welter. "The Cult of True Womanhood," p. 108.

18. Ashley. *Hospitals, Paternalism,* p. 27.

19. Greven, P. *The Protestant Temperament. Patterns of Child Rearing, Religious Experience and the Self in Early America,* New York: Alfred A. Knopf, 1977, p. 12.

20. Mill, J. and Mill, H. "The Subjection of Women in *Essays on Sex Equality,* ed. Rossi, A. Chicago: University of Chicago Press, 1970, pp. 143-144.

21. Ashley. *Hospitals, Paternalism,* p. 75.

22. Ibid., p. 76.

23. Ibid.

24. Dock, L. "Nurses Should be Obedient" in *Issues in Nursing,* Bullough, B. and Bullough, V. eds. New York: Spring, 1967, p. 96.

25. Jones, E. and Pfeffercorn. *The Johns Hopkins Hospital School of Nursing.* Baltimore: Johns Hopkins Press, 1954, p. 76.

26. Ibid.

27. Greven, P. *The Protestant Temperament,* p. 37.

28. *Websters II,* p. 529.

29. Welter. "The Cult of True Womanhood," p. 104.

30. Goodrich, A. "Education, the Nurse and Life," in the *Society of the NY Hospital Commemorative Exercises 50th Anniversary, New York Hospital School of Nursing 1877-1927,* p. 41.

31. Ibid.

32. Woodham-Smith, C. *Florence Nightingale,* p. 13.

33. O'Malley, I.B. *Florence Nightingale 8120-1956.* London: Thorton Butterworth, 1931, p. 197.

34. Welter. "The Cult of True Womanhood," p. 104.

Broken Wills and Tender Hearts: **167**
Religious Ideology and the Trained
Nurse of the Nineteenth Century

35. Dock, L. and Nutting, M. *History of Nursing*, Vol. 2, New York: Putnams, 1907-1912, p. 387.
36. Welter. "The Cult of True Womanhood," p. 106.
37. Woodham-Smith, C. *Florence Nightingale*, pp. 234-236.
38. Barritt, E. "Florence Nightingale's Values and Modern Nursing Education," *Nursing Forum*, 12 (1973), p. 34.
39. Kalisch & Kalisch. *The Advance of American Nursing*, p. 100-103.
40. Jones & Pfeffercorn. *Johns Hopkins School*, p. 68.

NURSING, SEXUAL HARASSMENT, AND FLORENCE NIGHTINGALE: IMPLICATIONS FOR TODAY

Vern and Bonnie Bullough

Sexual harassment was first publicly identified as an issue in women's working lives at a speakout held in the spring of 1975 in Ithaca, New York, when many women offered testimony as to how sexual harassment had affected them personally both in education and employment. The speak out was sponsored by Cornell University's Human Affairs Program and by a fledgling grass-roots organization, Working Women United Institute (later Working Women's Institute), dedicated to equal employment opportunities for women, decent working conditions, and most important, the elimination of sexual harassment on the job.[1]

The Working Women's Institute defined sexual harrassment at that time as

> any sexual attention on the job which makes a woman uncomfortable, affects her ability to do her work, or interferes with her employment opportunities. It includes, degrading attitudes, looks, touches, jokes, innuendos, gestures, and direct propositions. It can come from supervisors, co-workers, clients and customers.[2]

168

This original definition is very similar to the one later adopted by the Equal Employment Opportunity Commission for guidelines which stated that sexual harassment included "unwelcome sexual advances, requests for sexual favors, and other verbal or physical conduct of a sexual nature."[3]

Though almost all women regard certain kinds of male responses to them as demeaning and objectionable, it was not until such behaviors were defined and labeled unacceptable that women (including nurses) felt freer to report and to act on such behaviors.

Harry Hazel, for example, after discussing reports on sexual harassment in education concluded that such practices occurred in hospitals and schools of anesthesia in approximately the same proportion as on college campuses or in a business setting.[4] He based his statement upon observations and personal experiences. Bonnie W. Duldt in 1982 offered some concrete data in her report on a survey of registered nurses attending a baccalaureate program in nursing on a part time basis. Of the 89 who returned their questionnaire over 60% had experienced sexual harassment in the preceding year to the extent that it distracted them from their nursing tasks, impaired their decision making, complicated their relationships with their spouse or lover, or even in some cases made them physically ill. Male physicians were the most common initiators of harassing action.[5]

In a more comprehensive study Grieco sent a questionnaire to 1,733 nurses (both LPN's and RN's) with a mailing address in Boone County, Missouri, the site of the University of Missouri and its nursing school, as well as a Veterans Administration Hospital, and several other state and private hospitals. He requested nurses to respond to any incidents of harassment during their entire career and included patients on a list of possible harassers. A total of 496 responded of which 462 were usable. Some 26% of the respondents reported incidents of harassment with younger nurses more likely to report such incidents than older ones. Grieco hypothesized that older nurses were more likely to have forgotten incidents of harassment early in their career. The data also implies that older nurses are less likely to be harassed than younger ones. While patients were listed as being harassing in 87% of the cases, physicians were the next most likely group (67%) and other male employees fell further down the scale. Grieco concluded that not only was sexual harassment a frequent occurence in nursing, but that it was probably higher in nursing than in any of the other traditionally female occupations.[6]

Once sexual harassment is recognized as a reality in nursing today, particularly that practiced by male physicians and co-workers, it also became clear that it was not a new phenomenon. In fact, it is the thesis of this paper, that the reality of sexual harassment was a major force in determining many of the directions taken by early nursing.

Though it seems clear that what women regard as harassment is often not perceived as such by men, it clearly is a reflection of power. In fact outbursts of sexual harassment seem most likely to occur when a woman's action is perceived as a threat to male power. There is, however, more to it than this. MacKinnon, one of the major theory makers in this feld, characterized sexual harassment as "dominance eroticized." She wrote

> The sense that emerges from incidents of sexual harassment is less that men mean to arouse or gratify the women's sexual desires, or vent their own, and more that they want to know that they can go this far this way any time they wish and get away with it. The fact that they can do this seems itself to be sexually arousing. The practice seems an extension of their desire and belief that the woman is there *for them*, however they may choose to define that.[7]

Put in this way harassment seeks to sustain both male workplace power and male power to treat women as

sexual objects. But associated with this is also a male
effort to trivialize what a woman does. As Schur has
written:

> Visual objectification and occupational
> trivialization tend to reinforce one another.
> Furthermore, the two processes appear in
> combination in the now-prevalent pattern of
> "display jobs"--work roles in which perceived
> female attractiveness is treated as being
> highly salient. Such salience is understandable
> in certain occupations such as actress or
> model (and, with less "respectability,"
> striptease artist or pornography star). Yet the
> "display job" phenomenon now greatly
> transcends these standard categories. Women's
> "looks" continue to be treated as a relevant
> employment criterion in a wide range of
> situations, despite the usual denials that this
> is happening. There appears to be a persisting
> tendency without our present gender system
> for many if not most jobs held by women to
> become, in some degree, display jobs. To the
> extent this continues to occur, we have
> further evidence that the objectification and
> trivialization of women have far from
> disappeared.[8]

Since nursing in its origins was a challenge to males
in the workplace, particularly physicians, harassment
would seem to be an inevitable part of the nursing
role. The problem that early nurses had was to
develop effective coping mechanisms.

Traditionally women have lived far more
circumscribed lives than men. In western culture, at
least, women have, until recently, been under the
jurisdiction of men, either fathers, husbands,
brothers, or adult sons who were supposed to protect
them. In fact, this was the distinction between good
women and bad women which has also been so much
of the dichotomy of being a woman. Good women
were wives, daughters, sisters, mothers, women who
were under the protection of men, while bad women

were prostitutes and other women who did not adhere to the need for male protection or proper chaperons. Rape, in fact, through much of western history was regarded as a crime against property rather than the individual--the crime was using another man's property rather than a crime of assault against the female victim.

Until the eighteenth century, these restrictions, while debilitating, did not handicap the economic function of women since most work was in the home and most people lived in rural areas, in villages, or in small towns. As cities increased rapidly in population, the restrictions put on women were less and less functional, particularly as they ventured into the cities. Ned Ward in his *Secret History of the London Clubs* (1709) indicated what happened to women who went out in the city on their own. One group of young men known as Mohawks went out nightly to beat up on people, stand women and girls on their heads so that their skirts would fall down (underparts were not yet worn), and other such boisterous activities. Others, such as the Bold Bucks specialized in rape, the Blasters in exposing themselves to passing women, and the Fun Club in practical jokes (often on women). All the clubs had sexual overtones and their bulletin boards listed famous madams and noted prostitutes.[10]

What was emerging was a new restriction of women's freedom, namely the establishment of limits on the places where women could go. A woman who violated such a constraint was said to "ask for" any violence she might suffer. Though women were not raped any more frequently in the nineteenth than in the eighteenth century (at least as far as the court records are concerned), they now had to bear the guilt of believing they invited rape or harassment by their conduct. This led to detailed questioning of women rape victims designed as much to find out what they had done to cause their own trauma as to catch and identify the rapist. To protect themselves women had to accept that the potential of sexual

violence made certain areas unsafe for them and
limited the scope of their behavior.[11]

What could women do to make themselves
less prone to attack or harassment? The nineteenth
century gave a two fold answer to this. First, women
were to avoid doing certain things and going in
certain places, and second, they could protect
themselves by acting like ladies. Though the term
lady originally implied a certain social class, by the
nineteenth century it also conveyed the way in which
a proper women, regardless of social class, was
supposed to act in order to prevent unwanted
invitations which would result if she gave the wrong
impression. Acting as a lady required a woman to
present an image of proper gentility. Hannah Moore,
the early nineteenth century bluestocking teacher,
dramatist, writer, and essayist, described the ideal
gentle woman as one who

> had been accustomed to have an early habit
> of restraint exercised over all her appetites
> and temper; she who has been used to pent
> [confine] bounds of her desires as a general
> principle, will have learned to withstand a
> passion for dress and personal ornaments; and
> the woman who has conquered this propensity
> has surmounted one of the most domineering
> temptations which assail the sex. Modesty,
> simplicity, humility, economy, prudence,
> liberality, charity, are almost inseparable, and
> not very remotely connected with an habitual
> victory over personal vanity.[12]

Though ladies were different from ordinary women,
it was possible with proper training to become a
lady.

> It was her purity, contrasted with the
> coarseness of men, that made women the head
> of the Home (though not of the family) and
> the guardian of public morality.[13]

Fashion helped in forging this new kind of
women by popularizing bustles and hoops, wasp
waisted corsets and trailing skirts, and other items of

clothing which limited freedom of action. The tight lacing especially made many women more delicate than they otherwise might have been since it made it more difficult to breathe as well as to move. Since feminine delicacy was so admired, many women who were not delicate by nature tried to become so by design. In short becoming a lady put restrictions on what a woman could do. It also had its compensations.

A lady, for example, was not without power, and in fact in some ways it served as a power base that women otherwise might not have had. The simple fact that ladies were believed to be made of finer fabric than their male counterparts, allowed them to deal with those moral causes which grew out of their concerns for their family and for others. Ladies were prominent in the anti-slavery movement, in the campaign to outlaw regulated prostitution (more difficult because it dealt with sex), in campaigns to bridle male licentiousness (read harassment of the females), the efforts to extend educational opportunity to women as well as to provide better care for the sick and the mentally ill.[14]

Obviously, it was difficult for a lady to enter the labor market but on the other hand women as a group did so in increasing numbers, particularly in the last part of the nineteenth century. In the United States, for example, the rise of the cotton textile industry in New England radically altered working and living patterns for large numbers of women. Thousands of young, single women left the home of their parents to work in the growing mill towns such as Lowell, Mass., the leading factory town in the middle decades of the nineteenth century. Here they were continually reminded that they were ladies. As Nathan Appleton, one of the original organizers of the Waltham-Lowell mills, argued, it was necessary to protect the virtue of his women workers and to this end he established boarding houses "under the charge of respectable women with every provision

for religious workship."[15] Women were required to
live in company boardinghouses, attend regular
church services, abstain from alcoholic beverages,
observe a 10 p.m. curfew, and not have men in their
rooms.[16] Boarding House keepers were regarded as
surrogate parents while the women workers were
more or less treated as minor children. Though there
was some rebellion against this attitude, particularly
in the later part of the century, apparently most of
the women were not particularly upset at the
restrictive rules because they were rather similar to
those under which they lived at home. Though they
were working women, they also wanted respect, as
ladies and were hostile to those among them who did
not act as a lady.

> A girl, suspected of immoralities, or serious
> improprieties, at once loses caste. Her fellow
> boarders will . . . immediately leave the
> house, if the keeper does not dismiss the
> offender. In self-protection, therefor, the
> patron is obliged to put the offender away.
> Nor will her former companions walk with
> her, or work with her; till at length, finding
> herself everywhere talked about, and pointed
> at, and shunned she is obliged to relieve her
> fellow-operatives of a presence which they
> feel brings disgrace.[17]

Being a lady was continually emphasized,
often by comparing the role of the lady with the
man.

> He is made more strong, that he may protect
> and defend; she more lovely, that he may be
> willing to shield and guard her, and that
> physical difference which, in one state of
> society, makes woman the slave of man, in
> another makes him, her worshiper . . .. In
> that station where woman is most herself,
> where her predominating qualities have the
> fullest scope, there she is most influential,
> and most truly worthy of respect. But when
> she steps from her alloted path into that of

the other sex, she betrays her inferiority, and in the struggle would be inevitably subdued.[18]

IMAGE AND THE DEVELOPMENT OF NURSING

Florence Nightingale obviously was a lady and although she was concerned with areas with which a proper lady should be concerned, she also did unlady like things. Though ladies had fought for the right to speak about issues, even in public, and volunteer work was accepted and encouraged, Nightingale went where no proper lady had previously gone and in the process violated the gender norms of the day. This threatened male power and made her subject to harassment. She reacted as a lady should. The most symbolic action took place at Scutari when after her services were rejected by the surgeons, she simply sat in the hospital with her nurses until her services were requested. Like a proper lady she also worked behind the scenes for her causes, using men to carry out much of the public aspect of her work. In fact, it was only by acting as a lady that she was able to accomplish what she did.

Anxious to protect nurses from harassment, she also insisted that they act as ladies. Still proper ladies did not work for a living, and the Nightingale nurses did. But then ladies in the past had not done what Nightingale did. She, in effect, was extending the concept of the lady to the work place in order to protect nurses. This required that nurses, regardless of their social class, be educated to act as ladies by Nightingale as well as by most of the other early nursing leaders. To emphasize the special nature of these women, even secular nurses came to be called sisters. The very title aroused the chivalric feeling in the male to be protective rather than harassing.

Whether Nightingale was consciously designing techniques to deal with male harassment or whether such techniques were inculcated so deeply in

the middle class women of the day that they were
second nature to her is nowhere written down, but
her actions emphasize she was. She very much
recognized that nurses were invading and even
challenging the male on his own turf. In 1867, she
wrote to Mary Jones, her close friend and head of
St. John's House as well as a colleague who had
supplied six of her original nurses for Nightingale's
use in the Crimea:

> The whole reform in nursing both at home
> and abroad has consisted in this: to take all
> power over the nursing out of the hands of
> men, and put it into the hands of one female
> trained head and make her responsible for
> everything (regarding internal management
> and discipline) being carried out.

She added:

> Usually it is the medical staff who have
> injudiciously interfered as "master." How
> much worse it is when it is the Chaplain . .
> . Don't let the Chaplain want to make himself
> matron. Don't let the Doctor make himself
> Head nurse.[19]

Nightingale recognized that lady like behavior
would not always save a nurse from being harassed.
She wrote, for example, that in military hospitals

> every night, of every year, every military
> hospital contains a certain number of non-
> commissioned officers who are more or less
> the worse for drink . . . people think that the
> discipline in military hospitals will be strict,
> it is not; it is worse than in civil hospitals.[20]

Nightingale was not just concerned about military
hospitals and in her letter she went on to report
stories about porters hanging around the stairs of St.
Thomas's and how they made themselves
objectionable to the probationers. In fact, the
problem of dark stairs received much attention in her
discussion of hospitals. In short, women were being
in places that many men judged as unacceptable.
Male physicians and surgeons had the same concepts

about the proper role of women and were themselves
likely to harass nurses. Nightingale mentioned some
of the worst offenders by name.

In a sense Nightingale as an older women and
a lady could escape much of the harassment. Age
itself is somewhat protective or it might be that age
simply gives a woman more skills in avoiding
harassing situations. It is also equally possible that
males are less likely to harass older women unless
they were conceived of as threatening male authority
and nurses did threaten the authority.

Nightingale developed three methods for
coping with sexual harassment. Although they have
not previously been described in such terms, looking
at them as coping methods to deal with harassment,
makes them far more logical to us today than if
examined out of this context. First she insisted on
the importance of good character, i.e., morality, or
in simple terms, evidence of a lady like character.
Obviously most of her recruits came from the
working classes but she wanted them to act like
ladies. A second method was to establish a protective
system for the Nightingale nurses centered in the
nursing home. Nursing homes were in her mind the
only place where the nurses could be protected since
neither military nor civilian hospital officials and
administrators, all men, would intervene in any case
where a nurse would allege harassment against a
physician or surgeon. The third method she adopted
was supervision. On and off duty, students were
watched closely by the matron and sisters to ensure
that they did not succumb to the temptations of the
world. Discipline for those who strayed was strict.
Flirtation, for example, was punished by instant
dismissal. Only by struggling to raise the moral level
of nurses could "nursing be raised from the sink."[22]

Even this did not save nurses from
harassment, particularly from male staff members. It
certainly did not save nurses who were perceived as
not being respectful enough to physicians. Recently
Judith Moore has recounted some of the harassing

situations faced by 19th century nurses in three
situations, two at King's College Hospital in London
and the other at Guy's Hospital between 1874 and
1882.[23] Though Moore classifies her cases as part of
the struggle of nurses for professional recognition,
they clearly would better be described as examples of
sexual harassment. Sister Aimee Parry, the Sister
Matron at King's hospital, for example, felt it was
part of her duty to protect both her nurses and
patients from unprofessional conduct by physicians.
Thus she felt she had to act when one of her nurses
reported the harassing conduct of Thomas Crawford
Hayes, the hospital's assistant obstetric physician. The
nurse reported that Hayes

> gets worse and worse in the way in which he
> treats the women. He uses such dreadful
> language to them and makes fun to their
> faces of their ailments. The women feel it
> very much, and one woman left yesterday,
> saying she had never been so insulted, that
> nothing would induce her to come back to
> the hospital.[24]

Though such conduct had been noted before, nothing
had been done and when Sister Aimee protested, she
was discharged for her zeal and for infringing upon
the rights of physicians.

Sometimes the lady nurses went to great
lengths to avoid confronting the harassing male
physicians directly lest they be thought unladylike
but the results were the same. Margaret Lonsdale, a
matron at Guy's Hospital, observed what she
regarded as callous and hurtful treatment of patients
by a physician, Walter Moxon. Rather than confront
Moxon about the situation which disturbed her, she
wrote a letter to her mother and then asked her
mother to forward the letter to Moxon. This effort
to be lady like utterly failed because Moxon began
a campaign against her and all female meddling. As
one commentator wrote at the time:

> The staff do not object to lady pupils, so
> long as they conduct themselves as ladies, not

> as agents of a system of espionage where
> truth is held lightly, nor as meddlesome
> busybodies who interfere with the well being
> of the patients.[25]

Removing the language of circumlocutions from this
statement, nurses are welcome as long as they do not
question the physician at any time and only do what
the physician indicates they should.

NURSES IN AMERICA

American nurses faced the same problem.
One Civil War nurse, Hannah Ropes, wrote that the
battles between the soldiers are "nothing compaed
with the fights I have with the stewards."[26] Again,
the very requirements that nurses be over thirty
seemed to be an effort to avoid the most obvious
kinds of harassment. Still, as Georgeanna Woolsey,
one of the famous Woolsey sisters, reported:

> No one knows, who did not watch the thing
> from the beginning, how much unfeeling
> want of thought these women nurses endured.
> Government had decided that women should
> be employed, and the army surgeons . . .
> determined to make their lives so unbearable
> that they would be forced in self-defense to
> leave . . .. Some of the bravest women I have
> ever known were among the first company of
> army nurses. They saw at once the position of
> affairs, the attitude assumed by the surgerons
> and the wall against which they were
> expected to break and scatter; and they set
> themselves to undermine the whole thing.[27]

When a group of women under the leadership
of Louisa Lee Schuyler turned their attention after
the Civil War to public charitable institutions, they
believed that a woman's presence would uplift these
institutions from the cesspools in which they often
found themselves, at least in the public mind.
Nursing then was conceived as an attempt to

challenge the medical system which was failing, and
nurses were to not only minister to the sick using a
model of unselfish and virtuous femininity, but also
improve the hospital internal management.[28]
Obviously nurses in the process became fair game for
the physicians. Bearing the brunt of this physician
harassment were the nursing administrators since
most graduate nurses went into private duty. It was
an unequal battle and one where the nurses on the
battlefield had few allies. Physicians and hospital
administrators, often the same person, welcomed the
new nursing schools but then demanded control.
When the nursing administrators resisted, they were
often harassed until they left. A good example is
Elizabeth Conde Glenn (1859-1920), who established
a school of nursing at Rockford City Hospital in
1889 and when she attempted to exercise some
control, the physicians opposed her. She was forced
to resign. Esther Voorhees Hasson (1868-1942) the
first superintendent of the Navy Nurse Corps clashed
with the male authorities who harassed her and
demanded her resignation. One of the things to
notice about the early nursing leaders, particularly
those in a hospital situation, was how many of them
had comparatively short terms in any one institution.
They adopted a solution which nurses have since
often adopted for dealing with an impossible
situation, that is, moving on to another job. They
might ultimately end up being harassed in the new
job but at least they had escaped, if only
temporarily, from the problems under which they
had worked.[29]

Collectively they also continued to utilize the
same solution as Nightingale had advocated. Nurses
should be ladies, they should live in protective
dormitories, they should wear non-provocative (and
even at times non-functional) uniforms, and
morality, devotion to duty, and self-sacrifice was to
be emphasized. Though nurses emphasized obedience
to the physician as commander-in-chief of the
hospital, the one thing they most tried to prevent

was interference in the control of the nursing school.[30]

Since the majority of registered nurses during the last part of the nineteenth century and first part of the twentieth worked in private duty settings where they were mainly their own boss, they could avoid most of the kinds of harassment which plagued their institutional sisters. As late as 1927, it was reported that 73 percent of the hospitals which had schools of nursing connected with them had no graduate nurses; by 1937 that number had decreased to 10 percent.[31] This only emphasizes that in spite of nursing efforts, the physicians had a great deal of control over nursing education and harassment of those nurses who tried to change things was a standard complaint. The lack of graduate nurses in most hospitals also emphasized the age inequality between the older physicians and the student nurses, a factor which prevented nursing from gaining a power base to challenge the physician. Still harassment was widespread and demeaning. It was the demand of the physicians that they be obeyed at all costs even above the welfare of the patient and it was a continual put down of the skills of the nurse. Put in this way, many of the situations which traditionally have been looked at as physicians' attempts to retain power, are also efforts to put nursing down. In short, efforts today which would be defined as harassment.

The uppity nurse with an independent mind is a theme of much medical literature dealing with nursing. In 1921 when Charles H. Mayo, the famed founder of the Mayo clinic, wanted to estabish a new category of sub-nurse who would not be so "uppity" and give more service, his hidden agenda obviously was the elimination of nurses who would question physicians. Good nurses in his mind were born, not made, and such nurses would be self-sacrificing in helping out suffering humanity, and take the orders of physicians without question since the physician knew so much more than they did.[32] Though Mayo's suggestions never were implemented, and nursing continued to upgrade itself, auxiliary nursing personnel did develop but not quite in the way in which Mayo wanted.

As nurses entered the hospital in force in the 'thirties and after World War II, the traditional means of dealing with harassment changed. Nurses' homes increasingly became a thing of the past, control of nursing education fell more and more under the control of nurses, particularly as it moved into the collegiate and university setting, and the traditional shortage of nurses due to a rapidly expanding role in the 50's, 60's, and 70's, forced changes in the way in which physicians looked upon nurses.

Individual harassment of nurses became much less likely, but a far more subtle form of harassment continued, namely the putting down of nurses collectively. Often such articles appeared in medical journals such as Thomas Hale's put down of nursing education in a 1968 issue of the *New England Journal of Medicine* emphasizing the need for more diploma programs.[33] This same concept keeps reappearing usually with physicians leading the charge. The latest put down of the profession is the proposal of the AMA and its allies in hospital administration to establish a registered care technologist (RCT). Who will control the training and education of this new technologist? Obviously, the assumption is that it would be the physician.

There has been a long tradition of harassment of nurses, both individually and collectively. Florence Nightingale had her solution which was essential to her time period, but not to ours. Recognizing that much of what Nightingale was trying to do was deal with the problem of harassment, however, makes her more understandable to us than ever before. We have worked hard over the past few decades to eliminate the notion that women cannot go where they want to go or do what they want to do. This nineteenth century notion is no longer accepted and neither is the nineteenth century concept of the role of women.

Nightingale's solutions are not ours but she acted the way she did because that was the way she had to act to be successful. We act differently because times are different and we do not appreciate being put down as just a crazy bunch of women. Perhaps by facing the long history of harassment in nursing, we can finally find a solution in the 1990's to a problem which Nightingale struggled with over a hundred years ago. It is only by coming to terms with the problems of sexual harassment, however, that it will be possible.

FOOTNOTES

1.   M. Dawn McCaghy, *Sexual Harassment: A Guide to Resources* (Boston: G.K. Hall, 1985), pp. ix-x.

2.   This is the definition given in a flyer distributed by the Working Women's Institute, and quoted by McCaghy, *Sexual Harassment*, p. 1.

3.   D.E. Ledgerwood and S. Johnson-Dietz, "The EECO's Foray into Sexual Harassment: Interpreting the New Guidelines for Employer Liability," *Labor Law Journal* 31 (1980), 741-44.

4.   Harry Hazel, "Sexual Harassment and Nurse Anesthetists," *American Association of Nurse Anesthetists (AANA) Journal*, 49 (June 1981), 277-79.

5.   Bonnie W. Duldt, "Sexual Harassment in Nursing," *Nursing Outlook*, 30 (June 1982), 336-43.

6.   A Grieco, "Scope and Nature of Sexual Harassment in Nursing," *Journal of Sex Research*, 23 (1987), 261-65.

7.   Catherine A. MacKinnon, *Sexual Harassment of Working Women* (New Haven: Yale University Press, 1979), p. 162.

8. Edwin M. Schur, *Labeling Women Deviant: Gender Stigma and Social Control* (New York: Random House, 1984), p. 142.

9. For discussion of rape at various periods in history, see Vern L. Bullough, *Sexual Variance in Society and History* (Chicago: University of Chicago Press, 1976), passim.

10. See Ned (Edward) Ward, *The London Spy*, ed. Arthur Hayward (New York: George H. Doran, 1927). Other popular accounts of the London clubs include Jack Loudan, *The Hell Rakers* (Letchworth, England: Books for You, 1967), and Daniel P. Mannix, *The Hell Fire Club* (New York: Ballantine Books, 1959).

11. This is the argument of Anna Clark, *Women's Silence, Men's Violence: Sexual Assault in England, 1770-1845* (New York: Pandora, 1987). Such limitations on movement and location itself did not, she states, exist before.

12. Quoted in Fred K. Vigman, *Beauty's Triumph* (Boston: Chrisophter Publishing House, 1966), p. 48.

13. William R. Taylor and Christopher Lasch, "Two Kindred Spirit: Sorority and Family in New England, 1839-1946," *New England Quarterly* 36 (March 1963), 35.

14. See Carroll Smith Rosenberg, "Beauty, the Beast, and the Militant Woman: A Case Study in Sex Roles and Social Stress in Jacksonian America," *American Quarterly* 23 (1971), 562-84. See also Vern L. Bullough, Brenda Shelton, Sarah Slavin, *The Subordinated Sex* (Athens, Ga.: University of Georgia, 1988), passim.

15. Nathan Appleton, *Introduction of the Power Loom and Origin of Lowell* (Lowell: B.H. Penhallow, 1958), pp. 15-16.

16. See Thomas Dublin, *Women at Work* (New York: Columbia University Press, 1979), p. 78).

17. Henry A. Mills, *Lowell as It Was and As It*

Is (Lowell: Powers and Bagley, 1845), pp. 144-45.

18. Dublin, *Women at Work*, pp. 129-30.

19. Letter from Florence Nightingale to H. Bonham Carter, 1 October, 1869, Florence Nightingale Collection in the Greater London Record Office, and quoted by Malcolm S. Newby, "Problems of Teaching Nursing History--1," Occasional Papers, *Nursing Times*, 22 Nov. 1979, 123.

20. Letter from Florence Nightingale to H. Bonham Carter, 1 October, 1869, in Florence Nightingale Collection in the Greater London Record Office, 14 (5), and quoted in M.E. Baly, *Florence Nightingale and the Nursing Legacy* (London: Croom-Helm, 1986).

21. Baly, *Florence Nightingale*, pp. 108-110.

22. Cecil Woodham-Smith, *Florence Nightingale 1820-1910* (New York: McGraw-Hill, 1951), p. 352.

23. Judith Moore, *A Zeal for Responsibility: The Struggle for Professional Nursing*, 1868-1883 (Athens, Ga.: University of Gerogia Press, 1988).

24. R. Few, *A History of St. John's House* (Norfolk Street, Strand, n.d.), pp. 21-22, as quoted by Moore, *A Zeal for Responsibility*, p. 115. Few's pamphlet is in the Greater London Council Archives, H.I/St/SJ/A39/39.

25. Moore, *A Zeal for Responsibility*, pp. 68-69.

26. John R. Brumgardt, ed., *Civil War Nurse: The Diary and Letters of Hannah Ropes* (Knosville: The University of Tennessee Press, 1980), pp. 69-70.

27. Quoted from Anne L. Austin, *The Woolsey Sisters of New York--1868-1900* (Philadelphia: American Philosophical Society, 1971), p. 112.

28. See, for example, New York State Charities Aid Association, *Report of a Committee on Hospitals on a Training School for Nurses to*

be Attached to Bellevue (New York: 1877).
29.   This statement is based upon a survey of biographies in *American Nursing: A Biographical Dictionary*, edited by Vern L. Bullough, Olga Maranjian Church, and Alice Stein (New York: Garland, 1988).
30.   See Lavinia L. Dock, "The Relation of Training Schools to Hospitals," a paper given at the International Congress of Charities, Correction, and Philanthropy at the Chicago World's Fair in 1893 and published in *Nursing the Sick*, edited Isabel A. Hampton (Chicago, 1893), and reprinted in Bonnie Bullough and Vern L. Bullough, *Issues in Nursing* (New York: Springer, 1966), pp. 96-97.
31.   *Facts About Nursing* (New York: The Nursing Information Bureau of the American Nurses Association, 1938), p. 5.
32.   Genevieve Parkhurst, "Wanted--100,000 Girls for Sub-Nurses," *The Pictorial Review* (October, 1921), and reprinted in Bonnie Bullough and Vern L. Bullough, *New Directions for Nurses* (New York: Springer, 1971), 87-94.
33.   Thomas Hale, "Cliches of Nursing Education," *The New England Journal of Medicine* 28 (April 18, 1968), 879-886. The article was reprinted in Bonnie Bullough and Vern L. Bullough, *New Directions in Nursing*, pp. 94-110.

STUDENTS WANTED: WOMEN NEED NOT APPLY (A HISTORICAL REVIEW OF IDEAS ON WOMEN'S PLACE IN HIGHER EDUCATION DURING THE NIGHTINGALE ERA)*

Janice Cooke Feigenbaum

> Women often strive to live by intellect. The clear, brilliant, sharp radiance of intellect's moonlight rising upon such an expanse of snow is dreary, it is true, but some love its solemn desolation, its silence, its solitude--if they are but allowed to live in it.[1]

Writing these exquisite words in "Cassandra" in 1952, Nightingale highlighted the cravings of some women for a thought provoking and intellectually satisfying education. In effect, she was advocating the need for society to counteract a pervasive theme that has dominated Western thought from ancient through contemporary times. This idea essentially emphasizes that women should not participate in higher education, especially in programs established for men. While this basic concept has been the underlying motif, its form has changed significantly. Many of these alterations occurred during the Nightingale Era.

This belief influenced Nightingale throughout her life, and continues to dominate nursing's quest for professionalization as its strives to promote quality health care. This author, however, suggests that this thought may partly account for nursing's "obstinate,

188

Students Wanted: Women Need Not Apply (A   189
Historical Review of Ideas on Women's Place
in Higher Education During the Nightingale Era)

perverse and adamantine resistance to change"[2] as it has attempted to become collegiate and have the baccalaureate degree the minimal requirement for professional nursing.

PURPOSES OF THE STUDY

The purposes of this historical study were to pose and explore three interrelated questions.

1. How was the theme of women's place not being an acceptable part of higher education manifested in the United States at the time of Nightingale's birth on May 12, 1820?
2. How did the theme change in the United States during Nightingale's life, which ended on August 13, 1910?
3. How has this theme influenced the progress of educational programs for nurses in the United States?

METHODOLOGY OF THE STUDY

This project, an historical analysis, used primary and secondary sources to explore various ideas on women's place within higher education. A limitation of this study is that the majority of ideas discussed excluded large portions of society. In effect, the affluent classes provided the norms for their originators, while they ignored the underprivileged groups or considered them too hopeless and helpless to contemplate.[3]

Another limitation is that this study excludes the ideas of individuals, such as John Dewey, who actually advocated higher education for women.

DOMINANT IDEAS REGARDING WOMEN PRIOR TO 1820

Western thought has been dominated by the perspective that women are basically inferior creatures who can never be equal with members of the superior male species. Writing *A History of Western Philosophy* in 1945, Bertrand Russell seems to have documented one of the earliest sources of this view when he discussed the writings of Timmaeus, a Greek astronomer and philosopher who lived during the fourth century B.C.

Reviewing Timmaeus' work, Russell wrote that he believed

> The creator . . . made one soul for each star. Souls have sensation, love, fear and anger; if they overcome these, they will live righteously, but if not, not. If a man lives well, he goes, after death, to live happily forever in his star. But if he lives badly, he will in the next life, be a woman.[4]

This negative view of women persisted for centuries and the earliest European settlers of America brought it with them. It usually was extended to the realm of education since women were not acknowledged to be in need of it.

In his *Emile*, Jean-Jacques Rousseau, a French writer and philosopher who lived from 1712-1778, expounded his views on the educational processes necessary for both boys and girls.

> A woman's education must be planned in relation to man. To be pleasing in his sight, to win his respect and love, to train him in childhood, to tend him in manhood, to counsel and console, to make his life pleasant and happy, these are the duties of woman, for all time, and that is what she should be taught while she is young.[5]

He further explained that women were incapable of benefiting from higher education since the

Students Wanted: Women Need Not Apply (A   191
Historical Review of Ideas on Women's Place
in Higher Education During the Nightingale Era)

quest for abstract and speculative truths, principles, and axioms in the sciences, for everything that tends to generalize ideas, is not within the competence of women.[6]

In Book V, Rosseau spelled out his ideas in detail, emphasizing that boys and girls should have different educational programs which should "always follow nature's indications."[7] He encouraged mothers to teach their daughters the skills of developing one's attractiveness,[8] sewing, embroidery, lacemaking, simple arithmetic,[9] singing and dancing,[10] and how to avoid the sins of "idleness and disobedience."[11] He believed, however, that girls should be given the opportunity to exercise and play games in the garden since "women need enough strength to do everything they do with grace." He added "women ought not to be robust like men, but they should be robust for men, so that the men borne from them will be robust too."[12]

In effect, Rousseau was advocating that girls be educated by their mothers regarding household skills and management, and that higher levels of education be avoided because it would make them unfit to be wives and mothers. He wrote, "A brilliant wife is a plague to her husband, her children, her friends, her valets, everyone."[13]

Nightingale was extremely sensitive to the limitations placed on women due to society's acceptance of Rousseau's ideas. In "Cassandra," she questioned "Why have women passion, intellect, moral activity--these three--and a place in society where no one of the three can be exercised?"[14] She further recognized the reality that in "conventional society, which men have made for women, and women have accepted, they must have none, they must act the farce of hypocrisy, the lie that they are without passion--and therefore what else can they say to their daughters, without giving the lie to themselves."[15]

Yet, Nightingale believed women had to play the major role in providing health care and this had to be based in theoretical and practical knowledge. Thus, she finished writing *Notes on Nursing* in 1859 by emphasizing,

> Would not the true way of infusing the art of preserving its own health into the human race be to teach the female part of it in schools and hospitals, both by practical teaching and by simple experiments, in as far as these illustrate what may be called the theory of it?[16]

BACKGROUND OF THE NIGHTINGALE ERA (1820-1910) IN THE UNITED STATES

Rousseau's ideas on education dominated Western thought when Nightingale was born and they continued to influence the founders of programs of higher education for women in the United States. The dawn of these opportunities slowly emerged as the nation experienced major changes during the Nightingale Era.

During the 1830s, a number of the northeastern industrial states introduced programs of free elementary education for children. In 1821 the Emma Willard School opened as the first endowed institution for women. The Hartford Female Seminary was begun in 1832 by Catherine Beecher. Both hoped to educate women "as a means of preparing them for family duties."[17]

Then, in 1836 Mary Lyons established Mt. Holyoke Female Seminary. Her curriculum "emphasized religion as a part of the school's training,"[18] since a graduate was hoped to be "a handmaid to the Gospel and an efficient auxillary in the great task of renovating the world."[19] In 1833, Oberlin College became the first coeducational instution of higher education. Women, however, were admitted only so they could learn the skills needed to be supportive wives of ministers.[20]

Women's access to higher education continued to expand between the 1850s and the 1870s. Solomon explained that during this period "several models developed: the private women's college, the religiously

Students Wanted: Women Need Not Apply (A   193
Historical Review of Ideas on Women's Place
in Higher Education During the Nightingale Era)

oriented coeducational college, the private coordinate
women's college, the secular coeducational instution,
both public and private, and the private single-sex
vocational institution."[21] By 1900, approximately 80%
of the professional schools, universities and colleges
admitted women.[22]

While these programs were developing, the
first three hospital schools of nursing opened in the
United States in 1873, the Bellevue Hospital School of
Nursing, the Connecticut Training School for Nurses
and the New England Hospital School of Nursing.
Then, in 1899, Teachers College of Columbia
University launched a program in "Hospital
Economics" for graduate nurses to take a one year
program of study to qualify for the position of
superintendent of a hospital or training school."[23]
Finally, on March 1, 1909, the first preservice school
of nursing opened under the auspices of an
educational institution, the University of Minnesota.
The aim of this program was to produce nurses who
would qualify for positions as head nurses in
hospitals.[24]

However, even though women, including
nurses, in the United States, had gained access to
instutions of higher education by the end of the
Nightingale Era, it has been argued that a major factor
in the development was due to the financial problems
of the universities who needed students to pay tuition
and fill their classrooms. High levels of opposition to
their presence on campuses continued, based on the
assumption that women really did not belong within
higher education.

REFINEMENT OF THE THEME

Thus, even as opportunities for access to
higher education for women began to appear,
Rousseau's ideas seemed to be their guiding light.
During the initial period of this study's era, his
philosophy was further enhanced by the Christian

ideal of True Womanhood. Barbara Welter has discussed this puritanical view that promoted the idea that the female species must strive to emulate the prescripts of piety, purity, domesticity and obedience.[25]

Welter surveyed "almost all of the women's magazines published for more than three years during the period 1820-60 and a sampling of all those published for less than three years," plus many books, diaries, memoirs, personal papers, and autobiographies.[26] She stated that a major debate of this era was whether or not "a 'finished' education detracted from the practice of housewifely arts."[27] This is also evidenced by the fears of "bluestockings" were commonly found in such literature.[28] In effect, women who were involved in the fight for women's rights were often viewed as "only semi-women, mental hermaphrodites."[29]

Welter further explained that one of the major ways that women fulfilled the criterion of domesticity was through the role of a nurse. "Nursing the sick, particularly sick males, not only made a woman feel useful and accomplished, but increased her influence."[30]

Thus, during much of the Nightingale Era, both the new and existing programs for females in high schools as well as in higher education, emphasized the needs of women's separate sphere of life. Many did not allow women the chance to study the same curricula as men since it was believed that the male form of higher education would limit a female's abilities to tend to her womanly duties.

As more and more women gained access to higher education, the nature of the theme was then significantly altered during the 1870s and bolstered with new arguments based on "scientific discoveries." Charles Darwin's Theory of Evolution was interpreted to mean that women were "relegated to a permanently inferior condition, physically and mentally. In this view, women were too far behind men in human evolution ever to catch up."[31]

Students Wanted: Women Need Not Apply (A   195
Historical Review of Ideas on Women's Place
in Higher Education During the Nightingale Era)

This notion was taken one step further and strongly advanced by the dubious writings of Edward H. Clarke, M.D. Clarke was a member of the Massachusetts Medical Society, fellow of the American Academy of Arts and Sciences, and Late Professor of Materia Medica of Harvard College.[32] In 1873, he published a book, *Sex in Education*, as part of the Medicine and Society in America series. Ironically, he subtitled his work, *A Fair Chance for the Girls*. Clarke identified the purpose of this text to be to bring "physiological facts and laws prominently to the notice of all who are interested in education."[33]

While emphasizing that "man is not superior to woman, nor woman to man,"[34] Clarke grounded his ideas on the notion that men and women

> are different, widely different from each other, and so different that each can do, in certain directions, what the other cannot; and in other directions, where both can do the same things, one sex, as a rule can do them better than the other.[35]

Thus, throughout his text, he emphasizes his "physiological motto . . ., Educate a man for manhood, a woman for womanhood, both for humanity."[36] This concept was based on his "scientific understanding" of the physiology of females.

> Woman, in the interest of the race, is dowered with a set of organs peculiar to herself, ... If properly nurtured and cared for, they are a source of strength and power to her. If neglected and mismanaged, they retaliate upon their possessor with weakness and disease, as well of the mind as of the body.[37]

Actually, this idea holds a kernel of truth; men and women are physiologically different. The problem occurred when Clarke jumped to the conclusion that the cause of problems to the female reproductive system was the educational programs, especially co-educational ones, being offered to girls.

Thus, emphasizing the physiological principle that "the system never does two things well at the same time [, since the] muscles and the brain cannot functionate in their best way at the same moment,"[38] Clarke developed a scheme for educating girls. First, he advocated that "during the period of rapid development, that is, from fourteen to eighteen, a girl should not study as many hours a day as a boy."[39] He recommended that a boy can tolerate six hours of study per day, while a girl can endure only four, since "if she puts as much force into her brain education as a boy, the brain or the special apparatus will suffer."[40] Secondly, every fourth week, the girl should take a rest from her studies and exercise. "The diminished labor, which shall give Nature an opportunity to accomplish her special periodical task and growth, is a physiological necessity for all, however robust they may seem to be."[41]

Ultimately, Clarke's alleged research conclusions appear to affirm the long-held belief that women's brains and bodies could not withstand the pressures of education, especially if it was patterned after the male model. Further, a compelling aspect of Clarke's ideas was that he emphasized that for the good of society, women clearly had "to save their energies to fulfill their biological function as childbearers."[42] In effect, how could any female take a chance on becoming sterile by studying?

The trend of these notions was advanced further by the work of one of the founders of American psychology, Granville Stanley Hall. He wrote 14 books and more than 400 other publications spelling out his "theories of childhood, adolescence, senescence, instincts, religion, and human destiny."[43] Hall was the first to receive an American doctorate (Ph.D.) in psychology,[44] and he attempted to build a new science based on Darwin's ideas. The result was his theory of psychic recapitulation.[45]

> Hall accepted Clarke's ideas and added that "one of the gravest dangers is the persistent ignoring by feminists of the prime importance of establishing normal periodicity in girls, to the needs of which everything else should for

Students Wanted: Women Need Not Apply (A   197
Historical Review of Ideas on Women's Place
in Higher Education During the Nightingale Era)

a few years be secondary."[46]

Based on his theory, Hall developed his educational scheme for children. He recommended that at puberty, educational programs should be distinct and separate for boys and girls. He further emphasized that

> The leaders of the new education for girls recommend training them for self-support. . . This assumption is radically wrong and vicious, and should be reversed. Every girl should be educated primarily to become a wife and mother.[47]

Hall certainly sounds like Rousseau!

Hall further used "eight good and independent statistical studies [, which he did not cite,] to show that the ideals of boys from ten years on are almost always those of their own sex, while girls' ideals are increasingly of the opposite sex, or also men."[48] In effect, Hall seems to be illustrating the effects of the hidden curriculum on women, or the reality that male images dominate the learning experiences offered to children.[49] He, however, blamed the girls for this occurrence, instead of looking for other reasons.

Hall further identified many negative effects of having boys attend schools primarily filled with girls and female teachers. He declared, "This feminization of the school spirit, discipline, and personnel is bad for boys."[50] Thus he recommended that the education of girls must be different and apart from that of boys. He advocated the idea that after puberty, girls should attend schools in the country and be allowed "a sacred time of reverent exemption from the hard struggle of existence in the world, mental effort in the school,"[51] since their health for their "whole life depends upon normalizing the lunar month."[52] Seen as documenting both Clarke's and Hall's theories were declining marriage and birth rates among college educated women.[53]

At the turn of the century, the nature of the theme was again significantly changed. Speaking at a quarter-centennial meeting of the Association of

Collegiate Alumnae in Boston during 1907, Charles Van Hise, President of the University of Wisconsin, discussed the negative effect that the large numbers of women taking liberal arts courses had on male college students. This problem has been called the "sex repulsion theory."[54] First, Van Hise emphasized that women were allowed on campus only because of financial considerations, and "with much reluctance."[55] He explained this stemmed primarily from "fear that the intellectual standards of the instutions would deteriorate if women were admitted."[56] He also noted that there was much concern regarding the effect women would have on the standards of graduate work by explaining,

> The president of one large state university says that the presence of women does tend to lower the standard of graduate work, for the simple reason women do not incline to research. While I should hesitate to assent to this statement, it does appear to be a fact that the percentage of women who are willing to work at the same subject six hours a day for three hundred days in the year is much smaller than among men.[57]

Van Hise, however, continued by describing the double bind women have encountered within institutions of higher learning. This is that whatever their level of accomplishment, the women were seen as exhibiting problematic behaviors. Thus, he observed that "the average scholastic record of the young women in the state universities has been higher than the average of that of young men."[58] Though he was not pleased by this reality, he went on to explain that this occurs because of women's "close adherence to the work assigned under the feeling that they must make good records . . . (possibly because) women upon the whole are less independent in their work than the men."[59]

Van Hise identified as a major problem women caused on campus that as "certain courses have become popular with the women so they greatly outnumber the men." As a result, "there is a tendency

Students Wanted: Women Need Not Apply (A   199
Historical Review of Ideas on Women's Place
in Higher Education During the Nightingale Era)

for the men not to elect these courses, even if they are otherwise attractive to them."[60]

The solution to this problem was viewed as the creation of sex segregated separate classes and courses of study. Van Hise himself advocated that institutions of higher education

> provide for natural segregation by the development of professional courses, such as engineering, agriculture, commerce, and law, for men, and other courses, illustrated by home economics, for women.[61]

He justified his proposal by stating, "The woman who has studied the fundamental sciences leading to these subjects and becomes trained in their application to the home, is educated in a profession as dignified as other professions. When a woman becomes thus educated she will find the direction of her home a high intellectual pleasure rather than wearisome routine."[62] This rationale again seems to be a return to Rousseau's ideas.

Van Hise's thesis was taken one step further by the work of Edward Thorndike, Professor of Educational Psychology at Teachers College, Columbia University. He had published *Theory of Mental and Social Measurements*, an elementary statistics handbook, in 1904.[63] Concurrent with the development of intelligence tests, Thorndike was able to illustrate the "differences in mental variability" between the sexes.[64]

Facts did not confuse him since he admitted that

> "what little scientific study of the differences between the sexes in intellect and character there has been . . . (shows) the average man differs from the average woman far less than any men differ one from another."[65]

He accepted this by explaining that "the upper extreme of one sex always overlaps the lower extreme of the other."[66] He added that "of the hundred most gifted individuals in this country not two would be women, and of the thousand most gifted, not one in twenty."[67]

He concluded that "postgraduate instruction, to which women are flowing in large numbers, is, at least in its higher reaches, a far more remunerative investment in the case of men."[68]

INFLUENCE OF THE THEME ON NURSING

It is in this setting that nursing developed and these unscientific and erroneous assumptions were accepted by many Americans, including multitudes of nurses and physicians. It is a wonder that women have been able to withstand the pressures from the variations of these ideas (which are still held by many) and been able to suceed in higher education. Its dominant presence influenced nursing's struggle to become professional and find a firm standing for its basic preparation within academe. Nutting seemed to understand the constraints of her position and the influence of this theme when she wrote in 1906:

"All good nursing included the constant use of some of the finest and most exquisite of housekeeping arts [and that] hospital management consisted of expert housekeeping on an enlarged scale."[69]

She later acknowledged the negative effect this theme was having on the recruitment of talented students to nursing programs. She explained that "the existing prevalence of a sentiment which looks upon nursing as an easily-acquired homely art, in which preparation for which, nature leads the way," seems to discourage many of the best candidates from entering nursing.[70]

Thus, it appears that the theme long prevented nursing from becoming collegiate at the beginning level. It further stalled progress in nursing educators meeting the rigorous demands of academe. In 1980, Lucy Kelly and Joan Baker discussed this problem by acknowledging that

until recently, a degree at the Master's level for School of Nursing faculty was considered

Students Wanted: Women Need Not Apply (A 201
Historical Review of Ideas on Women's Place
in Higher Education During the Nightingale Era)

the final 'necessary' degree in many universities. With that degree, acquisition of tenure and promotion to associate or full professor or even higher positions were possible. Hardly anyone expected School of Nursing faculty to pursue, let alone achieve, doctoral level preparation.[71]

In effect, this reality seems to be an illustration of the persistence of a basic theme of Western society, namely that women really do not belong within the fields of higher education. However, if they do enter it, they should remain within programs established primarily for women so they may attend to feminine pursuits, such as nursing.

In spite of this, the reality is that many women, including nurses, have accomplished much within higher education. The question now is, how might the profession as a totality finds its place within academe so it may assert itself within society and gain recognition as a profession equal to others who gained this status long ago. Hopefully, once this is achieved, all nurses will have a place in society where they can exercise "passion, intellect and moral activity."[72]

*The writer's thinking regarding this topic has been catalyzed by the work of five women. They are Maxine Seller, a Professor of History of Education at the State University of New York at Buffalo, Jane Roland Martin, author of *Reclaiming a Conversation: The Ideal of the Educated Person*, Barbara Miller Solomon, writer of *In The Company of Educated Women*, Sheila Rothman, author of *Woman's Proper Place*, and Mary Roth Walsh, writer of *Doctors Wanted--No Women Need Apply*.

NOTES

1.   Nightingale, F. "Cassandra." (1852) pp. 33-52 in R. Herbert (Ed.) *Florence Nightingale: Saint, Reformer or Rebel?* Malabar, Fla.:

Robert E. Krieger Publishing Company, 1981. The quotation is from p. 40.

2. Button, H. and Provenzo, E. *History of Education and Culture in America*. Englewood Cliffs, N.J.: Prentice-Hall, 1983, p. xvi.

3. Norton, M. "The Paradox of 'Women's Sphere'." pp. 139-149 in C. Berkin and M. Norton (Eds.) *Women of America--A History*. Boston: Houghton Mifflin Company, 1979, p. 139.

4. Russell, B. *A History of Western Philosophy*. New York: Simon and Schuster, 1945, p. 145.

5. Rousseau, J. *Emile* (A. Bloom, Trans.). New York: Basic Books, Inc., Publishers, 1762/1979, p. 328. For a background to these ideas see Vern L. and Bonnie Bullough, *The Subordinate Sex: A History of Attitudes Toward Women*, New York, Penguin Books, 1974.

6. Rousseau, *Emile*, pp. 386-387.

7. Ibid., p. 363.

8. Ibid., p. 365.

9. Ibid., p. 368.

10. Ibid., p. 373.

11. Ibid., p. 369.

12. Ibid., p. 366, emphases added.

13. Ibid., p. 409.

14. Nightingale, "Cassandra" p. 34.

15. Ibid.

16. Nightingale, F. *Notes on Nursing: What It Is and What It Is Not*. New York: Dover Publications, Inc., 1960/1969, p. 140.

17. Button, H. and Provenzo, E. *History of Education and Culture in America*, p. 139.

18. Ibid.

19. Woloch, N. *Women and the American Experience*. New York: Alfred A. Knopf, 1984, p. 127.

20. Solomon, B. *In the Company of Educated Women*. New Haven: Yale University Press, 1985, p. 21.

21. Ibid., p. 47.

22. Button, H. and Provenzo, E. *History of*

Students Wanted: Women Need Not Apply (A   203
Historical Review of Ideas on Women's Place
in Higher Education During the Nightingale Era)

Education and Culture in America, p. 140.

23.   Marshall, H. *Mary Adelaide Nutting.* Baltimore: Johns Hopkins University Press, 1972, p. 99.

24.   *American Journal of Nursing.* "Department of Nursing Education." x:1 (October 1909), p. 9.

25.   Welter, B. "The Cult of True Womanhood: 1820-1960." *American Quarterly* 18 (1966) 151-174, p. 152.

26.   Ibid., p. 166.

27.   Ibid., p. 166.

28.   Ibid., p. 167.

29.   Ibid., p. 173.

30.   Ibid., p. 164.

31.   Solomon, B. *In the Company of Educated Women*, p. 56.

32.   Clarke, E. *Sex in Education: Or a Fair Chance for Girls.* New York: Arno Press, 1873/reported 1972, Title Page. For a discussion see Vern Bullough and Martha Voght, "Women, Menstruation, and Nineteenth Century Medicine." *Bulletin of the History of Medicine*, 47 (1973) 66-82.

33.   Clarke, *Sex or Education*, p. 6.

34.   Ibid., p. 13.

35.   Ibid., p. 13.

36.   Ibid., p. 19.

37.   Ibid., p. 33.

38.   Ibid., p. 40, emphases added.

39.   Ibid., pp. 154-155.

40.   Ibid., pp. 156-157.

41.   Ibid., p. 157.

42.   Solomon, B. *In the Company of Educated Women*, p. 56.

43.   Strickland, C. and Burgess, C. "G. Stanley Hall: Prophet of Naturalism." pp. 1-26, Introduction to *Health, Growth, and Heredity.* New York: Teachers College Press, 1965, p. 1.

44.   Ibid., p. 5.

45.   Ibid., p. 8.

46.   Hall, G.S. "Childhood and Adolescence." (1904) pp. 99-113 in C. Strickland and C.

Burgess (Eds.) *Health, Growth, and Heredity.* New York: Teachers College Press, 1965, p. 107.

47. Hall, G.S. "The Ideal School as Based on Child Study," (1901) pp. 114-136 in C. Strickland and C. Burgess (Eds.) *Health, Growth, and Heredity.* New York: Teachers College Press, 1965, p. 131.

48. Hall, G.S. "Coeducation in the High School." pp. 179-187 in C. Strickland and C. Burgess (Eds.) *Health, Growth, and Heredity.* New York: Teachers College Press, 1903/1965, p. 182.

49. Martin, J. "The Ideal of the Educated Person." *Educational Theory* 31:2 (1981), 97-109, p. 107.

50. Hall, G.S. "Coeducation in the High School." p. 183.

51. Ibid., p. 182,

52. Ibid., p. 181.

53. Ehrenreich, B. and English, D. *For Her Own Good: 150 Years of the Experts' Advice to Women.* Garden City, N.Y.: Anchor Press, 1978, p. 128; Goodsell, W. *The Education of Women: Its Social Background and Its Problems.* New York: Macmillan Company, 1923, pp. 37-38; Solomon, B. *In the Company of Educated Women.* p. 39.

54. Solomon, *In The Company of Educated Women.* p. 60.

55. Van Hise, C. "Educational Tendencies in State Universities." *Educational Review* 34 (December 1907), 504-520, p. 509.

56. Ibid., p. 510.

57. Ibid., p. 511.

58. Ibid., p. 513.

59. Ibid., pp. 513-514, emphases added.

60. Ibid., p. 515.

61. Ibid., p. 520.

62. Ibid., p. 517.

63. Button, H. and Provenzo, E. *History of Education and Culture in America*, p. 243.

Students Wanted: Women Need Not Apply (A   205
Historical Review of Ideas on Women's Place
in Higher Education During the Nightingale Era)

64. Goodsell, W. *The Education of Women: Its Social Background and Its Problems*, p. 73.
65. Thorndike, E. *Individuality.* Boston: Houghton Mifflin Company, 1911, p. 30, emphases added.
66. Ibid.
67. Thorndike, E. "Sex in Education." *Bookman* 23:2 (April 1906): 211-214, p. 212.
68. Ibid.
69. Nutting, M.A. Unpublished notes in the M.A. Nutting Collection. New York: Teachers College Library. Undated.
70. Nutting, M.A. "How Can We Attract Suitable Applicants to Our Training Schools?" *American Journal of Nursing* XIV:B (May 1914): 601-610, p. 603.
71. Kelly, L. and Baker, J. "Women in Nursing and Academic Tenure. *Journal of Nursing Education* 19:2 (February 1980), 41-48, p. 41.
72. Nightingale, F. "Cassandra" p. 34.

NURSING ETHICS EDUCATION IN VICTORIAN AMERICA - 1873-1890

by

Ellen Giarelli

The study of ethics education in American nursing training schools has historical significance in that it provides an understanding of how nurses coped with a position of power in a society where women were considered powerless. Such a study uncovers the foundations of the profession's ethical standards and the values held by the founders of the first schools and reveals the relative importance of teachers, superiors and textbooks to the development of the student's professional ethics. This paper will describe Victorian nursing ethics education by briefly presenting some of the cultural determinants of the students' qualifications for caring, and by concentrating on some of the training school experiences such as role model relationships, the use of textbooks and moral problems encountered by nursing administrators.

America in the nineteenth century was in cultural turmoil, under siege of Victorian social attitudes and ideas. Although conventionality and prudery were the bywords for this era, in fact it was an age of cultural revolution constant change, variety and self-criticism with overtones of moral certainty. Attempting to make peace with a rapidly changing life, people embraced ideals such as rigid control of public and private behavior and gender stereotyping to keep some sort of stability. An ideal of womanhood was constructed that few women could fully achieve. Convinced of the nature of evil, the Victorians found it everywhere and advised temperance, chastity and piety.

Highly critical of living people and existing institutions, it liked to endow hypothetical creatures with a lavish assortment of virtues. Most dramatic were the virtues bestowed on the ideal women and the new profession of nursing which did not escape the influence of Victorianism. The nurse was to be pious, pure, submissive and domestic and by these cardinal virtues she was judged as the weed, or the flower, of "true womanhood." Physically inferior to man, she was to be protected. Alleged as morally superior, she was the keeper of all that was good and pure. She was to be gentle, quiet, and refined. Her hypothetical sphere of influence was uniquely separate, defined by certain behaviors and its boundaries mostly structured for confinement. Women were provided with an internally consistent justification for the behaviors prescribed by Victorian Society . . . by accepting piety, purity, submissiveness and domesticity.[1] Inevitably ethics and etiquette in early training were rooted in these ideals of womanhood.

Piety or religion was the essence of Victorian women's virtue. Believed to be endowed with a peculiar ability to know goodness, a woman had the responsibility of bringing faith and religion to all her encounters. Piety and purity were related virtues. Purity specifically referred to chastity before and outside of marriage and the absence of taste for sexual pleasures. In the absence of purity, a woman was considered unfeminine and unfit for the company of decent men and women. Purity in women would also assure purity in man and it followed that an unchaste woman was evil. Purity, an important virtue for women, became a social responsibility.

Essential to this system were dominance and submission, power and control. All women were expected to be submissive. Their public and private relationships with others were structured with some degree of obedience. Ideal women were supposed to yield to their fathers, husbands, pastors and the dictates of social norms. Dutiful daughters and servants of their church, they were not to rebel against their fate as submissive wives. Femininity became synonymous with submission and it was a useful tool which lubricated social encounters. An adroit female learned to use submissiveness as a means of power by couching suggestions and requests in terms that denied her knowledge or physical skills. For example, the nurse during the Civil War quickly learned that her success at work depended on her ability to convince the surgeons of her powerlessness and therefore pose no threat.

Throughout the nineteenth century the image of the nurse oscillated with her expediency. Consequently, the image of the "ideal" nurse became inextricably and opportunistically linked to religious imagery, military imagery, the ethic of work and the ideals of womanhood.

QUALIFICATIONS FOR CARING - THE TRAINING SCHOOL ADMISSION PROCESS

Though the curriculum in the early nursing schools did not give the teaching of moral philosophy the place of importance that some other educational institutions did, it was because the pupil was expected to enter the school with a certain degree of moral integrity based on Christian values and the ideals of womanhood. This is evident from the admission process. Concerned with changing the once held belief that nurses were commonly recruited from the lower class and of questionable morality, the Committee on the Training School for Nurses Attached to Bellevue Hospital, for example, tried to control for the good character of the applicants and recommended that the trainees be:

Daughters and widows of clergymen, professional men and farmers throughout New

England and the Northern States . . . and who
received . . . good education [at] common
schools and academies and [were] dependent
on their own exertions for support.[2]
Later applicants at Bellevue, Connecticut
Training School for Nurses, Waltham Training School,
and others were required to bring with them a
testimonal of good character from their clergyman, a
certificate of health from their physician and, later, a
third letter testifying to dental health. Personal
interviews presumed to evaluate the applicant for
obedience, submissiveness to teaching and discipline,
capability of self-sacrifice, heartfelt sympathy for the
patient, sobriety, honesty, punctuality and cleanliness.[3]
Through this process the student learned that she was
expected to possess a catalogue of virtues.

The applicant's sexuality and relationships with
men were subject to scrutiny. Women whose husbands
were living were not received nor were women
separated from their husbands. Only single and
widowed women were qualified for admission. At first
glance one might assume that the women's personal
responsibilities to family and home were being
considered as a reason for their elimination, but this
was not the case as women were not questioned about
children. Rather the sexuality of the prospective
student was the issue since also excluded were young
women still under paternal control, apparently because
they lacked the proper "temperament" or were not yet
inclined to commit themselves to rigourous work.
Sexually inactive women were most valuable to the
school, hospital and patient. Lack of sexual activity
made it easier to protect her purity, restrict her social
activity, control her free time and allow her to be in
close proximity to her employer and at ready call if a
patient or doctor was in need of her services. No
provisions were reportedly made for the children (if
any) of students who were required to live in housing
supplied by the hospital.

While striving to change the negative image of
the nurse, the founders of the early training schools
designed the ideal practitioner, and increased the

catalogue of expected virtues as the years went on. Conformity of applicants was desired, from uniformity of temperament to a reasonable standard of weight and height. Any kind of deformity was prohibitive and a very tall or short stature, a tendency to sleep or tread heavily and a chronic cough were serious drawbacks. In a profession pledged to care, that practiced acceptance of anothers differences and aligned itself with the Christian virtue of charity, it is startling to see the degree of intolerance it had for the differences or shortcomings of its members. Applicants learned that independence and individuality were not necessarily desired qualities, but rather, good order and discipline were the ideal. Schools sought to retain only those nurses without degrading character traits. The spirit of self-sacrifice had to prevail as the ethical principles that governed the school were to be those that governed the individual. A work ethic was sparked in the new pupil who learned that order and obedience although not directly related to the restoration of a patient health, were the traits of a good nurse. The new American nurse was to be quite a bit different from the English model as proposed by Nightingale; she was not to be educated to be a leader but rather to be a worker.

Even the founders of Bellevue Training School, who were well known for their good intentions, deviated from what was supposed to be a model Nightingale program of instruction. For example, readings of the classics, novels, and spiritual books were not included as part of the curriculum in the early training schools at Bellevue, New York Hospital, Massachusetts General Hospital, Pennsylvania Hospital and others. American nursing students were to be as ethical as their English counterparts, but were not given the time during training to cultivate their personal values.[4] The only aim from the Nightingale model neither adopted nor applied in the early training schools, was the fourth, "The ability to act independently with wise judgement."[5] Independent action was neither taught in class nor in practice. The critical skill of making value judgements was not taught or evaluated.

TEXTBOOKS

The first nurse educators and students were not without guidance in standards of conduct. Popular English texts on the nursing of the sick were available to students and educators, such as the very well read *Notes on Nursing: What it is and What it is Not*, by Florence Nightingale, *Handbook for Nurses for the Sick*, by Zepherina P. Veitch, *A Manual for Hospital Nurses and Others Engaged in Attending on the Sick*, by Edward J. Domville and *Handbook for Hospital Sisters*, by Florence S. Lees.[6] Ethics content was scant and usually included as part of the introduction, preface or opening chapter of the text. Writers of the early nursing books dedicated from one to six pages out of fifty to two hundred to a topic they considered fundamental to the success of the nurse. Content on ethics in the first books was difficult to extract from the text because points of manners, relationships and duty were scattered throughout discussions of the benefits of silence, proper ways of emptying chamber pots, cold air ventilation and other practical points. The mingling of ideas illustrated how nurses perceived their training and practice as an intimate, sometimes inseparable union of morality, etiquette and action.

A popular approach used in textbooks of the period, divided the discussion of nursing ethics into duties toward (1) self, (2) patients, (3) fellow nurses and servants and (4) superiors. The student nurse was asked to view her responsibilities in terms of relationships; an approach that was personal, uncomplicated and easily understood. Interestingly, what was considered intellectually bankrupt, outmoded and simplistic by early twentieth century standards of pedagogy, contemporary feminist psychologists would compliment as being germane to the true nature of female emotional and cognitive learning styles. That is, the Victorian women's relationships defined her existence. They were her *raison d'etre*. The concept of

"Relationships" formed the skeleton of early instruction in ethics and etiquette in training schools and the nurse clothed herself in moral do's and don'ts depending on these relationships. For example, personal intimacy, which was considered natural and generally desirable among women during the late Victorian period, was excluded from the discussion of expected moral conduct.

In all early texts another virtue, sobriety, was deemed indispensable and encompassed food, drink, dress, and conduct. Essentially, the nurse was to be temperate, moderate and serious in demeanor and lack an inward state or an outward show of extremes while being cheerful, good tempered and contented.

The first American training schools soon published and printed their own textbooks. Several became available during the later half of the 1870s and the early 1880s. They adopted some of the styles and formats of their English predecessors but gave them their own peculiar stamp of American individuality. Towards the end of the century American authors began to qualify content as "Hospital Etiquette," and "Etiquette when Nursing Privately" and in Harriet C. Camp's, *A Reference Book for Trained Nurses*, 1889,[7] the first chapter was entitled, "The Ethics of Nursing." This appears to be the first formal reference to the new discipline. Students and instructors of nursing would have to wait until 1900 for the first, exclusively, nursing ethics textbook.[8] Not all of the textbooks noted were uniformly used in training schools, but there is a record of some having been the most popular and widely acknowledged as good references. Bellevue's, *A Manual of Nursing* is important as it was one of the first manuals compiled by nurses and women who were members of the Committee on the Training School for Nurses at the hospital's training school, and it credited the English texts of Domville, Nightingale, Lees, and Veitch for ideas and borrowed content.[9] This and Connecticut's handbook were found on the reading lists of several other schools and were the first important publications on nursing by nurses in the United States. Following these early manuals was Clara Weeks', *A Textbook of Nursing*, hailed as the outstanding book of the decade before 1890 and considered the first "real" textbook in nursing.[10] Used by many schools of nursing in the United States during the 1880s and 1890s, its content in practical nursing and nursing ethics is representative of what was taught in many late Victorian training schools. In regard to the content of etiquette and ethics, all texts used a "duties" approach, identifying the responsibilities of the nurse to the patient, physician and superiors, and to herself. Camp further delineated the duties of the nurse to her peers, hospital or school. Duties to the family, friends and servants of the patient were typically included when the student was expected to undertake private nursing.

The bulk of content on ethical responsibilities reflected expectations of appropriate social behavior and reflected the "Christian" virtues considered essential to nursing. Rather than instructing the student in critical thinking on moral issues in nursing and medicine, they attempted to infuse the moral vein of the student with emphatic nursing "do's and don'ts" and fast principles to live by. Many of the opinions on dress, manners and disposition were the same as those espoused in the contemporary tomes on etiquette, such as *Sensible Etiquette*, which was especially well read and considered to give popular views and customs of New York society.[11]

Weeks, however, made no reference to God, and she also used the image of the nurse as "angel of mercy" to illustrate a relic of the "by-gone times"[12] when nurses had but a sentimental vision of themselves and their duties. Her omission of the references to Christian virtues and the "holy calling" was significant during these early years of nurse training when religion played an important role in women's lives and moral reform was a designated aim of the public hospital.

FOUR STANDARDS OF NURSING

From the content of the English and American

textbooks and the available data on training schools' curriculum, four standards of the profession were identified as expected of all nurses. These were 1) confidentiality, 2) loyalty, 3) caring/doing no harm and 4) hard work. All the early textbooks advised the student on the value of protecting the patient's reputation and public image. Confidentiality was loosely described by several prescriptive behaviors in the context of hypothetical situations. The ethic was irregularly defined but usually included the nurses obligation to withhold information from the patient and her obligation to refrain from divulging personal or family business. Confidentiality, as an ethic of nursing was sometimes stated as such but often described in the context of the social ill manners of "gossiping" and slander. Social custom of the "best society" required that, "No honorable man or virtuous women can hear evil spoken of others in their absence without forming this opinion of the utterer (a sneak and liar). Gossip and tale bearing were regarded as a personal confession either of malice or imbecility."[13] A loyal nurse was a virtuous nurse. Loyalty to the physician was universally recognized as an ethic of practice. All nurses were to be loyal to all physicians and absolutely obedient. There was a simple strength in the Bellevue's *Manual* which lacked repetitive caveats. It did not dwell on the materialness of obedient nurses, but emphasized that faithfulness was to the nurse what skill was to the physician.[14]

The ethic of caring and of doing no harm was featured prominently in the early literature. The nurses foremost duties were to restore a person to health with careful nursing care and assure that during this time no harm would be caused by her presence. The nature of nursing was defined. The ideal nurse was kind, gentle, quiet, clean and selfless. Her pure heart, strong hand, good breeding and simple manner contributed to the patient's recovery and aided nature in the healing process. Her very presence was to make the patient feel restful in the turmoil of sickness. On the other hand, it was believed that nurses demonstrating deplorable character traits could lead to a worsening of the patient's condition. Caring could be considered the foremost nursing ethic, as all others depended on the elemental premise of the nurse's existence.

It was also recognized that nursing was a business and the nurse was an important asset to the hospital and institutional nursing. Some values ascribed to the "ideal nurse" were germane to the nineteenth century work place, and constitute a work ethic that served the employer. Hard work for low pay was the reality of a job that had to be done by someone. Nursing educators reminded students that their time was not their own.

Efficiency and effective use of limited time were signs of excellence in the nurse. The authors of Bellevue's Manual, in an emphatic and simple tone, asserted that "punctuality and order are all important."[15] Other values and excellences of the ethical worker were: accuracy, endurance, cooperativeness, dependability, ability to accept criticism, respect for authority, versatility and of course, the ubiquitous, obedience. On the student evaluation form of the Bellevue Hospital Training School for Nurses[16] the ethic of work was amply represented (12 of 18 items or 67 percent) in critical behaviors such as punctuality, efficiency, thoroughness, obedience and accuracy. It appears that the virtue of obedience was more relevant to the work ethic than to the ethic of loyalty.

STUDENTS RELATIONSHIPS WITH ROLE MODELS

As indicated earlier, few schools in the nineteenth century had classes in which ethics was the exclusive content. Such content was usually included in classes on the sciences and medical arts or in assigned readings from textbooks. Most of the schools provided only a few hours of formal instruction each week. There undoubtedly were exceptions, since except for ideas about curriculum presented in textbooks, curriculum content in nursing ethics during classroom lectures was not regularly recorded. Still, if the notebook of Bellevue student George L. King,[17] which contained extensive and meticulously detailed notes of lectures from various physicians is any example, principles for ethical nursing conduct were not included.

The essence of nursing was taught at the bedside. If the content of ethics and etiquette in the training school curricula were the modelling clay, then the teacher was the sculptor of the student's ultimate education. The first classroom instructors of nursing theory were almost exclusively physicians. At Bellevue Hospital in 1875, a series of forty-two lectures were given to the nursing students. All were delivered by physicians, except one, "Bedside Manipulation or Rubbing."[18] At New York Hospital, in 1881, a similar state of affairs existed.[19] When physicians were often called upon to summarize the ideal of nursing for senior students and graduate nurses, often in commencement addresses, they presented good nursing in a nutshell from the physician's point of view.

Ethics education depended on role modeling, experiences in relationships and informal instruction. Since a large part of the student's training occurred while practicing at the patient's bedside, it would follow that the ethics of the profession would also be conferred while interacting with clients, peers and superiors during clinical experiences. Head nurses were the first line of contact between the student and the training school while on the hospital wards. They provided the most direct and consistent transmission of preferred behaviors through supervision, evaluation, command and expression of authority. Mindful of the desire to provide moral guidance for students and patients and acting on the prevalent belief that a better class of woman would be the better teacher and supervisor, training school authorities preferred the socially elite nurse for the position of head nurse, since she, quite naturally, would most likely demonstrate gentility, temperance and refinement.[20]

The character traits of the head nurse became the model character traits for the student. The astute probationer and junior quickly learned that "womanly refinement" was rewarded by recognition, responsibility, respect and success. The members of the Board of Managers, at Bellevue Hospital Training School, for example, agreed that the presence of a "lady" on the wards would be a positive influence on the students and nurses regardless of their lack of nursing theory or expertise. Some head nurses were often chosen from graduate nurse applicants or senior nursing students; it is likely that they had demonstrated to the school hierarchy womanly refinement and, to some degree, competence. The paramount concern was for the nurses' respectability, subordination and moral integrity and it was on these that the integrity of the training school rested. For example, Euphemia Van Rensselaer, one of New York City's social elite, while attending the training school at Bellevue Hospital, was given a position as supervisor over students and ward head nurses.[21] She was also offered the post of Assistant Superintendent before the usual two years of training was completed. Of her eligibility to be a nursing leader and therefore role model, the Board of Managers wrote:

> Miss Van Rensselaer knows the work, devotes herself to it from high religious principles, is strict in her discipline, [and] exerts an excellent moral influence throughout the school.[22]

Ethical mettle was tested during practice on the hospital wards when the student left the safety of the classroom and the ideology of her textbooks behind. It was during this time that role modeling by instructors and the actual ethics of the profession became most evident. First nursing experiences consisted of cleaning slop pots, washing patients, folding linen and wrapping bandages for hour after tedious hour. She worked up to fourteen hours per day, seven days a week and any notions of a glamorous profession quickly disappeared. Creativity was discouraged. Each nursing activity was guided by a strict set of rules and any attempt to change or even improve on the performance was considered disobedience.[23] Under these conditions of nursing practice, independent moral judgement could not flourish. Not surprisingly, the ideal nurse and the real nurse were quite different. While the ideal image served to design practice by the best, the actual nurse practiced within a system and in relationships that were often fraught with problems and contradictions. From their textbooks and classes students learned ideal ethical conduct, but it was from their relationships with the hospital, physicians, and other students that they became acquainted with the real world of patient care.

The relationship between men and women was the prototype for the relationship between hospital and nursing student and physician and nurse. Just as women were subordinate to men, nurses were subordinate to physicians. Sexism and the relationship of the nurse to doctor and nurse to hospital were inseparable. Aware of the forces of attraction between men and women in a society of strict sexual mores, one nervous nurse offered this caveat on the need for a strictly professional relationship.

> Any other will mean diaster to the nurse. By disaster I mean that any relation not professional will lead to misunderstandings, quarrels or perhaps marriage and in either case the nurse's usefulness as a professional nurse will be at an end.[24]

In the public sphere men were a threat to the moral integrity of women, and in the hospital arena, where the bounds of propriety could easily wear thin, physicians were the wolves in sheep's clothing. The relationship between physicians and nurses was as closely inspected, and then treated, just as the patient's disease was treated in the surgical amphitheater. The ethics of the relationship between nurses and doctors was in part influenced by the degree of insecurity felt by the physicians for their practice and their motive for participating in nurse training. A popular guide written for physicians by a physician in the late 1800s portrayed their profession as facing a hostile and skeptical world. Advice suggested that doctors concern themselves with expressing their competence and only secondarily with actually being competent.

In light of the prevalent fear by physicians of losing control over their practice, many physicians undoubtedly saw teaching of nurses as a way of restricting knowledge to a competitor and there was no effort to distinguish these physicians from truly progressive, professionally secure physicians. In summary, from the onset of nurse training, a confused ethical message was being sent to the pupil in training.

Another important relationship that supplied the informal ethics education was that among students. A new student had few peers. Under conditions of hard work, long hours and social isolation, the nurse was pushed to the limit of her physical and emotional endurance. Strict control of free time and working conditions left little time to develop friendships. Supportive emotional ties were discouraged in the shadow of burdensome work and the rank and file of a quasi-military environment. One nurse remembered that "The nurses were practical young women working themselves to death."[25]

Foremost of the nineteenth century, female friendships played a central emotional role in each women's lives. Women regularly formed emotional ties with other women that were deeply felt, long lived and casually accepted as part of American society.[26] In contrast, women in nursing training were warned to avoid close relationships with other nurses, as these would pose a distraction and reduce their efficiency. In spite of such warnings, supportive relationships developed outside of the accepted ideal for students. While some seniors exploited the juniors by making them do extra work, others protected them from rebuke if their work was unsatisfactory.[27] Still, the natural inclinations of the Victorian women to bond with other females was stifled by the training school routine and may have greatly contributed to the high attrition rate of students (as high as 50 percent). Working and living in an environment that was harshly realistic, the student was faced, daily, with challenges to her personal value system and newly conceived vision of ethical nursing. Feelings of sympathy were extinguished. Strength and health were taxed. Family and personal support systems were shaken or removed, and the student's ideal self-image was molded to fit into the real working world which taught her own inferiority. In such a situation the ethic of loyalty struggled to survive. Even the ethic of caring and doing no harm was diluted in the midst of overwhelming human suffering. Confidentiality fared no better when the nursing care of the last night's patient might have been the only common denominator in meager social lives of the students. The value of hard work must surely have been questioned when personal rewards, and institutional recognition were as minimal as their monthly pends.[28]

MORAL PROBLEMS ENCOUNTERED IN TRAINING SCHOOL

Outlets for tension and resolutions of internal conflicts were easy to find but not always appropriate. While training schools did make some small attempt to maintain the physical well-being of the students, they neglected their emotional and social needs.[29] Like harmonic movement, ideal and actual behaviors were resonating extremes. Students found release by acting out in ways opposed to the ideal.

Inspection of the records of students who attended training schools revealed a pattern of critical behaviors, problems, and punishments. Misbehavior among pupils ranged from sexual misconduct to substance abuse to violence. The most common problem. encountered in training schools, however, was disobedience and insubordination. Through the eyes of the Victorian "judge," these sins were both morally and economically objectionable. They were in direct opposition both to the accepted ideals of womanhood and to the work ethic. Even seemingly innocuous examples of improper behavior received swift rebuke. At New York Hospital, for example, some students were suspended after "putting some decayed cheese in a package, addressing it to Dr. Tilton and placing it on the table at which he stood to deliver his lecture . . ." "[The] perpetrators promptly came forward, [admitting they had] done it thoughtlessly in a spirit of fun and expressed regret."[30] Though the visual display of the doctor's reputation as the "big cheese" (albeit rotten), was, by today's standards, a relatively harmless manifestation of student frustration and release of tension, to school officials of the time, it cut to the core of the ideal relaitonship between physician and nurse and the unquestioned loyalty due the former. Punishment was in order.

Another problem faced by training school administrators was unreliability, and neglect of duties and responsibilities. Acts committed against patients and employers such as stealing, borrowing jewelry, striking patients, errors in medication administration and being absent without proper leave, besides being disobedient of one or another regulation, were regarded as conduct indicating unreliability and neglect of duties. An especially common problem was the finding of nurses asleep while on night duty. This usually resulted in a forced resignation, but when coupled with insolence or gross insubordination, students were simply dismissed. Incidents of striking, or otherwise harming a patient were found in training school records, especially at large insitutions such as Bellevue.[31] There is some evidence that the use of force was common and expected from male nurses who were selected, by virtue of their strength and size, to work on Insane and Alcoholic Wards within hospitals such as The Manhattan Hospital for the Insane on Wards Island, New York City.

Nurse propriety and sexuality were under constant scrutiny. The ideal of purity prevailed for male as well as female nurses. Any nurse caught breaking written or unwritten laws on sexual conduct was summarily withdrawn from the school's roster. At Bellevue, female nurses were dismissed for "immoral conduct," concealment of marriage while in training, and in one case, for falsely claiming to be a widow.[32] Romantic relationships with men were strongly discouraged and forbidden with doctors. The nurse was to forget both sex and self. The metaphor of "nurse as mother" was emphasized since when acting in the name of "motherhood," tasks that would ordinarily be distasteful, became acts of self-sacrifice.

Another indicator of immorality to society at the time was the prevalent use of simulants and other drugs.[33] It appeared to be a relatively common problem and was openly discussed in the nineteenth century hospital board room. Students found intoxicated while on duty, or "intemperate," or known to have a "drug habit" of morphia or opium, were discharged or forced to resign.[34] Since access to narcotics was as easy as a trip to the corner apothecary, and popular culture did not condemn self-medication while consumerism encouraged it, those who became nurses had to be aware of these changing expectations.

Lastly alcohol was the tonic panacea. Doled out to patients as a staple nutrient and as a palliative relief during the Civil War, it retained its place as a potion for the treatment of pain and discomfort. It was recommended, without hesitation by authors of leading medical textbooks as a cardiac tonic, a conservator of tissue capable of increasing and sustaining vital energy, and as possessing actual food value. By dismissing those who drank alcohol or used opiates while nursing, the Boards of Managers not only attempted to limit the influence of past practices, but exert a moral influence and mold young practitioners to accept efficiency as a work ideal. Like the young child in the family, ethical role modeling was confounded by the age old caveat - do as I say, not as I do.

In summary, because the ethical education of nurses in nineteenth century training schools was not outlined in a formal curriculum, its form and content were set by the cultural expectations laid out in the ideals of womanhood and the cardinal virtues of piety, purity, domesticity, and submissiveness. The primary teaching method was role modeling which was as varied as the personalities of the physician and head nurse instructors. In addition, the powerful demonstrators and reinforcers of the actual ethics of the profession were those found in the nature of the relationships among nurses and their peers, physicians, and the institutional hierarchy.

From the way the nurse-physician relationship was practiced, the student was forced to deny her power and knowledge and to become dependent. From her relationship with the institution she learned the overriding importance of the work ethic since the creation of an ideal worker was the prime aim of the institution in her training. How successful was such training? From the prevalence of problems such as insubordination, substance abuse, and neglect of duties, it is evident that there were numerous failures. One reason for the failure was the confusing message given to nurses and its contradictions to every day life. In an analysis of nursing ethics in the nineteenth century training school, we gain an understanding of the problems of working women in a bureaucratic society and of the difficulties that our predecessors had in dealing with some of the problems still facing us.

NOTES

1. Barbara Welter, *Dimity Convictions, The American Woman in the 19th Century*, (Athens, Ohio: Ohio University Press, 1976).
2. State Charities Aid Association, *Report of the Committee on the Training School for Nurses to be Attached to Bellevue* (New York: Cushing, Bardua and Co., 1872), pp. 25-26. The official title of the school was The Training School for Nurses Attached to Bellevue Hospital from 1873-1891. It was changed to New York

Training School for Nurses from 1891 - 1910 and finally became Bellevue Training School for Nurses in 1901.

3.   Sr. Dorothy A. Sheahan, "The Social Origins of American Nursing and Its Movement into the University: A Microcosmic Approach," Ph.D. Dissertation, New York: New York University, 1980, p. 158. Waltham Training School, *First Fifty Years of the Waltham Training School for Nursing*, 1935, (Typed, bound material) [Mugar Library], p. 27.
      W.G. Thompson, M.D., *Training-Schools for Nurses with Notes on Twenty-Two Schools*, (New York: G.P. Putnam's Sons, 1883), p. 14-17.

4.   Constance Schuyler, "The Nightingale Program for Educating Professional Nurses and Its Interpretation in the United States," *Historical Studies in Nursing*, M. Louisa Fitzpatrick, ed. (New York: Teachers College Press, 1978), pp. 31-54. Schulyer's article gives an excellent explanation of the difference between the Nightingale school in England and the American version, and an interpretation of the effective differences.

5.   Ibid., p. 39.

6.   Florence Nightingale, *Notes on Nursing: What it is and What it is Not* (London: Harrison and Sons, 1859); Zepherina P. Veitch, *Handbook for Nurses for the Sick* (London: J. & A. Churchill, 1872, Second Edition, 1876); Edward J. Domville, *A Manual for Hospital Sisters and Others Engaged in Attending on the Sick* (London: J. & A. Churchill, 1872); Florence S. Lees, *Handbook for Hospital Sisters*, (London: W. Isbister & Co., 1874).

7.   Harriet C. Camp, *A Reference Book for Trained Nurses*, (New York: Lakeside Publishing Co., 1889).

8.   The first nursing ethics textbook was Isabel H. Robb, *Nursing Ethics: For Hospital and Private Use* (Cleveland, Ohio: E.C. Koeckert

Publishers, 1900). Until then other American textbooks available were, such as, *An American Woman's Suggestions for the Sick-Room*, (New York: Anson D.F. Randolph and Company, 1876); Connecticut Training School's, *A Hand-Book of Nursing for Family and General Use*, (Philadelphia: J.B. Lippincott Co., 1878); Bellevue Training School's, *A Manual of Nursing*, (New York: G.P. Putnam and Sons, 1878); Clara S. Weeks', *A Text-Book of Nursing, for the Use of Training Schools, Families, and Private Students*, (New York: D. Appleton and Co., 1885); and Emily A.M. Stoney's, *Practical Points in Nursing for Nurses in Private Practice*, (Philadelphia: W.B. Saunders, 1896).

9. Minutes of the Committee on the Training School for Nurses At Bellevue Hospital, Committee on the Training School, October 11, 1876, p. 168, Bellevue Hospital Archives, New York. The committee moved "To appoint a special committee to examine the various books already published and decide which, if any they would recommend as textbooks for the Bellevue School," or consider writing their own, which they subsequently decided to do. In the preface of the newly compiled manual, credit was given to Nightingale's, *Notes on Nursing*, Lee's, *Hospital Sister*, Domville's, *A Handbook for Nurses*. The committee began to compile the text in 1877 as recorded in the, Minutes of the Board of Managers of Bellevue Hospital, April 4, 1877: "The Committee on Instruction for Nurses was about prepared to compile the Manual for Nurses."

10. Op. Cit. Weeks.

11. Mrs. H.O. Ward (pseudonym for Mrs. Clara Sophia Bloomfield-Moore) *Sensible Etiquette of the Best Society, Customs, Manners, Morals, and Home Culture* (Philadelphia: Porter & Coates, 1878).

12. Weeks, p. 15.

13.   Ward, p. 92, 146.
14.   *A Manual of Nursing*, p. 2.
15.   *A Manual of Nursing*, p. 2.
16.   Evaluation Sheet for the Training School for Nurses, Bellevue Hospital Archives.
17.   George L. King's Notebook, (1891), Bellevue Hospital Archives. King was a graduate of Mills Training School in 1891.
18.   Second Report of the Training School for Nurses Attached to Bellevue Hospital, (New York: Angell Book and Pamphlet Printer, 1875), p. 8.
19.   Committee Papers, Committee on the Training School for Nurses, Secretary/Treasurer Papers of the Society of New York Hospital, 1881. Medical Archives, The New York Hospital-Cornell Medical Center, New York.
20.   Nancy Tomes, "Little World of Our Own: The Pennsylvania Hospital Training School for Nurses, 1895-1907," *Journal of the History of Medicine*, 33 (1978), pp. 328-345. Rosenberg, p. 225).
21.   Minutes of the Meeting of the Committee on Surgical Wards for Women, Ward #18, Lady Board of Managers of the Training School for Nurses Attached to Bellevue Hospital (August 12, 1874, p. 76, Bellevue Hospital Archives.
22.   Ibid., (November 4, 1874), p. 91.
23.   Philip A. Kalisch and Beatrice J. Kalisch, *The Advance of American Nursing*, (Boston, Mass: Little, Brown and Co., 1978), p. 189.
24.   Sarah Dock, "The Relation of the Nurse to the Doctor and the Doctor to the Nurse," *American Journal of Nursing*, 17, (February 1917), 394.
25.   Mary Roberts Rinehart, *My Story* (New York: Rinehart and Co., Inc., 1931), p. 45.
26.   Carol Smith-Rosenberg, "The Female World of Love and Ritual: Relations Between Women in Nineteenth Century America," *A Heritage of Her Own, Toward a New Social History of American Women*, Nancy F. Cott, and Elizabeth H. Peck, Eds. (New York: Simon and Shuster,

1979), pp. 311-342.
27. Tomes, p. 475.
28. Nurses were allotted monthly stipends on the average of $10 per month. Some small hospitals were reputed to have received at least $21 per week, from patients, for services provided by the students. Kalisch and Kalisch, *The Advance of American Nursing* (Boston: Little, Brown and Co., 1986), p. 185.
29. The training schools provided for rest periods and eight hour blocks of sleeping time in addition to three meals per day, but they did not encourage social activities nor personal enrichment other than religious services and advocating of prayer.
30. Medical Archives, New York Hospital, Letter to Visiting Committee from George, Ludlam, Superintendent, New York Hospital, March 1902.
31. Record Book, Mills Training School at Bellevue Hospital, 1892-1906 and Record of Probationers, The Training School Attached to Bellevue Hospital, 1873-1886.
32. Record of Probationers, The Training School Attached to Bellevue Hospital, 1873-1886.
33. Drugs is a term that will be used to include narcotics and alcohol.
34. Record Book, Mills Training School, Bellevue Hospital, 1892-1908, and Record of Probationers, The Training School Attached to Bellevue Hospital, 1873-1886.

SECTION IV

NIGHTINGALISM AND REFORM IN PSYCHIATRIC CARE

NIGHTINGALISM: ITS USE AND ABUSE IN LUNACY REFORM AND THE DEVELOPMENT OF NURSING IN PSYCHIATRIC CARE AT THE TURN OF THE CENTURY

Olga Maranjian Church

This paper is part of a larger study which investigates the emergence of psychiatric nursing in the U.S. from 1882 forward. The use of the term Nightingalism is meant to imply, as the dictionary explains "ism", a devotion to a particular theory, doctrine or system. Recently, much has been said that would lead us to question whether and to what extent there was a Nightingale theory, doctrine or system but certainly at least in the United States there has been a perception and belief that there was. As Monica Baly has said "in history what people think is happening is often as important as what actually happened." I believe the challenge for historians has always been to separate out, as much as is humanly possible, the rhetoric from the reality, but to discount neither.

A few words about the primary source materials that I gathered may be of interest. Resources for data collected include the archives at the McLean Hospital in Massachusetts; the Sterling Library at Yale University in Connecticut; the Alan Chesney Archives at Johns Hopkins in Baltimore, MD; the History of Nursing Collection at Teachers College, Columbia University, NY; the Boston University Nursing

230 *Nightingalism: Its Use and Abuse in Lunacy,*
Reform and the Development of Nursing in
Psychiatric Care at the Turn of the Century

Archives, the Medical Historical Collection at John Crerar Library at the Illinois Institute of Technology, which is now part of the University of Chicago; and, last but not least, the (APA) American Psychiatric Association Archives in Washington, D.C.

In the early 19th century, individual attempts had not successfully transformed the attitudes of the general population nor had they left any lasting impression on the general approaches to psychiatric care. The prevailing rhetoric was one that promised a genteel and humane approach of moral rehabilitation. However, harsh treatments were in keeping with the persistent view of mental derangement as a hopelessly dehumanizing process which rendered its victims insensitive and irreversibly damaged.

One of the earliest lunacy reform efforts, and perhaps the best well known, is the crusade that was begun in 1841 by Dorothea Dix. Dix is credited with single-handedly surveying the existing conditions of the mentally ill in this country and abroad. She followed her observations with concrete proposals to the various governmental bodies, charging them with the responsibility for humane care of their mentally ill citizenry. Unfortunately, her efforts provided short term solutions to much longer lasting problems. Dix campaigned for better care by way of bigger facilities and was successful in instigating the construction of such buildings. However, as soon as these became overcrowded, the ideal of individualized care became impossible to achieve and these larger facilities became warehouses for custodial care.

The customary neglect with respect to society's responsibility for providing care for the mentally ill and the concerns of reformers such as Dix and others who would follow, is a part of the traditional conflict that is inherent to the very nature of how mental illness is defined and determined by a given society.

The elusive nature of mental illness is our first clue that it is not a static condition conducive to convenient labeling. In addition, it suggests that its ever changing character may have more to do with the

Nightingalism: Its Use and Abuse in Lunacy 231
Reform and the Development of Nursing in
Psychiatric Care at the Turn of the Century

definer of the disorder (society) than with those being defined (the afflicted). According to Magaro, "Theories of madness and their treatments are accepted and implemented according to whether or not the theories fit the thought of the current cultural milieu."[1] In any event, over the years much confusion has surfaced which had led to contradictions and misapprehensions of those who were the reported "experts" of their time on such matters. A brief survey of the attitudes and the ways in which mental illness was defined from the earliest times to the present day reveals that with some modifications, the process of enlightenment has been a circuitous one.

By the middle of the 19th century, social reformers as well as the alienists[2] in the medical community continued to be concerned about the need for development of the proper care for the physically and mentally ill citizens of their communities. This heightened concern prompted the formation of a new organization in 1880. Along with the alienists involved in the treatment of the insane were a group of like-minded "social workers," neurologists, and civic-minded laymen and women who joined together to formally organize the National Association for the Protection of the Insane and the Prevention of Insanity (NAPIPI).[3] Though acknowledging the organizations that were already in existence at the time, the members of this new group pointed to the inability of the established groups to cope with or control the real problems of increasing patient population and the general mismanagement of treatment settings. The two organizations which were specifically cited by NAPIPI were the Association of Medical Superintendents of Institutions for the Insane (later known as the American Medico-Psychological Association, which in turn became the American Psychiatric Association) and the Conference of Charities, a state level organization that was involved with various dependent populations.

In and out of existence during a period of six years, the NAPIPI, was a "Ralph Nader" type of organization, which preceded the Mental Hygiene Organization established in 1908. Through the brief time that it functioned, the NAPIPI sought to establish a coordinating body for the practices of those who were responsible for the treatment of the insane. This early example of a "whistle blowing" organization maintained keen vigilance in matters of institutional care. By agitating for legislative inquiries wherever the existence of abuses were known or suspected, the NAPIPI undoubtedly exerted a generally healthy influence in preventing and alleviating such abuses.

The major methods by which this organization proposed to meet its objectives were: to encourage observations of physicians, both general practitioners and alienists; to enlighten public sentiment regarding the possibilities for prevention and the management and home treatment of the insane; to urge legislation of progressive policies; and to further the notion of patients' rights while they were confined in the asylum. At public meetings professionals spoke about these issues and the inherent evils in the existing system of care.

In 1882 a Dr. Nathan Allen, speaking of lunacy reform, noted the conservative nature of the superintendents (physicians) in charge of the asylums and the "general defect in the present system . . . that is often arrayed against improvements or reform."[4] Allen noted that

> The history of all reforms shows that they scarcely ever started within the circle or institution in which the evils existed. The history of lunacy reform is not an exception. Insanity as a disease has fallen into the hands of a few interested parties, and these have had the entire charge of hospitals.[5]

The very nature of the NAPIPI's aims and methods challenged the existing organizations, and ultimately provoked and antagonized those in power. It is not surprising that eventually the many conflicts,

Nightingalism: Its Use and Abuse in Lunacy 233
Reform and the Development of Nursing in
Psychiatric Care at the Turn of the Century

both internal (among the professional members) and external, as well as the lack of enlightened public support, contributed to the demise of the NAPIPI.

As we know, almost a decade before this lunacy reform movement began, what has become known as the Nightingale System of training nurses became established in the U.S. with the three training schools in New York, Connecticut and Massachusetts in 1873. Nine years later in 1882, the "first formally organized training school within a hospital for insane in the world"[6] was opened at the McLean Asylum in Massachusetts, through the efforts of Dr. Edward Cowles.

Prior to his arrival at McLean in 1879, Cowles had briefly served as Superintendent at the Boston City Hospital. While there, Cowles,

> "with the assistance of Linda Richards, the first American woman in the United States to hold a diploma as a trained nurse, began the Training-School for Nurses at the Boston City Hospital . . . the first in the United States that was a part of the hospital organization itself, and independent of outside assistance."[7]

This organizational structure was not in keeping with what was thought of as the "Nightingale System," and as such would serve as an early indicator of the domination and influence of training programs by hospital administrators and physicians.

Although Cowles spoke favorably about Nightingale as the "founder of Modern Nursing," he carefully avoided following the principle of autonomy in the establishment of the organization of the training programs both at Boston City and at McLean. He often spoke of nursing, and Nightingale as responsible for "that Noble Reform" and claimed that

> "No greater work has ever been done for the amelioration of human suffering and the saving of human life than this . . . She [Nightingale] has created an epoch for the hospitals while the asylums were still groping to find the way in which they first felt the

need of going."[8]

In Cowles' view, the training and employment of nurses served several vital purposes. First, the nurse was important in her role as a symbolic manifestation for medicalizing the asylum. Secondly, the female nurses provided "great value, and the moral and curative influence of their habitual presence in our wards for men is positive, and would not be willingly given up."[9] In addition, the nurse's "natural motherliness" was an important part of her role, and according to Cowles could be used to the patient's benefit. In his assessment of his experiment in establishing the training school program Cowles determined that

> What was wanted in the nurse was intelligence, sympathy and trustworthiness. It was seen that the secret of Florence Nightingale's success was in overcoming repugnance to the work of nursing by giving the nurse better knowledge of the nature of disease and how to relieve suffering."[10]

The candidates considered most desirable for entrance into the school at the McLean Asylum were between age twenty-one and thirty-five, of sound health and good character, and "required to be sober, honest, truthful, turstworthy, punctual, quiet, orderly, cleanly, neat, patient, kind, and cheerful."[11] Instructions were given by the Superintendent of the Training School (a nurse) and by Supervisors and Head nurses. Lectures and demonstrations were periodically given by the asylum medical staff.

In addition, the students were employed as assistant nurses in the wards of the asylum, and it is interesting to note that while the women students were paid twleve dollars per month during their first year and fifteen dollars per month during the second year for their clothing and personal expenses, the men who were in the program were paid twenty-three dollars per month during the first year and twenty-five dollars per month during the second year. Upon graduation the women would be paid twenty-five

Nightingalism: Its Use and Abuse in Lunacy 235
Reform and the Development of Nursing in
Psychiatric Care at the Turn of the Century

dollars per month and the men would receive twenty-seven dollars per month. The course was a two-year program, and when completed, and after a final examination, the graduates were issued "diplomas certifying to their period of training, their proficiency and good character."[12]

From its inception, Cowles was determined that in his school the students should be prepared in general for what he sometimes called "bodily" nursing inasmuch as he disagreed with the commonly held belief that

> "the asylums could furnish only the means of teaching the care of the insane, so that bodily nursing could not be adequately taught; and that the repugnance to mental nursing would forbid the finding of the right material for training as in the general hospitals."[13]

The importance of selecting appropriate candidates to the asylum work was carefully considered, and Cowles spoke on the subject of the natural talents of women as opposed to men in this field. Although he was to begin one of the first such organized training programs for men in 1886, his caution in the use of men as nurses was grounded in the idea that men "do not lend themselves so pliably as women to the spirit of the work."[14]

Speaking of the risks involved in teaching women who might be misguided into thinking of themselves as more than nurses, Cowles stated that most of the women sought honest and respectable livelihoods and had no such "higher motives." Acknowledging the misgivings of the medical community with regard to such inappropriate ambitions, he referred to the "timely caution" against "training the woman so that she becomes a sort of hybrid, which is neither nurse nor doctor."[15]

The following provides a glimpse of Cowles' motivation and inspiration for his training school for nurses.

> "The feeling is strong upon me that the importance of this nursing reform for the

236 *Nightingalism: Its Use and Abuse in Lunacy,
Reform and the Development of Nursing in
Psychiatric Care at the Turn of the Century*

insane is not yet half realized. The keen psychological interest an intelligent nurse will take (when taught to do it), in the mental operation of an insane patient, is something beyond even my very sanguine expectations. This puts a power into our hands for the moral treatment of our patients that opens wide possibilities in promoting their comfort and cure. One must believe this when he finds his nurses methodically and intelligently fitting their manner and speech to different patients, and with womanly gentleness, as well as with an effectiveness that comes from an almost unconscious knowledge (so to speak) of power to manage the varying mental states of the insane. The acute intuition of women, when trained to this work, becomes a most valuable instrument in our hands."[16]

Other physicians had other "decided opinions." A Dr. H.R. Storer for example maintained there were few pretensions to authority on "the subject of nursing, save those of Florence Nightingale,"[17] and ends his rationale for his own opinions by stating that:

Nursing as a science and an art still is left a matter of accident, taste, or individual experience . . . The medical profession, dependent, as we confessedly all are, on our practice, upon the discretion and assistance of the nurse or attendant, has been content to leave matters much as it had found them; fearing, from certain notable examples, the nurse, by endeavoring to advance, might exceed her sphere; that in attempting to do better, she would do more--too much, perhaps--unsexing herself by attempting all the duties of the opposite sex, for many of which, at certain times, she is physiologically unfitted, and on the other, injuring the patient by excessive kindness or mistaken zeal.[18]

Essentially, the message was one of concern not only for the client, but for the kind of women who

Nightingalism: Its Use and Abuse in Lunacy   237
Reform and the Development of Nursing in
Psychiatric Care at the Turn of the Century

would become involved in nursing or the practice of
medicine. It is important to note that in society at
large, there was great debate on "the woman problem,"
"what do women want," etc. and of course, the parallel
for nursing can be seen in the discussion by physicians
who referred to this as the "nursing problem."

As indicated elsewhere in this book, in 1893,
at the Columbia Exposition, papers were read at the
meetings of the International Congress of Charities,
Corrections, and Philanthropy, Secion IV, dealing with
Commitment, Detention, Care and Treatment of the
Insane. The World's Exposition played host to many
social scientists and educators, among whom were the
members of the American Medico-Psychological
Association, formerly the Association of Medical
Superintendents of Institutions for the Insane. The
president, Dr. J.B. Andrews, discussed the issue of
training asylum nurses as an element of progress and
suggested that the American Medico-Psychological
Association appoint a committee to prepare a definite
scheme and, so far as possible, a uniform method of
procedure for asylum training schools. His words were
not heeded immediately and it took another 13 years
of annual meetings before the Association membership
saw fit to appoint such a committee.

At the same time a newly emerging *group* of
nurses was also meeting in Chicago in 1893, most of
whom were Nurse Superintendents of Training Schools
for Nurses. As a group they were in no position to
take on the responsibility of asylum training, for they
had yet to organize the most fundamental core of
education for the practice of traditional nursing. As a
separate area of concern for nursing, asylum training
would have to wait.

In spite of such neglect, and influenced by the
"common sense" of the sociocultural considerations
inherent to a comprehensive approach to patient care,
some of the early nursing leaders did include the
wider realm of mental health in their rhetoric and
their definition of the scope of nursing practice. These
nurses recognized the importance of prevention and

the need for public involvement in health education. Although they advocated special preparation for psychiatric nursing, the acceptance of their ideas and suggestions was impeded by social and economic factors as well as by the circumstances from within and outside of nursing proper.

It was not until the 1906 annual meeting of the American Medico-Psychological Association that the value of training the attendants and nurses in asylums was discussed in detail. Implicit to the issues discussed was the need for the involvement of the medical superintendents in the training that was offered. Titles of the presentations reveal the topics discussed:

> Dr. George T. Tuttle, Waverly, Mass., read a paper entitled, *'The Male Nurse.'*

> Dr. C.R. Woodson, of St. Joseph, Mo., read a paper entitled, *'Night Nurses for the Insane.'*

> Dr. Edward B. Lane, Boston, Mass., read a paper, *'The Training School in the Insane Hospital.'*

> The paper of Dr. W.P. Crumbacker, Independence, Iowa, *'Musings Concerning Nurses in Hospitals for the Insane,'* was read by title.[1]

This "Symposium on Nursing" included a lengthy discussion following the formal presentations. An interesting issue was whether men or women would be better companions for the male patients. The underlying issue was not the competence of the female nurses in patient care, but rested on the impact of their responsibilities in being in charge of male attendants and male nurses.

The qualities of both male and female applicants to the training school were discussed fully by those in attendance, with all agreeing that the special requirements for nursing the insane required

Nightingalism: Its Use and Abuse in Lunacy 239
Reform and the Development of Nursing in
Psychiatric Care at the Turn of the Century

special material out of which to make such nurses.
There was general agreement that

> ... the amount of intelligence, tact, judgment
> and skill required to care properly for an
> insane person is infinitely greater than that
> required to care properly of even a surgical
> patient in a general hospital. There is need of
> missionary work with the public to teach the
> importance of intelligent care of the insane.[19]

Perhaps the most telling remarks from this
group of male physicians speak to their stereotypic
image of the nurse as the essence of *"pure sweet
woman."*

> ... a woman is a natural born nurse, the more
> gentle and womanly, the better the nurse. Now
> as the woman becomes a little mannish, as is
> the tendency of the present day, she spoils her
> usefulness as a nurse. The best male nurse is
> effeminate and is good accordingly as he
> approaches a woman in his characteristics.[20]

In closing the "Symposium on Nursing," Dr.
W.A. White made the motion, suggested by Dr.
Andrews 13 years earlier at the Colombian exposition,
to appoint a committee

> " . . . to be known as the Committee on
> Training Schools, whose duty shall be to
> prescribe a minimum requirement in a course
> of study in training schools for nurses in
> hospitals for the insane and that the diplomas
> issued by those hospitals in the judgement of
> the committee, satisfy the requirements, shall
> be accepted in other hospitals for the insane.
> The motion was duly seconded and carried."[22]

The first report from the Committee on
Training Schools for Nurses was submitted the
following year at the Annual Meeting of the
Association. It was accepted and adopted by the
association on May 8, 1907. Thus it was that a group
of five physicians, having been duly appointed by
their fellow alienists and having consulted with five
Superintendents of Training Schools for Nurses in

Hospitals for the Insane, determined by design who and what should be taught in the training programs. They defined the function of the nurse, from their perspective, as "to assist the physician in the care of his patients."[22]

The nursing perspectives and early efforts in psychiatric nursing education can be viewed by examining the work of Effie Jane Taylor, who was the nurse in charge of the Nursing Department of the Henry Phipps Psychiatric Clinic of the Johns Hopkins Hospital which opened in 1913 under the direction of Dr. Adolph Meyer. This center would soon become "generally recognized as one of the great centers of psychiatric research and education, not only of this country but of the world."[23]

> Taylor, [a] graduate of the Johns Hopkins Hospital School of Nursing, and long a member of the faculty of that school, . . . did post graduate work in both private and state mental hospitals in New York, Rhode Island and Massachusetts, preparatory to organizing and directing the nursing service of . . . [the] Phipps.[24]

Most important to the development of the psychiatric nursing movement was the fact that at the time the Phipps opened its doors at Johns Hopkins it

> . . . was the first general hospital to offer such a course under the direction and control of its own faculty. Miss Taylor developed and guided a course in psychiatric nursing composed of lectures, quizzes, demonstrations, ward experiences, as well as clinics and conferences. The course extended throughout the three-year training period.[25]

Taylor adapted Meyer's psychobiological approach to her work in nursing education. She sought to integrate the basic concepts from general and mental nursing to establish a more comprehensive knowledge base from which all nursing care could be delivered.

Nightingalism: Its Use and Abuse in Lunacy 241
Reform and the Development of Nursing in
Psychiatric Care at the Turn of the Century

Taylor's broad scope of concern for preparing mental nurses was inherent to her psychobiological orientation. But she would not find immediate satisfaction in achieving any consensus on what she saw as important in mental nursing education. The basic problem was one "of defining the place of the nurse and determining what knowledge she needs to possess in order to function in her capacity and meet her responsibility in the community."[26]

For Taylor, the nurse must be in a decision-making position. She stated that "the nurse is instructed to think for herself and use her own judgment, keeping in mind how she would wish a thing done were she the patient herself, or a member of her family."[27] Taylor had anticipated a new era for mental nursing, as had Cowles when he spoke of Nightingale's noble reform. Yet the role that the 'trained' nurse played in the improvement of conditions for psychiatric care continued to be minimal. It was clear to Taylor that the mental institutions and the policies which guided them confined and restricted opportunities for the development of the nurse and the care she might provide.

The solution for Taylor was a broader and firmer educational foundation for preparing mental nurses. However the prevailing medical/curative ideology would continue to limit the development of a scientifically and academically broader perspective for nursing schools. Though there were enlightened leaders, their followers were few compared to the consensus that apparently ruled.

HISTORICAL IMPLICATIONS

The development of psychiatric nursing as a response to the development of psychiatric care in the United States is an example of the traditional relatonship between nursing and medicine. The powerful influence of the curative/medical model ideology on the evolution of psychiatric nursing and the current acknowledgement of the limitations of such a model has given rise to recent challenges and changes within psychiatric care.

The work of Edward Cowles reveals the medical authority's desperate need for organized educational programs for asylum caretakers to become informed caregivers. This examination of the awareness within the early psychiatric-medical establishment of nursing reform, inspired by Nightingale's work, and its promise of an economically expedient solution for filling caretaking needs, provides historical *antecedents* that serve as meaningful parallels to economic issues today. The recent proposal by organized medicine to create "registered care technicians" who would work under their authority is yet another example of the unresolved perpetual tensions between nursing and medicine.

In examining the use and abuse of Nightingale's work in the transformation of asylums to hospitals one is struck by the blatant disregard of the original intent of "that Noble Reform" and the ongoing struggle to make it a reality.

NOTES

1. P.A. Magaro (ed.). *The Mental Health Industry: A Cultural Phenomenon.* New York: Welsey - Inter-Science Publishers, 1978, p. 4

2. This term was used to describe the early psychiatrists (19th and early 20th century) who were believed to be treating persons who were mentally alienated.

3. *Papers and Proceedings of the National Association for the Protection of the Insane and the Prevention of Insanity.* New York: G.P. Putnam's Sons, 1882.

4. N. Allen, M.D.: Insanity and Its Relations to the Medical Profession and Lunatic Hospitals.

Nightingalism: Its Use and Abuse in Lunacy 243
Reform and the Development of Nursing in
Psychiatric Care at the Turn of the Century

In *Papers and Proceedings of the National Association for the Protection of the Insane and the Prevention of Insanity.* New York: G.P. Putnam's Sons, 1882, p. 21.

5. Ibid.
6. Sixty-fifth Annual Report of the Superintendents of the McLean Asylum for the Insane to the Trustees of the Massachusetts General Hospital for the year 1882.
7. Testimonial dinner to Dr. Edward Cowles on his retirmeent from the McLean Hospital (written comments by John B. Chapin, M.D., Superintendent of the Pennsylvania Hospital for the Insane. Printed in the *American Journal of Insanity*, July: 116, 1904).
8. E. Cowles, M.D.: Nursing reform for the insane. *American Journal of Insanity*. October: 176, 1887.
9. Sixty-ninth Annual Report of the Trustees of the Massachusetts General Hospital and the McLean Asylum, 1882, p. 43.
10. Seventh Annual Report of the McLean Asylum Training School for Nurses, 1889, p. 6.
11. Ibid., p. 12.
12. Ibid.
13. Ibid.
14. E. Cowles, M.D. Nursing Reform for the Insane. *American Journal of Insanity*, (Oct., 1887): 187.
15. Ibid., p. 191.
16. Ibid.
17. H.R. Storer, M.D. *On Nurses and Nursing with Especial Reference to the Management of Sick Women.* Boston: Lee and Shepard, 1868, p. 16.
18. Ibid.
19. Proceedings of the American Medico-Psychological Association, Sixty-second meeting, June 12-15, Boston, Massachusetts (1906), reprinted in *Transactions of the American Medico-Psychological Association*, 13:206, 1906.

20. Ibid, p. 207.
21. Report of the Committee on Training Schools for Nurses, American Medico-Psychological Association, May, 1907, p. 2.
22. Ibid., p. 3.
23. A. Deutsch. *The Mentally Ill in America: A History of Their Care and Treatment from Colonial Times*. 2nd ed. New York: Columbia University Press, 1937, p. 297.
24. _____ "Some Specialist." *American Journal of Nursing*. 30: 66, 1930.
25. K.C. Buckwalter and O.M. Church. "Euphemia Jane Taylor: An Uncommon Psychiatric Nurse." *Perspectives in Psychiatric Care*. 17:126, 1979.
26. E.J. Taylor. "What Progress Are We Making in Mental Hygiene and Mental Nursing?" *International Congress of Nurses*. 94, 1925.
27. E.J. Taylor. "Nursing in the Henry Phipps Psychiatric Clinic." *Johns Hopkins Hospital Bulletin*, 26:10, 1915.

WOMEN'S PROPER PLACE: THE DEVELOPMENT OF PSYCHIATRIC NURSING AT BELLEVUE HOSPITAL

Joan Sayre

This study examines the historical context of the development of professional autonomy among psychiatric nurses at Bellevue Hospital. The specialization of psychiatric nursing originated at Bellevue, as at many other hospitals, from a perceived social need to upgrade standards of care for the mentally ill. In the late 19th century, the role of "mental nurse" was defined as that of adjunct to both physician and hospital administrator. The nurse was to use her natural feminine qualities of tact and kindness to provide the proper moral environment for recovery of the mentally disturbed.

As social attitudes toward psychiatric patients changed and new therapies developed, nursing functions remained basically custodial, despite efforts by nursing leaders to professionalize. Although the psychiatric nurse gradually became more autonomous, especially after 1940, medical dominance and bureaucratic policies have continued to restrict opportunities for the development of this field. Thus despite a substantial body of knowledge and educational programs which prepare practitioners at the masters level, role definition for the psychiatric nurse remains problematic.

The development of psychiatric nursing is examined in the context of Bellevue Hospital, an institution with a world-wide reputation in psychiatric care. Bellevue is also representative of large municipal almshouses which underwent major transformations with the development of scientific medicine and the need for cost effective care. Bellevue Hospital, like the specialization of psychiatric nursing which it fostered, is not an isolated entity but a reflection of historically determined social values and interests about the care of the mentally ill, the status of women and the development of professionalism. Placing psychiatric nursing in a specific historical context helps to clarify the past policies and social attitudes which continue to influence its development.

THE DIVISION OF LABOR IN PSYCHIATRIC CARE

This study is based on the premise that changing conceptions about the nature of mental illness have resulted in changes in treatment, as in the early 20th century when the integration of Freudian psychoanalytical concepts into American psychiatry inspired a psychological reconception of the etiology and treatment of what had previously been defined as an inherited organic deficiency. As new therapies emerge, they are incorporated into the role definitions of mental health professionals in terms of the division of labor for the care of the mentally ill. Psychiatrists, as the elite group, assume the most responsible and prestigious roles in diagnosis and treatment management in whatever therapeutic modality is dominant at the time. As a subordinate group, nurses thus are assigned the tasks which the physician rejects, such as patient hygiene and nutrition, medication administration and the maintenance of order on psychiatric wards.

An examination of the division of labor in mental health care is important in understanding problems psychiatric nurses have had with role definition and professional autonomy. Although other professional groups such as physicians and social workers claim exclusive possession of essential skills and are granted a scope of practice largely free of bureaucratic controls, the work of psychiatric nurses is closely regulated by hospital administrators. In addition, physicians who historically have had almost complete autonomy limit nurses' functioning by controlling access to clients and treatment information. When an individual becomes a patient of a particular psychiatrist, other health professionals who may be qualified to provide needed health care services must have the doctor's permission to gain access to the patient. Much psychiatric nursing care consists of procedures which carry out the physician's written orders.

In practice, of course, the physician's control is not total, as his successful interventions depend on the cooperation of other professionals as well as hospital support services. However, nurses who seek to expand their practice domain to include psychological interventions soon realize that psychiatrists continue to maintain a monopoly over mental health care.

The findings of this study indicate that there were two major historical circumstances which prevented psychiatric nurses at Bellevue Hospital from claiming exclusive expertise in a specific area of mental health care. These are: 1) the interpretation of the Nightingale model for training schools by the founders of organized nursing at Bellevue which placed all authority for patient care completely within the physician's domain and defined the nurse as an assistant to the physician, and 2) the emphasis on good character as the prerequisite for effective nursing which originated from Victorian ideas about the proper place for women in society. The combination of the lack of a clearly defined sphere of authority for patient care, coupled with an emphasis on improving one's character rather than on changing the behavior of the patient, prevented

psychiatric nurses from developing their own
therapeutic modalities.

THE DEVELOPMENT OF PSYCHIATRY AT BELLEVUE HOSPITAL

Established in New York City in 1736,
Bellevue Hospital has a long history in the treatment
of the mentally ill. In its initial form as a Public
Workhouse and House of Correction, Bellevue
included one room measuring 23 by 25 feet which
contained six beds "for the care of the infirm, the
aged, the unruly and the maniac."[1] This infirmary
gradually developed into a separate hospital after a
series of yellow fever epidemics in the city and an
increase in the number of sick poor made expansion
of the unit essential. By 1816, the almshouse and the
hospital had been transferred to the present location
of Bellevue on Manhattan's east side. Nursing care
was entrusted to prisoners. When Bellevue Hospital
became an independent institution in 1826, almost
one half of the 184 patients in the hospital were
mentally ill.

After 1833, the office of the resident
physician became a political appointment and the
care of patients deteriorated. It was at this time that
Bellevue began to develop its reputation as a "snake
pit" for the insane. An investigating commission in
1837 reported that there were 265 patients on the
wards, over half of whom were insane, and that
conditions in the hospital were such as to "excite
feelings of the most poignant sympathy for its
neglected inmates."[2] As a result, provisions were
made for another hospital for the mentally ill, the
New York Lunatic Asylum on Blackwell's Island,
which was also supervised by Bellevue staff.
Conditions were not any better there. Charles
Dickens, on a lecture tour of America, visited the
hospital and observed that "the asylum is a gloomy,
painful place, above whose door one might have

expected to read the legend, 'Abandon all hope, ye who enter here.'"[3]

Bellevue still admitted the mentally ill for observation and transfer to longer term facilities. Care was minimal and often abusive, reflecting the social values of the first half of the 19th century which categorized the mentally ill as an alien and morally repugnant group. Earlier, more optimistic theories about the possibility of curing mental illness through discipline and restraint were giving way to a more pessimistic view that insanity was an ingrained brain disease, or perhaps even an inherited trait.[4] Many patients at Bellevue, for example, were given diagnoses indicating this fatalistic view, such as "degenerative insanity from imperfect brain evolution," or "insanity associated with constitutional neuroses."

Until the latter part of the 19th century, mental patients brought to Bellevue by relatives or by the police were penned in two basement wards, one for women and one for men. The violently disturbed and acutely alcoholic waited together with the less disturbed as lawyers and alienists (as psychiatrists were then called) debated their sanity. The hospital wards were cold, dirty and understaffed: patients often slept two to a bed and were treated with abuse or utter indifference.

THE DEVELOPMENT OF NURSING AT BELLEVUE HOSPITAL

In 1873 the New York state legislature passed a bill mandating that state appointed committees visit all public institutions to observe and report on patient conditions. A philanthropic group was formed, called the Local Visiting Association of Bellevue Hospital, to make regular inspections of the hospital in order to initiate and carry out reforms. A small group of upper class women, led by Mrs. William H. Osburn, toured the hospital for several months and concluded that "Bellevue is a hospital whose patients were neither nursed, fed nor clothed as humanity demanded."[5]

The committee was particularly disturbed by the nature of the nursing care which was provided by "illiterate women at a very low wage, who were assisted in larger wards by prisoners and convalescent patients happy to have found a home in the hospital."[6] In addition, medicines were casually given to patients to take as they liked, the food was unappetizing and only those who had money to pay for service were given any attention. The Visiting Association also discovered, to their horror, that "keepers of houses of prostitution obtained access to wards without difficulty to attempt to recruit female patients into their service."[7]

Deciding that the only way to change conditions was to improve nursing care, they proposed to establish a training school organized according to the model instituted by Florence Nightingale at St. Thomas's Hospital in London. The committee initially faced opposition from the Department of Charities as well as from physicians who feared that a training school would be only a short-lived experiment. They believed that the extreme nature of conditions pupil nurses would face on the wards would cause them to lose heart and hope long before their training was completed. However, support from sympathetic physicians and a successful fund raising drive persuaded the Commissioner of Charities to give permission for the use of six wards of the hospital by the Bellevue Training School. Six pupils were secured and a superintendent installed, Sister Helen, formerly of All Saints Sisterhood in London. The school opened in May 1873.

The most significant influence on the subsequent development of the nurses' role at Bellevue was the stipulation of the Visiting Committee that the training school adopt Nightingale's proposal for the supervision of pupil nurses. In a letter written to the Visiting Committee, Nightingale stressed the importance of the role of the nursing superintendent for the success of a training school. She specified a clear division of authority for the supervision of pupil nurses; namely that in all matters regarding the management of the sick, the nurse should be placed absolutely under the orders of medical men, while in all disciplinary matters, the superintendent was to have complete control.

Although this measure can be viewed as a means of protecting an area of autonomous functioning for nursing, what it actually accomplished was the subordination of the nursing staff to physicians. Nightingale herself made this state of affairs clear. In her letter to the Visiting Committee of Bellevue Hospital, she defined the lines of authority to which nurses were subject, stating that nurses are "not medical men . . . on the contrary, nurses are there . . . solely to carry out the orders of the medical and surgical staff."[8]

Even though the conduct of nurses was to be supervised by another nurse, the superintendent's function was defined as strictly regulatory. She was to assure that nurses behaved in such a way that their work was performed to the satisfaction of physicians. The provision that patient care was to be entirely controlled by the physician left little room for nurses to develop their own techniques. This meant, in theory at least, that standards for care were defined by the doctor and nursing care was to adhere to these standards.

In addition, nurses' training was defined not as an intellectual endeavor but as a matter of gaining practical skills during many hours of work on the wards. Thus administrators were able to use pupil nurses as a source of cheap labor. As a result, hospital administrators also had a vested interest in maintaining the subordinate, apprenticeship nature of nurses' training.

An important area of autonomy was preserved, however. The founders of the school stipulated that neither a medical officer nor any other male head should have the power to dismiss a nurse or a servant for bad conduct or neglect of duty. This became a considerable source of direct power over the quality of patient care, since pupil nurses eventually took over this function on most wards.

The minutes of the Medical Board reveal periodic challenges to the authority of the nursing superintendent. In 1902, for instance, the Hospital Superintendent communicated his disapproval of the division of responsibility for the governance of nurses which this practice created. He felt that since as the hospital superintendent he was in charge of all staff, he should be permitted to prevail in a conflict with the nursing superintendent about a nurse's performance. The nursing supervisor held her ground however, and wrote a reply instructing the physician to refrain from questioning her judgement and interfering in the management of the training school.[9]

Conditions for medical and surgical patients began to improve after the training school was established. However, the situation of the hospitalized mentally ill remained poor. The reality of conditions for these patients was brought to public view by a sensationalized account of abuses called "Ten Days in a Madhouse," published by the *New York Post* in 1887. A woman reporter operating under the alias of "Nelly Bly" pretended to be mentally ill and had herself admitted to Bellevue for the purpose of exposing patient abuse.

In her article, she described such indignities as being certified insane without being properly examined and enduring lack of heat, poor food and verbal abuse from the staff. Although she found that some nurses were kind, the *Post's* management editorialized that "there can be no excuse for the heartless conduct of the nurses who are paid by the city to be kind and considerate, in telling patients that because they are charity ward, they should not expect good treatment . . . in keeping nervous, suffering women up all night merely because they want to read novels to each other, . . . in tramping up and down corridors like troopers, and in subjecting tender patients to cold and the dangers of pneumonia."[10]

The public clamor over such exposes and the rapid increase in the numbers of mental patients admitted to Bellevue resulted in the opening of the "Insane Pavilion" in 1879. However, care still did not improve. No resident physician was assigned to this department and most of those called nurses were recruited from the semi-recovered alcoholic patients and were paid a meager wage. A year after the Insane Pavilion opened, the State Charities Aid Association requested that the training school extend its work in the hospital to take charge of the whole of Bellevue, especially the "cells for the insane and alcoholic."[11] The nursing superintendent was unwilling to assume this responsibility, giving as her reason the lack of a physician to give instruction to the nurses. Pupil nurses were also reluctant to go to the Insane Pavilion. In 1880 only two from a class of 67 volunteered for this study. Finally in 1886, four nurses from the school were assigned to these wards.[12]

By 1903, conditions had improved. The Insane Pavilion was now referred to as the "Pavilion for the Alleged Insane" in recognition of the stigma attached to the mentally ill, and the sign "Insane Pavilion" was removed from the front of the building. Pictures were hung on the walls and half a dozen indestructible artifical palm trees brought in, as it was believed that such objects exerted a tranquilizing influence on disturbed mental conditions. Restraining devices and many of the window bars were removed and clean toilet facilities were installed. Severe cases of mental illness were separated from the less disturbed, and recalcitrant alcoholics, who were thought to be morally corrupt rather than ill, were sent to the work house.[13]

Physicians received credit for these reforms, although an occasional tribute to a nurse can be found in the literature. One "Jane Nash" was praised as an extraordinarily gifted nurse who was "a moving spirit in the clinical work of the physicians."[14] This tribute to the emotional, rather than the technical gifts of a nurse is indicative of the way in which the work of nursing was viewed.

THE IMPORTANCE OF CHARACTER IN NURSING

As Susan Reverby has pointed out, "the emphasis in early nursing was not on character instead of skills, but on character *as* the skill thought to be critical to the reformation in both nursing and hospital care."[15] The trained nurse originated as a means of reforming and purifying the hospitals,[16] a circumstance related both to hospital conditions in the 19th century and to Victorian ideals about the nature of womanhood.

Bellevue was not unique in the poor quality of its patient care. Hospitals in the 19th century were generally unsanitary and disorganized. Nursing duties were minimal and the low-paid, untrained nurses were reputed to rely on intoxicating beverages to enable them to endure their work. Nurses were also often accused of loose sexual behavior with male patients. In this context, Nightingale's belief that character was the essential element separating the trained nurse from her often disreputable predecessor is quite understandable.

The idea that it should be women, rather than men who should understake the task of organizing and sanitizing hospitals is also understandable in terms of the Victorian ideal of proper womanhood. Men and women were assumed to be so different that their very characters were thought to operate on separate principles. Men were seen as aggressive and selfish; the role of women was to correct these deficits through their own selfless, maternal purity. This moral influence over men was to compensate women for their lack of direct power in the world. Furthermore, since power was viewed as corrupting in nature, a woman's dependency and powerlessness was thought to be necessary if she were to retain her moral character and carry out her refoming mission.[17]

However, many women did not want to be socially and economically dependent upon men. Some women wished to be released from what they saw as domestic idleness and confinement and to be allowed to share "in the productive work of the world."[18] Nightingale wrote about the "poor lives of women"[19] and chastised those who demanded a woman's privileges of "inaccuracy, weakness and muddleheadedness."[20] She also protested against the sentimental view of nurses as ministering angels, which she described as "worse than useless."[21] She defined nursing as what nurses do, the hard work they undertake to improve their work and character, and not as any sanctified image of nursing.

The sentimental glorification of the domestic dependency of women continued to influence attitudes towards women's work. Thus although the image of Nightingale and her trained nurses as self-sacrificing, ministering angels was a distortion of both Nightingale's character and of the actual work of nursing, it was probably necessary for the establishment of nursing.

This overriding emphasis on character is revealed in the records of the Bellevue Training School. Applicants were carefully screened for their moral suitability, as illustrated in the following description of the type of woman considered most suitable for nurses' training:

> "They are conscientious women who aspire to some higher and more thoughtful labor than household service or work in shops. These women, preferrably daughters or widows of clergymen, professional men and

farmers, from New England and the Northern states, come from a race with a ready wit, quick perceptions and strong powers of observation. Let her acquire the indispensable habit of obedience and you have all the elements for making a good nurse."[22]

Perspective pupils were required to submit both a certificate of good health from a physician and a certificate of good moral character from a clergyman. Once a student was admitted, periodic evaluations were made about such characteristics as obedience, neatness, order, temper, intelligence, judgement, diligence, deportment, common sense, trustworthiness and punctuality. Students were also observed as to whether they got along with patients and fellow nurses, whether they took reports well, or were inclined to gossip. When they graduated, students received two certificates, one testifying to their nursing ability and the other to their character.[23]

This focus on character development in nurses' training was an important factor preventing the development of a body of knowledge and practice for psychiatric nursing. As the perspective on causes and treatments of mental illness changed at the turn of the century, psychiatric nursing did not develop. Insanity came to be increasingly defined as a brain disease, not a moral affliction, and physicians turned away from patient management to the institution of scientific treatments. City hospitals like Bellevue were in the process of evolving from almshouses for the poor to modern, business-like medical enterprises. But as physicians and hospitals focused on the development of treatments for the mentally ill, the role of the psychiatric nurse remained custodial.

In the materials in the Bellevue archives from 1880-1920 relating to the curriculum of the training school, there is little mention of specific psychiatric nursing skills. Students were taught various procedures for physical care such as bandaging, managing trusses, application of leeches, cookery for the sick and the art of ventilation. Discussion of the care of psychiatric conditions was brief and consisted primarily of stressing the importance of making observations about disorders of consciousness, such as delusions, hallucinations and delirium. There were warnings to "never be off guard for an instant" when dealing with the mentally disturbed. The use of tact was frequently recommended; being tactful seemed to involve deceiving the patient about his true circumstances, as in the example of a nurse telling a newly admitted patient that the screams he was hearing from the wards were nothing to be alarmed about as they were only noises the carpenters were making while repairing the building.[25]

There were a few surprisingly modern suggestions made in a 1894 textbook of nursing developed at Bellevue Hospital.[26] These included the futility of arguing with delusional patients about their misconceptions and the insight that patient with hysterical neuroses did not have complete control over their physical symptoms. However, these kinds of suggestions were apparently not incorporated into a body of specific psychiatric nursing knowledge.

The intellectual expectations of pupil nurses graduating from the Bellevue Training School during this period can be summarized in the remarks of Dr. W. Van Buren in his address to the 1879 graduating class:

> "With knowledge of all kinds comes a sense of power . . . and a certain temptation to do wrong, namely to abuse this power by unwarranted self-assertion. Self-assertion, however, is not a feminine trait and I have little fear that you will be assuming medical functions . . . The unreasoning devotion of the true mother to her child is the model of the quality of self-abnegation you are called upon to exercise."

There were many interrelated factors which prevented psychiatric nurses at Bellevue Hospital from developing an autonomous area of nursing functions; the stigma of mental illness and pessimistic theories about its treatment which created a reluctance among nurses to care for these patients; the poor conditions in Bellevue as a 19th century public hospital for the care of the indigent; the economic exploitation of pupil nurses as a source of low cost labor; male dominance of the field of medicine and their resistance to competition from women, and the lingering ideal of Victorian womanhood and the sanctity of the family which upheld a paternalistic society. However, it was because nurses were so immediately useful and effective in meeting these needs that organized nursing was established. It was to be over fifty years before psychiatric nursing at Bellevue Hospital would begin to come into its own.

NOTES

1.   Walsh, J.A., Director, Public Relations, Bellevue Hospital. Undated. Bellevue Hospital Archives.
2.   Ibid., p. 2.
3.   Giles, D. *A Candle in Her Hand: A Story of the Schools of Nursing of Bellevue.* N.Y.: Putnam, 1949, p. 159.
4.   Porter, R. *A Social History of Madness.* N.Y.: Weidenfeld and Nicholson, 1987, 20-21.
5.   Hobson, E. *First Annual Report of the Visiting Committee for Bellevue Hospital and Other Public Hospitals of New York City.* February 1, 1874, Bellevue Hospital Archives.
6.   Ibid., p. 18.
7.   Ibid., p. 8.
8.   Agnes L. Brennan to William Polk, M.D., President, Medical Services Board, dated May 31, 1889 (N.Y.). Bellevue Hospital Medical Board Minutes. Bellevue Hospital Archives.

9. Bly, N. "Ten Days in a Madhouse," *New York Post* (October 19, 1887).

10. Giles, D. *A Candle in Her Hand*, p. 161.

11. Ladies Board of Managers Minutes, January 23, 1880, p. 3. Bellevue Hospital Archives.

12. Ladies Board of Managers Minutes, February 5, 1886, p. 5. Bellevue Hospital Archives.

13. Giles, D. *A Candle in Her Hand*, p. 241.

14. Starr, J. *Hospital City.* N.Y.: Crown, 1958, p. 244.

15. Reverby, S. *Ordered to Care: The Dilemma of American Nursing, 1885-1945.* N.Y.: Cambridge, 1987, p. 42.

16. Ibid., p. 39.

17. Murray, J. *Strong Minded Women.* N.Y.: Pantheon, 1982, p. 24.

18. Ibid., p. 261.

19. Ibid., p. 303.

20. Ibid., p. 304.

21. Ibid., p. 305.

22. Report of the Hospital Committee of the State Charities Association. p. 27, December 23, 1872. Bellevue Hospital Archives.

23. Second Annual Report of the Training School for Nurses, p. 19, February 1, 1875. Bellevue Hospital Archives.

24. Weeks-Shaw, C.S. *A Textbook of Nursing for the Use of Training Schools, Families, and Private Students.* N.Y.: D. Appleton, 1894, p. 333.

25. Bly, N. "Ten Days in a Madhouse."

26. Weeks-Shaw, C.S. *A Textbook of Nursing*, p. 333.

27. Sixth Annual Report of the Training School for Nurses. p. 10, January 1, 1879. Bellevue Hospital Archives.

SECTION V

NIGHTINGALISM: IMPACT AND RELATIONSHIP WITH SECULAR RELIGIOUS ORGANIZATIONS

SISTERHOOD IS POWERFUL: SISTER-NURSES CONFRONT THE MODERNIZATION OF NURSING

Jean Richardson

The last three decades of the 19th century witnessed the modernization of American medicine. This process transformed the practice of medicine and altered the role of various actors and institutions involved in the delivery of health care.

Before the Civil War Catholic (and to some extent Protestant) religious orders were the major providers of nursing care in hospitals. In the post Civil War period Catholic nursing orders and Catholic hospitals were forced to confront the rise of scientifically based, professionalized medical practice and the rise of professional nursing. For the most part, the sister-nurses suceeded in mastering the radical transformation in health care while preserving their traditional clerical orders and the institutional autonomy of their hospitals. Since historians have written little about the sisters' successful adaptation to these changes, the Sisters of Charity in Buffalo, N.Y.'s response to the late 19th century's changes might serve as a case study of what was taking place.

Elizabeth Seton founded the Sisters of Charity of St. Joseph at Emmitsburgh, Md. in 1809, the first indigenous Catholic women's order in the United States. It was patterned after the Daughters of Charity founded by St. Vincent De. Paul in France

261

and adopted the latter's mission of working with the sick poor.[1] In 1823, the Sisters of Charity took charge of the Baltimore Infirmary, marking the beginning of Catholic religious women's involvement in hospital work in the United States. Since that time, the Sisters have been in the forefront as nurses and as pioneers of the Catholic church's efforts in establishing general hospitals, maternity hospitals and other specialized health care facilities.[2]

In Buffalo, N.Y., the Sisters of Charity established the city's first hospital in 1848. The Buffalo Hospital of the Sisters of Charity (Sisters Hospital) was established as a general hospital open to all irrespective of faith and was the teaching facility for the then fledgling Buffalo Medical School. Subsequently the sisters founded Buffalo's first maternity hospital, foundling and widows' asylum (1852); the city's first institution for the insane and addicted (1860); and the first emergency hospital (1884). Though the early Buffalo institutions founded by the Sisters were governed by all male lay and cleric boards, the Sisters, at least from 1860, had full executive and administrative control over their institutions.[3]

From the opening of their hospitals and asylums the sisters provided all the nursing care and sister supervisors oversaw the operation of the hospitals. Thus, the sisters were both managers and workers in their institutions. Premodern nursing consisted chiefly of administering medications, managing patient nutrition and hygiene, cleaning the hospital wards and washing linen and clothing.[4] Though the sisters played a vital nursing role with the Civil War,[5] transformation of medical practice which took place during this period threatened the status and role of sister-nurses in the post-war period. The medical knowledge and experienced gained in the war, the discovery and acceptance of germ theory, and the development of anesthesia had radically transformed medicine by the late 19th century. The new medical profession envisioned an elaborate specialization of functions, all requiring trained personnel. Nurses trained in the appropriate technical procedures were to play a vital but subordinate part of a medical "team." The mission of hospitals also changed to meet a growing demand by middle class patients. They ceased being sick houses for the poor and became places of healing and recovery with a more upscale clientele. The modernization of nursing paralleled this modernization of medicine.[6] The demand for trained nurses encouraged the establishment of nursing schools with the first three institutions opening as early as 1873.[7]

This transformation of medical practice, the rise of nursing, and the change in hospital's social role in the latter 19th century challenged the sister-nurses on three grounds: (1) modernization/professionalization, (2) secularization of social institutions, and (3) expansion of male domination. Catholic sisterhoods, running medical institutions all over the United States, confronted these challenges in a variety of ways.

The Buffalo Sisters of Charity adapted to these challenges while retaining their role as nurses and maintaining their status as decision making, authority wielding members of the medical community. Below we will first describe each of the three challenges, then we will discuss the actions the Buffalo Sisters of Charity took to meet each challenge.

The first challenge was the modernization of medicine and the growth in professional nursing. The establishment of secular nursing schools threatened to make the traditional training received by the sister-nurses obsolete.

The Sisters of Charity had developed their premodern nursing expertise from their experience in addressing the recurrent epidemics, chronic illnesses and frequent injuries afflicting early urban populations. Individual sister-nurses were trained in an apprenticeship system with experienced sister-nurses informally teaching new sisters what they had learned from experience. They also received informal clinical instruction from physicians.[8]

By the last two decades of the 19th century sister-nurses were fast becoming the least technically trained nurses in the country.[9]

The second challenge, secularism, reflected the prejudices and agendas of the predominantly Protestant leaders of American medical modernization. The Protestant elite drive for secularization of social institutions was both an expression of the rise of secular-social thought and dislike of dependence or connection with Catholic welfare institutions. For most Protestant elites the latter expression was probably more important. Many of Buffalo's Protestant elites had been embarrassed by the sisters' success in establishing the city's first network of health care facilities and they attempted, unsuccessfully at first, to get a secular city hospital into operation.[10] It was not until 1858 that they successfully established the nonsectarian, 'secular' hospital, Buffalo General Hospital. Its founders clearly intended this institution to compete with Sisters Hospital, its Catholic competitor.

It was the changes taking place in medicine and in the care of the sick which allowed secular hospitals a chance to displace their premodern sectarian counterparts. Even when church hospitals survived they often did so by becoming more secular, as clerical administrators and workers often gave way to nonsectarian professionals. The Buffalo sisters resisted the secularization of their hospital even while modernization radically altered what that institution did and how it did it.

The third challenge, the expansion of male domination was a recurrent theme in the history of Catholic women's institutions. The Sisters of Charity controlled 19th century Buffalo's only women-run network of social institutions, acting as autonomous decision makers. Neither the Diocese nor the local medical establishment was able to dictate to the sisters in the latter's institutions. Increasingly, however, the physicians assumed a more commanding role than had been true in premodern medicine, and since they were almost always male, the Sisters of Charity faced the prospect of losing the autonomy that they had held from the hospital's very founding.[11]

Before the changes in medical care had taken place the Sisters of Charity were totally responsible for managing and providing nursing care in their institutions. Though the sisters worked in collaboration with the physicians serving the hospital, apart from the prescription of medications and decisions on surgery, implementation of physicians ideas depended on the Sister Superior's approval. The physicians attending Sisters Hospital respected the sisters' authority and cooperation best characterized the relationship between the sisters and the physicians.[12]

The key to the success of the Sisters of Charity responding to all three challenges is found in the nursing school they established in 1889.[13] By modernizing their nursing practice through the establishment of their own scientifically based school of nursing, the Sisters could ward off secularization as well as limit the intrusion of male dominance.

The available historical records are sketchy about the origin of the Sisters Hospital Nurses Training School, but based on what is available, it seems that the initiative came from physicians associated with the hospital. An unsigned account by one of the hospital's physicians describes their efforts to lobby the Sister Superior, Sr. Florence O'Hara, to organize a nursing school for the sisters. The account aptly describes the changes in nursing care. The account written November 1890 begins:

> Drs. Mynter and Heath visited Sr. Florence . . . to confer with her in a friendly way about the wants of the Sisters Hospital . . . and to propose a remedy. They were not finding fault with the Sisters . . . but there was a want of proper nursing at the Hospital. The system of nursing of twenty years ago was not up to the wants of the present time. In former years they had 'the class of patient'

known as 'the coughers' at the hospital and
the sisters' nursing was all that was desired,
for these patients needed but care, good food,
comfort [and] kind-heartedness. But surgical
cases of today require trained nurses, who
knew how to act in an emergency and who
knew not only what to do, but why it was
done--technical knowledge was necessary.[14]

Drs. Mynter and Heath claimed the nurses presently
at the hospital did not even know how to use a
thermometer. The account continues:

Sr. Florence depended for nursing upon
such as she could get--who knew nothing
about nursing. The wages for a trained nurse
were, of course high . . . yet the class of
patients the hospital receives now pay for
better than the cougher formerly received at
the hospital. Rarely [Dr. Mynter] sent a
patient there who was not a good paying
patient. There is a trained female nurse there
who remains [at the Hospital when] she
cannot get a good paying position [elsewhere],
when she can . . . she goes.[15]

As a remedy to these difficulties, the Sisters
Hospital physicians proposed that a training school be
started at the hospital for the sisters. Drs. Mynter
and Heath expressed their willingness to train "a
good number of young sisters as those sisters
advanced in age are wedded to their ways."[16] The
physicians were also willing to train sisters for all the
Sisters of Charity hospitals not just the one in
Buffalo. The account ends with the physicians
declaring, "We want to build up the Sisters Hospital
so that a surgeon or physician may consider it an
honor to be attached to the Sisters Hospital."[17]

Clearly Drs. Mynter and Heath judged that
the sister-nurses lacked modern nursing skills. Also,
the two doctors were concerned about maintaining
their own standing within the medical community as
well as the hospital's reputation. Mynter was on the
faculty of Niagara University's Medical School, while
Heath had been one of the first faculty members at

the school.

Catholic Niagara University had opened its medical school in 1883 in Buffalo. Its establishment was "prompted by a desire to advance the standard of medical education" and not as rival to the well established Buffalo Medical School. In fact, Niagara University contended its medical school was superior to the Buffalo Medical School and above mere competition.[18]

The competition between the two medical schools was preceeded by the far more venerable rivalry previously mentioned, namely Buffalo General Hospital and Sisters Hospital. Faculty at the Buffalo Medical School had teaching privileges at both hospitals until Niagara University's Medical School opened. When it did, Sisters Hospital associated itself solely with Niagara University's Medical School and drew its medical staff from Niagara University's medical school faculty.[19]

In short, ethnic/sectarian rivalry within Buffalo's medical community now pitted the Protestant hospital and medical school against the Catholic hospital and medical school. This competition together with the hospital physicians' concerns about patient care gave Sr. Florence great incentive to upgrade the Sisters Hospital nursing staff.

Strict business considerations also pressured Sisters Hospital's leadership to adopt modern nursing practice since as operating costs rose so had Sisters Hospital's dependence on paying patients.[20] Moreover, paying patients demanded increasingly better care and might desert Sisters' Hospital, if Buffalo General Hospital offered better conditions or more "modern treatment." Buffalo General Hospital had been a pioneer in establishing a nursing school in 1877 and had greatly upgraded its standard of "modern nursing."[21] Sisters Hospital did not open its nursing school until twelve years later (1889), and had to do so in order to save its competitive position.

Initially the new Sisters Hospital Nursing School trained only sister-nurses, confining modern

nursing education to members of the order. Within
the first four years of the school's operation,
however, lay women were also admitted,[22] primarily
for economic reasons since the admission of lay
women to the sisters' nursing school gave Sisters
Hospital a source of inexpensive lay labor. In fact,
lay student nurses provided a labor source whose
stipends of $5.00 a month were comparable to the
low cost labor of the sisters.[23] This was important
because it was the low cost of labor provided by the
sisters which had, in part, enabled Sisters Hospital to
expand more rapidly than Buffalo General Hospital,
and originally to be more successful. Though the
records do not so indicate, it seems clear that one of
the reasons Buffalo General Hospital opened a
nursing school was to create a pool of student nurses
who could be put to work at lower cost then hiring
graduate nurses and enable the Hospital to cut
operating costs.

The admission of lay women as student nurses
did not affect the sisters' control of the school and
hospital. Despite gradually expanding lay involvement
in the hospital staff, the sister-nurses held virtually
all authority positions in the hospital, and constituted
the majority of the nursing school faculty. For
example, all head nurses in each ward were sisters
whether they were students themselves or graduate
nurses.[24] Clearly the sister-administrators were
determined to keep authority positions in the hands
of fellow sisters.

Most early training schools designated one
person both Superintendent of Nursing and teacher
of the student nurses. At the Sisters Hospital Nurses
Training School one graduate sister-nurse held both
of these positions and was known as the
Superintendent. Her duties focused on controlling
and supervising the lay nursing staff and lay nursing
education. Students were required to attend two
lectures a week given by the hospital's physicians.
Although all student nurses attended the lectures
together, the sister-nursing students received all
other training separately from the lay students. Their

teacher was not the Sister Superintendent of Nursing but another graduate sister-nurse, often the Sister Superior.[25]

In most American nursing schools the Superintendent of Nursing was responsible to a non-nursing board of lady managers, as at Buffalo General Hospital or to hospital medical professionals. At Sisters' Hospital the Sister Superintendent of Nursing was responsible to the hospital's Board of Directors which was entirely composed of sister-nurses. By retaining control over both the hospital's nursing school and over the wards the Sisters of Charity limited the secularization while permitting the modernization of nursing within their hospital.

Physicians at Sisters Hospital did, however, expand their control over patient treatment at the expense of the ward nurses. Physicians, however, still had to address conflicts with nurses through the sister administrators,[26] since the discipline of nurses was the exclusive province of the sister administrators. The sister administrators also retained control over physical plant management and general hospital affairs. Physicians, in sum, did not have the authority that physicians at other institutions may have had.

As the professionalization of nursing continued into the 20th century with the spread of the "registered nurse" concept, the Buffalo Sisters of Charity continued to adapt to this wave of modernization. In 1905 the Sisters Hospital School of Nursing was certified by the New York State Board of Regents to train registered nurses, one of the earliest New York State nursing schools to meet the Board of Regents certification standards.[27]

CONCLUSION

The Sisters of Charity responded to the challenges facing them by modernizing their own nursing practice and by establishing their own modern nursing school. Though they admitted lay students to their school, the sisters kept control of the school and insured that sister-students received modern training. They resisted secularization by keeping control over the hospitals general affairs, its physical plant, the training and discipline of sister-nurses. Lay nurses were not allowed to hold administrative posts. The sisters also limited the expansion of male domination. Male physicians had more control over patient treatment and more authority over nurses in the new system, but the sister hierarchy kept control over all disciplinary affairs relating to both sister-nurses and lay nurses. Sisters held on to all nursing administrative posts, and reported only to senior hospital administrator, all of whom were sisters. The sisters controlled all general hospital and physical plant management.

NOTES

The author is grateful to Sr. Elaine Wheeler, DC, archivist of the Daughters of Charity of St. Vincent De Paul Northeast Province, for her assistance.

1.   The Sisters of Charity of St. Joseph merged with the French Daughters of Charity of St. Vincent De Paul in 1850, and were thereafter known as the Daughters of Charity of St. Vincent De Paul. However in America, the popular name for the order remains the Sisters of Charity. Background on the Sisters of Charity appears in Madame De Barbercy, *Elizabeth Seton*, trans. & ed. Rev. Joseph Code (N.Y.: Macmillan Pub. Co., 1927); Mother Mary Fuller, SC, *Blessed Elizabeth Ann Seton Sister of Charity* (N.Y.: The Sisters of Charity Mount St. Vincent on the Hudson, 1968).

2.   Carlan Kraman, OSF, "Women Religious in Health Care, The Early Years," in *Pioneer*

Healers the History of Women Religious in American Health Care, eds. Ursula Stepsis, CSA and Dolores Liptak, RSM (N.Y.: Crossroad Pub. Co., 1989), pp. 22, 28.

3. Buffalo Hospital of the Sisters of Charity (BHSC), Minutes of Meetings of the Board of Trustees, 1849-1949, meetings of 24 January 1849-16 March 1860. With the exception of two sketches, Angela Redmond, DC, "The History of the Sisters of Charity in Buffalo, 1849-1945. (typewritten); Bernadette Arminger, DC, "The History of the Hospital Work of the Daughters of Charity of St. Vincent DePaul in the Eastern Province of the United States" (M.S. thesis, Catholic University of America, 1947), p. 74, the institutional history of Sisters Hospital has been neglected in secondary sources. Material for this study has been drawn from records at the Daughter of Charity of St. Vincent De Paul Northeast Province Archives, Albany, N.Y. and Sisters of Charity Hospital Archives, Buffalo, N.Y.

4. Doyle, "Nursing by Religious Orders in the United States," *American Journal of Nursing* 29 (July 1929): 781.

5. Mary Ewens, *The Role of the Nun in 19th Century America* (N.Y.: Arno, 1978), pp. 328, 222.

6. Susan Reverby, "The Hospital Disorder: A Critical History of the Hospital - Nursing Relationship, 1860-1945" (Ph.D. dissertation, Boston University, 1982), p. 73.; Richard Shryock, *The History of Nursing an Interpretation of the Social and Medical Factors Involved* (Philadelphia: W.B. Saunders, 1959), pp. 301, 310.

7. Isabel Stewart, *The Education of Nurses* (N.Y.: Macmillian Pub. Co., 1953), pp. 88, 90.

8. Doyle, p. 782; Mary C. Conroy, "The Transition Year," in *Pioneer Healers*, 145.

9. Ewens, pp. 273-274.

10.   Evelyn Hawes, *Proud Vision: History of Buffalo General Hospital.* (N.Y.: Thomas Crowell, 1964), pp. 1-2. David A. Gerber, *The Making of An American Pluralism: Buffalo, NY, 1825-60.* (Urbana, Ill: University of Illinois Press, 1989), p. 316.

11.   A good analysis of the transformation of health care can be found in Charles Rosenberg, *The Care of Strangers: The Rise of America's Hospital System* (N.Y.: Basic Books, 1987), chapters 4-9 and in Paul Starr, *The Social Transformation of American Medicine* (N.Y.: Basic Books, 1982), pp. 147-168.

12.   BHSC, Minutes of Meetings of the Board of Trustees, 1849-1949.

13.   *Sisters of Charity School of Nursing Handbook, 1984/1985.*

14.   Physician's account, 1890, BHSC papers, Box 11-27, 1-3, item 2. Daughters of Charity Archives, Albany, N.Y. (Handwritten.)

15.   Ibid.

16.   Ibid.

17.   Ibid.

18.   John Cronyn, "Establishment of the Medical Department of Niagara University," *Buffalo Medical Journal* 35 (May 1896): 781. "Niagara University Medical Department," *Buffalo Medical Journal* 30 (July 1891): advertisement.

19.   Buffalo Medical School, Minutes of Meetings of the Faculty, 1887-1907, meeting of 14 September 1883.

20.   BHSC, Minutes of Meetings of the Board of Trustees, 1849-1949; BHSC Auditor's Annual Financial Reports, 1880-1920.

21.   Hawes, p. 25.

22.   The slim documentary record for the Sisters Hospital Nursing School's early years does not indicate precisely when lay women were first enrolled. The school probably opened to lay women around 1891. Annual Report of

BHSC, 1901-1903, p. 44.

23. BHSC, Auditor's Annual Financial Reports, 1896-1920; James Walsh, *The History of Nursing* (N.Y.: P.J. Kennedy & Sons, 1929), pp. 245-246.

24. Annual Report of BHSC for Three Year, 1901-1903, p. 42; BHSC Auditor's Annual Financial Report, 1896-1920; New York State Department of Education, Training Schools for Nurses Annual Report, 1912, 1917-1920; New York State, Report of the New York State Board of Charities, Department of Inspection, 26 April 1904.

25. Ibid.

26. BHSC, Minutes of Meetings of the Medical Staff, 1900-1924, meetings of 16 May 1901, 4 November 1920.

27. Sisters of Charity Hospital School of Nursing Handbook, 1984/85; Susan Armeny, "Resolute Enthusastics: The Effort to Professionalize American Nursing, 1880-1915 (Ph.D. dissertation, University of Missouri, 1983), p. 451.

A FIERCE TENDERNESS: FLORENCE NIGHTINGALE ENCOUNTERS THE SISTERS OF MERCY

Mary P. Tarbox

INTRODUCTION

As a mature, educated woman in Irish society in the early 1800's, Catherine McAuley possessed the essential qualities of a charismatic leader of a religious order. Although she had not intended to estabish an Order when she launched a "social service" agency for young women in Dublin in 1827, the zealous encouragement of Archbishop Daniel Murray led her to develop the philosophical basis and personal standards for such a group. That group would evolve to become the Sisters of Mercy.

In the process of preparing for the establishment of an Order of active religious women, a phenomenon not familiar to the Irish or many other Catholics at the time, Catherine and two other colleagues entered the Presentation Convent for their novitiate year. At the completion of this "training," fifty-six-year-old Catherine received approval to establish the Sisters of Mercy in December, 1831. The *Rule and Constitution of the Order* became the guide which would lead this group of women to serve young, poor, Irish women. Their mission was clearly defined in these words of *The Rule*:

> The sisters admitted to this religious
> congregation besides attending particularly to
> their own perfection, which is the principal
> end of all Religious Orders, should also have
> in view what is peculiarly characteristic of
> this institute--that is, a most serious
> application to the instruction of Poor Girls,
> Visitation of the Sick, and Protection of
> Distressed Women of Good Character.[1]

The mission of the Sisters of Mercy was
clearly stated in this early description and continued
to guide their work throughout their growth to
become one of the largest Orders of religious women
in Church history. Their early venture into
"organized" nursing allowed them to enter the arena
of patient care in the homes of the Irish, urban poor
long before any other institution became involved.
The training of young sisters with an aptitude for
nursing became the basis for early education in a
service that had not yet seen formal education in any
other form. The characteristics of service, "calling,"
and formal training, were the factors which brought
this Order to the attention of Florence Nightingale
and would bring the sisters face to face with her in
the Crimean War.

THE IRELAND OF CATHERINE MCAULEY

Of significance in understanding the
relationship which developed between the "Irish"
Sisters of Mercy and the "British" Miss Florence
Nightingale is the society in which the Order was
founded and from which its members were recruited.
That society was just emerging from over a century
of Penal restrictions established by the British in an
effort to control the Roman Catholics who had been
disloyal not only to the Crown but, more
importantly, to the Church of England. From 1691 to
1829, Irish Catholics had been restricted in their
education, politics, participation in the judiciary,
parliament or armed services, and in their efforts to

purchase or inherit property.

As the Penal Laws were eased in the late 1700's it is evident that British motivation for such a move may have been as much influenced by the revolutionary activity in America and France as it was by any benevolent feelings toward the Irish. As the funding of British military efforts in the "colonies" became essential, Irish Catholics were "permitted" to circulate more of their money in property and possessions which had once been restricted. The British feared Irish aggression at a time when their military resources were otherwise engaged and they feared the spread of Catholicism even more.

Easing the Penal Laws also permitted Irish Catholic men to enlist or to be conscripted into the British Army when the ranks were in desperate need of reinforcements. Still, the long-term effects of a century of oppression remained in the resentment which many of the Irish held for the British. In addition, those most affected were essentially the uneducated, malnourished rural poor. These were the people for whom Catherine McAuley established the Sisters of Mercy; they would also be the soldiers the nurses cared for in the Crimean War.

The famine, which struck Ireland in 1845, and lasted for nearly five years, cost more than the lives of millions of people, especially when one considers the resentment which lingered in the minds of those who suffered under British oppression. In the next ten years, little progress was made in the living conditions of poor Irish Catholics and the military service offered one alternative to poverty or immigration. The army which would serve in the Crimea was made up of more than one-third Irish Catholic soldiers.[2]

THE MISSION OF THE SISTERS OF MERCY

As the Order of the Sisters of Mercy grew in the decades following its foundation, a characteristic

of the Order which would have long-lasting effects
was the system of establishing independent
motherhouses. Although each motherhouse was
founded by sisters who were called into service in a
new location, once established, the foundation
operated independently of the original motherhouse.
The Order followed established channels of authority
within the Church and consulted with the local
bishops, but the daily operation of the house itself
ran under its own rules, guided by *The Rule* of the
Order. Since the Sisters of Mercy who served in
Crimea came from different motherhouses, their
conduct was guided by *The Rule* of those houses.

The Order not only expanded rapidly
throughout Ireland but to England where it became
the first new Order to be founded there since the
Protestant Reformation. Nursing within the Order
was seen as a "calling" to serve others in the image
and likeness of Christ. Training was based on work-
experience and an aptitude for caring. The sisters
gained experience rapidly through their work in the
cholera and typhoid epidemics which swept through
urban Ireland and they were called upon to manage
public institutions. Their philosophy of nursing was
stated in the *Rule and Constitution* in the words of
Catherine McAuley:

> In all ages of the church, it has excited the
> faithful in a particular manner to instruct and
> comfort the sick and dying poor for in them
> is regarded the person of our Divine Master
> who has said . . . as long as you did it to one
> of these, my least brethren, you did it to me.[3]

The *Rule and Constitution* went on to offer other
guidance in the work of the sisters as nurses:

> Great tenderness should be employed and
> when there is not immediate danger of death,
> it will be well to relieve the distress first, and
> to endeavor by every practical means to
> promote the cleanliness, ease, and comfort of
> the patient.[4]

These words, which became the philosophical
basis for nursing within the Order of the Sisters of

Mercy would also become the basis for much of the controversy which occurred between the sisters and Florence Nightingale. Although Miss Nightingale actually attempted to gain some instruction in nursing from the sisters early in her efforts to become a nurse, the very dedication which she recognized in them would become a point of disagreement in her encounters with them in the Crimea.

THE CALL TO CRIMEA

The course of events which led to the outbreak of war in the Crimea continue to be debated as is so often part of historical exploration. In what most likely began as a reaction to the Russians' displacement of the Turkish Sultan as protector of Christian Shrines in the Holy Land, the Crimean War must also be recognized as a violent dispute over territory and trade in that region of Europe which was quickly becoming an essential channel to and from the Far East.[5] The controversy came to involve Great Britain, Turkey, France, Austria and Russia. In the fighting which occurred on the Russian Peninsula of Crimea, in the Black Sea,[6] most of the soldiers found themselves in a clash of ideas which were not clearly understood in an environment which was very clearly different from their own homelands and experiences.

The British army faced the enemy ill-prepared for war, with little experience in battle and even less in such a foreign territory so far from England. There was also little national support for their efforts as well as severe shortages in supplies, equipment, and inevitably, in morale. In an army where the officers were of a clearly defined upper class and the enlisted men of the lower class, disagreements occurred between the ranks as well as on the field. In a foreign location, without adequate food and supplies, the casualties were as much the result of illness as of injuries sustained in battle. A wounded soldier was much more likely to die of disease contracted in the "hospital" than of the injury incurred in battle.

These conditions did not go unnoticed by the soldier in the field or the reporter at his side. William Howard Russell was a "pioneer" war correspondent on location in the Crimea and his reports, published in the *London Times* brought the war home to the citizens of England. Letters from soldiers confirmed Russell's descriptions and the combination of the two brought outrage from the members of British society who were appalled by the "incompetence and confusion" reported by all of these "correspondents." In October, 1854, the conditions reported by Russell brought the reactions of the British citizens to culmination in a cry for assistance from civilian sources.[7]

The response to these reports, in addition to those which had proceeded and continued to arrive, was widespread and decisive. The public response was to raise money for support which became the "Times Fund." The institutional response came in the form of suggestions that someone do something to provide care on the scene. The response was many faceted, ecumenical, and rapid. On October 11, 1854, the first suggestion was made to Sidney Herbert, Minister for War, that Florence Nightingale should lead nurses to the scene.[8] Though the composition of the first party of nurses was meant to be small, according to Nightingale,[9] the make-up of the first group was the result of many offers of assistance from both Catholics and Protestants.[10]

The Roman Catholic Hierarchy of Britain took little time in recognizing the opportunity to include Catholic sisters in the nursing services for the Crimea. Not only did they offer experience, discipline, and dedication, but the sanction of the British Crown in permitting the sisters to serve would be a boost to the acceptance of Catholicism within England. Including the sisters in this service would bring them into favor with the British public who had remained suspicious of religious Orders and

convents. This positive image may have also helped
curtail any continued punitive legislation.

Bishop Thomas Grant made the first request
for assistance from Mother Mary Clare Moore of the
Sisters of Mercy in Bermondsey, England.[11] Within
three days, the six sisters from that convent, lead by
Mother Moore, were on their way to the Crimea by
ship. Although eager to serve, they agreed to work
with Florence Nightingale and awaited her arrival in
Paris before continuing to Turkey. The politics of
religion cannot be ignored in the sequence of events
which occurred within the days that followed.[11]

Nightingale was given government
authorization to assemble a contingent of nurses
which she would lead in service to the British Army.
The process involved in granting Nightingale official
authorization took only a matter of days but
developed as the result of political maneuvering.
Because he was a close friend, Sidney Herbert was
the first person Nightingale contacted in making her
offer to help although she did this by corresponding
with his wife, Elizabeth Herbert.[12] At the same time,
Herbert had responded to his wife's suggestion that
he ask Nightingale to lead the nurses. Their
correspondence passed in the mail and they met
within days to discuss plans for the party of nurses
with Nightingale in charge. Herbert described his
confidence in Miss Nightingale in this
correspondence:

> . . . your personal qualities, knowledge, your
> power of administration and among greater
> things, your rank and position in society give
> you advantages in such a work which no
> other person possesses.[13]

Although it was thought that only a few
nurses were necessary to assist Nightingale in her
task, the first party was composed of thirty-nine
nurses.[14] This group understood that Nightingale was
in command and that their work would be strenuous
and hazardous.

The journey to Scutari on the Bosporus was
long and miserable. There was no welcome on their

arrival and their intentions were held as suspect. The military authorities resented the dispatching of females to a combat area, particularly under the aegis of "civilian" officials in London. Although the military officers did not challenge Nightingale's authority, they did confine that authority to Turkey, while the fighting continued in the Crimea, many miles away![15]

Nightingale's relationship with the Sisters of Mercy began while on the ship transporting them to the war. The sisters for the most part remained in their quarters after the ship left France, but they experienced the same wretched travel conditions and sickness which afflicted most of the other travelers including Nightingale.[16] Through their on-going interactions, it became clear that Nightingale would command the party, even though the Bermondsey sisters were accustomed to the leadership of Mother Mary Clare Moore. Mother Moore agreed to remain as the "spiritual" superior of the sisters while Nightingale commanded the nursing details.[17]

This agreement would become a significant factor in Nightingale's relationship with the Sisters of Mercy, since authority became a question of contention as other groups arrived and disagreed with the established arrangement. As a result of their cooperative efforts, however, Mother Moore became a friend and confidant of Nightingale as they worked together in a difficult situation.

A much less cooperative course of events followed the arrival of a second party of nurses in the Crimea in December, 1854. Not only was this group not compiled by Miss Nightingale, but it arrived without her previous knowledge, and before questions of authority had been settled. Mary Stanley, the leader of the group, was a friend of Nightingale's but had proceeded to gather the group under her own direction. Stanley also received encouragement and direction from Sidney Herbert as well as others. Her group of forty-seven women included Sisters of Mercy from Ireland.[18] Nightingale was furious with Sidney Herbert for his part in this maneuver and wrote to him of her dissatisfaction.[19] Although her fury with Herbert settled soon, her displeasure with the members of the second party did not.

The factors which played into Nightingale's anger included not only the lack of communication about the group but the question of authority over the number of Catholic sisters who were among its members. The Mother Superior of the sisters from Ireland had made no agreement to abide by Nightingale's authority nor was she about to give up her own. She had come at the request of the Archbishop of Ireland and would heed only his command.[20] Reverend Mother Mary Francis Bridgeman presented a entirely different personality than that of Mother Clare Moore and she continued to challenge Nightingale throughout her tenure in the Crimea.

Mother Bridgeman, for example, insisted on maintaining the chaplain who had been assigned to the sisters. She also, unlike Mother Moore, refused to curtail the sisters' efforts in "spiritual" instruction as they cared for the physical needs of the soldiers. Nightingale expressed her frustration with Mother Bridgeman (Brickbat) in the following correspondence:

> The Roman Catholic question remains unsettled. Brickbat, the Revd. Mother of Kinsale, refusing to let five of her nuns come here without her to be under our Revd. Mother (Mother Moore) thereby showing that she has some second view besides nursing-- and I refusing to let our little society become a hotbed of RC intriquettes--Of course we shall have a R.C. storm--But our Revd Mother, heart and hand together is doing her best to stop it.[21]

The religious designations were essential in balancing the parties and in determining compensation. Nightingale's meticulous records may be some indication of the importance she placed on these identified characteristics.[22]

Reverend Mother Bridgeman never met the expectations of Nightingale to the extent that Reverend Mother Moore did. The two religious women were of very different personality and of very different circumstances as well. The influence of religion and politics influenced this relationship as it had so many others in the course of the historical events which led to this conflict.

Remembering the history of Irish-Anglo relationship gives one some understanding of the deeply entrenched feelings which existed between the Irish religious women and the upper class English lady who considered herself in command. Reverend Mother Moore was of Irish descent and though she had been in the original congregation of Sisters of Mercy, she had spent the last several years establishing a foundation in England and learning to work within a society which held different views of the Catholic Church and its authority. Reverend Mother Bridgeman on the other hand arrived from Ireland after having been asked by Church authorities to assist in a cause that involved her countrymen in fighting for British trade privileges and economic advantages which would have little effect on them as individuals or as a society. Mother Bridgeman's focus on spiritual needs was important in the eyes of her fellow Irish and most certainly as tangible as any other benefits she could assure them for their gallant efforts.

Gilgannon points out the commonality of the motivation of the two Sisters of Mercy as they fulfilled their mission of service and adhered to the *Rule and Constitution* of the Order. She also notes that Mother Moore was perceived by Nightingale as one who wanted peace at all costs and Mother Bridgeman as one who wanted authority at the cost of peace.

The conflict between Florence Nightingale and Mother Bridgeman was continually fired by factors which Gilgannon attributes to the "personification of Irish Catholicism" in the form of Mother Bridgeman and the "embodiment of English

Protestantism" in Nightingale.[23] Their unyielding views are brought to life in this correspondence with Sidney Herbert:

> You know the difficulties which have already arisen. More recently a charge of converting and rebaptizing before death has been made reported by me to the Senior Chaplain, by him to the Commandant, by him to the Commander-in-chief. I have exchanged the suspected nun. So sure am I that, give them rope, and they will hang themselves . . .[24]

The circumstances of Mother Bridgeman's defiance of Nightingale was eased only when Mother Bridgeman and five of her sisters were sent to Balaclava to work in the General Hospital. There, though they remained under Nightingale's formal authority, they escaped being under her watchful eye!

The perceptions of Nightingale's relationship with the Sisters of Mercy in the Crimea must not be confined to her interaction with only one group of sisters. Had she only worked with Mother Clare Moore the perception would be one of cooperation, mutual respect, and admiration. Nightingale describes her high regard for Mother Clare Moore in this letter written after the sister's departure from Crimea:

> You were far above me in fitness for the General Superintending both in worldly talent in administration and far more in the spiritual qualifications which God values in a Superior. My being placed over you in our unenviable reign of the East was my misfortune and not my fault.[25]

Mother Clare returned to Bermondsey and led the nursing sisters there in the operation of St. John's and St. Elizabeth's Hospital.

Mother Francis Bridgeman received no such praise from Miss Nightingale. Moreover, although the sisters from Ireland who arrived with the second party did indeed carry out heroic actions in their efforts to care for the sick and wounded, their work did not receive the same recognition from

Nightingale. Mother Francis Bridgeman recalled in her memoirs the following points of contention:

1 - Unity of the church was not upheld. The Sisters of Mercy and their chaplains were not allowed freedom.
2 - Material provisions were not adequate. Human needs were not met.
3 - Nightingale should not have tried to unify nuns from various motherhouses.
4 - It was a mistake to place sisters under a secular supervisor, especially if a Protestant.[26]

Although the Crimean War became that event which propelled Florence Nightingale into the public eye, it did not do the same for the Sisters of Mercy. Their efforts were recognized by some and went unnoticed by most. In characteristic humility, the sisters have not focused on any one event which was more significant than others in their development. They did, however, record their work in the private memoirs of individual sisters. Their relationship with Nightingale is revealed as one which was complex and ambivalent and, as worthy of exploration as any other aspect of Nightingale's life.

This paper has attempted to shed some light on their encounters, in view of the many factors which influence such relationships, and to recognize that much is to be told and even more to be learned about our heritage as nurses.

NOTES

1. *Rule and Constitution of the Religious Sisters of Mercy.* (Baltimore: John B. Piet, 1982) p. 3.
2. Gilgannon, Sr. M. *The Sisters of Mercy as Crimean War Nurses.* (Notre Dame, Indiana: University of Notre Dame, 1962, Dissertation) p. 129.
3. *Rule and Constitution* p. 6.
4. *Rule and Constitution* p. 9.

5.   Gilgannon, *The Sisters of Mercy as Crimean War Nurses*, p. 1.
6.   Goldie, S. ed. *"I have done my duty":* *Florence Nightingale in the Crimean War*, p. 7.
7.   Goldie, *"I have done my duty"*, p. 17-19.
8.   Gilgannon, *The Sisters of Mercy as Crimean War Nurses*, p. 37.
9.   Goldie, *"I have done my duty"*, p. 21. (Letter from Florence Nightingale to Mrs. Bracebridge, 15th October, 1854).
10.   Gilgannon, *Sisters of Mercy as Crimean War Nurses*, p. 68-69.
11.   Gilgannon, *Sisters of Mercy as Crimean War Nurses*, 39-40.
12.   Goldie, *"I have done my duty"*, p. 19.
13.   Goldie, *"I have done my duty"*, p. 24, (Letter from Sidney Herbert to Florence Nightingale, 15th October 1854).
14.   Palmer, I. *Florence Nightingale and the First Organized Delivery of Nursing Services*, p. 8.
15.   Gilgannon, *Sisters of Mercy as Crimean War Nurses*, p. 239.
16.   Gilgannon, *Sisters of Mercy as Crimean War Nurses*, p. 79-83.
17.   Gilgannon, *Sisters of Mercy as Crimean War Nurses*, p. 73-75.
18.   Gilgannon, *Sisters of Mercy as Crimean War Nurses*, p. 123 & 135.
19.   Goldie, *"I have done my duty"*, p. 50. (Letter from Florence Nightingale to Sir Sidney Herbert, 15th December 1854).
20.   Goldie, *"I have done my duty"*, p. 54.
21.   Goldie, *"I have done my duty"*, p. 62-63. (Letter from Florence Nightingale to Sir Sidney Herbert, 4th January 1855).
22.   Palmer, *Florence Nightingale*, p. 8.
23.   Gilgannon, *Sisters of Mercy as Crimean War Nurses*, p. 366-367.
24.   Goldie, *"I have done my duty"*, p. 90. (Letter from Florence Nightingale to Sir Sidney Herbert, 15th February 1855).

25. Goldie, *"I have done my duty"*, p. 261. (Letter from Florence Nightingale to Reverend Mother Bermondsey, [Mother Mary Clare Moore] 29th April 1856).
26. Gilgannon, *Sisters of Mercy as Crimean War Nurses*, p. 364-373.

REFERENCES

1. Gilgannon, Sr. Mary McAuley. *The Sisters of Mercy as Crimean War Nurses*. Notre Dame, IN: University of Notre Dame, Unpublished Dissertation. 1962.
2. Goldie, Sue M. ed. *"I have done my duty": Florence Nightingale in the Crimean War: 1854-1856*. Iowa City, IA: University of Iowa Press, 1987.
3. Palmer, Irene S. *Florence Nightingale and the First Delivery of Nursing Services*. Washington, D.C.: American Association of Colleges of Nursing. 1985.
4. *Rule and Constitution of the Religious Sisters of Mercy*. Baltimore: John B. Piet, 1892.
5. Tarbox, Mary P. *The Origins of Nursing by the Sisters of Mercy in the United States: 1843-1910*. New York: Teachers College, Columbia University. Unpublished Dissertation. 1986.

DEAREST REV'D MOTHER*

JoAnn G. Widerquist

INTRODUCTION

F.B. Smith in *Florence Nightingale Reputation and Power* characterized Nightingale as a cold woman, unable to understand or maintain friendships. In the first chapter he summarized his assessment of Nightingale:

> Outside the family Miss Nightingale used auxiliaries to obey her orders and reinforce

*This research was supported by an Open Faculty Fellowship grant from the Lilly Endowment. It is based primarily on collections of Nightingale's correspondence at the British Library, Wellcome Institute in London, the Greater London Record Office and the Nightingale School of Nursing Library. The original letters from Nightingale to Reverend Mother Mary Clare Moore are located primarily in the convent of the Sisters of Mercy. There are copies in the British Library and Wellcome Institute for Medical History, London. Goldie compiled summaries of Nightingale's letters published as *A Calender of Letters of Florence Nightingale*. For simplicity one reference is cited.

her self-esteem; she dropped them when they rebelled or lost their ability to service that esteem. She yearned for intimacy, to fuse herself with idealized others, yet she retained a profound sense of her psychological distance from other human beings, a contradiction, as I shall outline later, that permeated her dealings with such confidants as Sidney Herbert and Mary Jones, the superintendent of a High Church nursing sisterhood. Florence Nightingale's sexual relationships remained infantile. She never permitted herself to become unguardedly dependent upon anyone. Throughout her career she made public emotional investments in others, in shared great plans and objects, and when the others' commitment wavered or their contribution disappointed her, as invariably they did, she ostentatiously withdrew the outlay and reinvested it in herself. In all her ventures she played by turns the role of trusting acolyte and the only begetter who was always let down.[1]

Research into Nightingale's spirituality at least partially refutes this assessment. Her friendship with Mother Mary Clare Moore revealed a relationship different than those described by Smith. This paper examines that relationship. A prolific letter writer and crusader for reform, Nightingale had long correspondence and association with a variety of 19th Century people such as Mary Stanley; Dr. Edward Manning; members of her family including Aunt Mai Smith and her sister; nurses such as Misses Lees, Torrance, and Pringle; various physicians; government officials like Sir Sidney Herbert; and numerous others. Often because of Nightingale's strong opinions and forceful manner, these associations ended in disagreement or alienation, though some were reconciled in later life. Few expressed the sense of caring on Nightingale's part as her letters to Reverend Mother Mary Clare Moore of the Sisters of Mercy. Nightingale opened her heart and spiritual struggles to Mother Mary Clare Moore.

She trusted and loved "Rev'd" Mother enough to be vulnerable to her. This paper explores their relationship: the caring and respect Florence Nightingale had for Rev'd Mother and illustrates a "gentler" Nightingale than that described by Smith.

Despite their common nursing experience and concern for its practice, Nightingale and Mother Mary Clare Moore's relationship was essentially a private one. Except in the Crimean War Moore never worked in the public arenas in which Nightingale engaged, and although she gave private advice, never publicly challenged Nightingale. Their friendship dealt primarily with personal matters: each other's health and their devotion to the "religious" or spiritual or life as each felt called to it. Nightingale continued to ask Moore's advice throughout their association and did not hesitate to publicly aid her friend and the Bermondsey Sisters of Mercy when she saw the need. Theirs was a mutually sustaining relationship, especially for Nightingale who subordinated the authoritarian side of her personality out of great respect for a spiritual mentor and friend.

SPIRITUALITY

How in a time characterized by sectarianism, religious prejudice and distrust could these two women of different faiths and national origin find so much common spiritual ground? In part, the answer lies in Nightingale's open approach to religious belief. Although born into a Unitarian dissenting family, baptized Anglican, and motivated, as many Victorian women were, by religious fervor, Nightingale was not Unitarian, Anglican, Evangelical or Roman Catholic in any orthodox sense. Her beliefs were eclectic and heterodox. The essence of Nightingale was her spirituality. It was the force which drove her life and contributed to the development of early modern nursing. Walter Principe's definition of spirituality applies to Nightingale:

Spirituality is the way a person understands and lives, within his or her historical context, that aspect of his or her religion, philosophy, ethic, or viewpoint that is considered the loftiest, the noblest, the most calculated to lead the ideal or perfection sought by the person.[2]

Nightingale's personal spirituality upheld a lofty ideal of God as Absolute, the Perfect, the Spirit of Truth. In Nightingale's belief one pursued perfection in order to remodel the world; or as Nightingale frequently stated, "Mankind creating mankind." For her "religion was the tie between the perfect and the imperfect."[3] She believed in finding God's laws, physical and moral that would teach mankind how to live in perfect harmony with the Creator. Nightingale believed that the character of God could be known through His laws and that the character of persons could be used to bring others and society to perfection. She also believed that persons could communicate directly with God.[4]

In contrast F.B. Smith describes Nightingale by saying, "She fed on an unyielding, unremitting drive to dominate her associates and opponents and to this end she defined issues and goals, distinct from theirs . . ."[5] In truth, she drove associates relentlessly at times and was insensitive to their needs and failures. Yet, rather than the desire for power or domination, her private writings expressed an unremitting drive to perfection which, despite her efforts, she could not attain. The problem was that Nightingale demanded this drive from others. In a religious essay, Nightingale wrote "Happiness equals perfection. On the road to perfection is to be on the road to Happiness."[6] She also said two essentials of happiness were "sympathy in good works and oneness with God."[7]

Nightingale's beliefs illustrate the rational and mystical sides of her nature; in other words, practical work and communion with God to perfect society. These two natures often could not mesh neatly. Mother Moore provided a safe outlet for Nightingale's struggle and gave her sympathy filling

Nightingale's expressed need, or "want," asked for but rarely found.

SETTING FOR THE FRIENDSHIP

The Crimean War was the first covered by a war correspondent. William Russell's articles to the *London Times* described the horrifying conditions for the wounded or sick British soldier, contrasting them with the French soldiers who were nursed by the Sisters of Charity. His poignant plea, "Why have we no Sisters of Charity?[8] brought many responses-- group and individual, governmental and religious. Bishop Thomas Grant of Southwark made one of the first responses on the part of a religious group. He negotiated the arrangements for the Sisters of Mercy led by Reverend Mother Mary Clare from Bermondsey Convent, Southwark to send a contingent to the Crimea. Nightingale was to be in charge of organizing female nursing in the military establishment.

The position of the Roman Catholic Church in English society during this time influenced Bishop Grant's actions. Reinstated following the Emancipation Act of 1829, the church was viewed with considerable suspicion and intolerance from most parts of English society. The Catholic Church authorities were concerned to relieve suffering but were also looking to enhance the image of Roman Catholics as patriotic members of the British Empire.[9]

The Crimean War occurred concurrently with the Oxford Movement during which English Anglicanism lost many prominent members to the Roman Catholic Church such as John Henry Newman and Edward Manning. The Oxford Movement was both anti-Catholic and anti-Protestant at the same time but it brought a spirit of revival that "passed through both religious communities like a quickening gale."[10] Other non-conforming religious groups were also challenging the Anglican Church. All this religious ferment within and around the State church contributed to distrust and sectarian dissension. In this heightened religious atmosphere bigotry and proselytizing were common in the army and the hospitals of the Crimean War.

F.B. Smith says "Miss Nightingale had the advantage in the government's view of being safely Protestant but otherwise religiously neuter"[11] and therefore acceptable as a lady superintendent of nurses. She was, however, more religously eclectic than neuter; she was deeply religious, although she never really found a home in any organized church. In the midst of, and perhaps because of, all this sectarian turmoil, Nightingale was committed to secular nursing. In these circumstances it seems remarkable that Nightingale and Rev'd Mother Mary Clare became colleagues and friends.

Florence Nightingale met Moore with four Sisters of Mercy on October 22, 1954 in Paris while waiting to leave for Scutari with thirty-two other nurses, lay and religious. Thus began a warm relationship which provided spiritual support to Nightingale for many years. They arrived in Constantinople on November 4th, 1854, the day after the horrible battle of Inkerman. The battle of Balaclava on October 25 and the battle of Alma on September 20 had already overwhelmed the available medical personnel. The group proceeded on to Scutari, the only base hospital at the time, under an agreement from the War Office issued by Sir Sidney Herbert, Secretary at War. A second group of nurses, also arranged by Sir Sidney Herbert but with somewhat different policies, arrived December 21, 1854. The composition of this group included fifteen Sisters of Mercy from Ireland. The Bermondsey nuns were usually referred to as the English Sisters of Mercy. Ironically, Mother Mary Clare was, however, from Ireland.[12]

Mother Mary Clare Moore was born Georgiana Moore in Dublin in 1814 into a pious Protestant family, who, following the death of the father in 1823, became Catholic. The Protestant background she shared with Nightingale may explain some of the natural affinity the two women later developed.

Georgiana Moore joined with Mother Mary Catherine McAuley, the foundress of the Sisters of Mercy, as one of the original seven nuns in 1833. She is described as:

> tall and slender with prominent dark eyes, "more Anglo-Irish than Irish," being naturally lively and sometimes even as an excitable temperament and quite energetic. She acquired remarkable self-control though she never overcame a tendency to irritability. Always strict with herself, she had, especially early, a tendency to be rather exacting with others, but she displayed mature judgment.[13]

In 1839, at age 25, she was lent to the Bermondsey foundation in Southwark. She returned very briefly to Ireland in 1841 for six months. In 1854 she was 40 years old and had fifteen years experience as the superior for Bermondsey. Moore gained her nursing experience during cholera epidemics in Dublin and London and developed strong leadership skills before going to Scutari. Nightingale was 34 with one year of experience as a superintendent of a nursing home for gentlewomen; she needed every bit of Rev'd Mother's experience.[14]

FLORENCE NIGHTINGALE AND REV'D MOTHER

The correspondence of Florence Nightingale with Mother Mary Clare Moore in many ways resembled other of the great letter writing Victorian women. They discussed their everyday activities including recipes from Alexis Soyer, chef during the war, their health, such as advice from Nightingale to Moore not to brush out any more gutters in cold weather, the concerns of persons important to them and above all spiritual or religious matters. Nightingale and Moore, furthermore, corresponded against a backgrop of war and reform in which both played roles not common to the average woman of the time.

The correspondence began in 1855 when Nightingale left Scutari and Moore to consolidate her leadership of hospitals in the Crimea and continued through 1868. Gaps occurred indicating letters missing and/or lack of communication at times. Only a very few of Moore's letters remain although inferences as to their contents can be made from Nightingale's letters. Several letters to Sr. M. Gonzaga, one of the original four Sisters who accompanied Moore to Scutari, including one apparently written after Moore's death, add to the understanding of the relationship between Rev'd Mother and Nightingale.[15] Another group of letters concerning a conflict between Dr. Manning and the Bermondsey Sisters late in the 1860's exists in the Nightingale correspondence with family members, friends, and associates. The situation concerned the nursing by Sister M. Gonzaga and others at the Great Ormonde Street Hospital. The "affair," as it has been called by Sr. Shane Leslie in *Forgotten Passages*, provides clues to problems between nursing and hospital administration, an interesting area warranting further research.[16]

Portions of all of the letters illustrated Nightingale's respect and care for Rev'd Mother; only a few examples can be included. Nightingale nearly always addressed her letters "Dearest Rev'd Mother" and closed them with "ever my Dearest Rev'd Mother's grateful and loving Florence Nightingale" or "my dearest Rev'd Mother's grateful and affectionate child, FN." The first letter from Nightingale to Rev'd Mother is dated 19 November 1855 after she left Scutari. In it Nightingale said, "you have been one of our chief main-stays and without you I do not know what would have become of the work."[17] She occasionally discussed other nurses and sisters with Mother Mary Clare in these letters.

When Moore was preparing to return to England because of ill health, Nightingale wrote on 29 April, 1856:

> Your going home is the greatest blow I have had yet. But God's love and gratitude go with

you, as you well know. You know well too
that I shall do everything I can for the
Sisters, whom you left with me--but it will
not be like you--your wishes will be our law.
And I shall try and remain in the Crimea for
your sakes as long as any of us are there
. . . I do not presume to express praise or
gratitude to you, Rev'd Mother, because it
would look as if I thought you had done the
work not unto God but unto me. You are far
above me in fitness for the General
Superintendency, both in worldly talent of
administration and far more in the spiritual
qualifications which God values in a Superior
. . . I will ask you to forgive me for
everything or anything which I may
unintentionally have done which can ever
have given you pain. Remembering only that
I have always felt what I have just expressed-
-and that it has given me more pain to reign
over you than to you to serve under me.[18]

The war ended on March 20th, 1856, but
many staff stayed until all the sick and wounded
were gone. Finally in July 1856, when the remainder
of the sisters were leaving and Nightingale was
winding up her service at Barracks Hospital Scutari,
she wrote:

By the time you receive this you will have
the last of the sisters . . . Dearest Reverend
Mother, I am sure that no one, even your
own children, values you, loves you and
reveres you more than I do--Take care of
your precious health, do. In closing this work
I can never sufficiently express how much I
feel all that you and your sisters have been to
it.[19]

Many writers deplore the lack of recognition
and reward accorded the Sisters which their war
service warranted. But apparently Nightingale
understood Rev'd Mother on this subject because
when Lord Panmure, Secretary for War and member
of the House of Lords, sent cheques to the Sisters in
January, 1857 they "generously declined this gift for

themselves but expressed the desire to distribute it amongst the poor and sick in their district, and the government agreed."[20]

On 23 July 1856, Nightingale in a letter to Sr. Mary Gonzaga wrote of her intention to visit Bermondsey upon her arrival in England and then sneak quietly out of the way.[21] On the morning of August 6, 1856 Nightingale appeared alone and unannounced at the Convent in Bermondsey to visit with the sisters before proceeding to the Nightingale home in Lea Hurst on August 7th.[22] Contact with the Bermondsey Sisters was her initial concern in England.

Nightingale solicited Rev'd Mother's opinions about persons and events during the war years, a practice she continued throughout the correspondence. In a letter of 12 May 1864 Nightingale referred to some disconcerting correspondence with a Jesuit father. She shared her foibles thus:

> Since I wrote to you I have a note from that Jesuit Father I mentioned to you and what I ask you now is whether I should have it unanswered or whether I should write and tell him it was all a mistake. I really lose all confidence in my own judgment as to the routine of life am always in scrapes. Poor Lord Herbert used to laugh at me and tell me I was so overcivil that I was always in scrapes from overcivility. But really the scrapes I get into are those of a person always going about doing insulting rude things. My impulse was not to answer this Father's note, but I remember Dr. Manning was or pretended to be hurt, that I did not answer one of his, which really required no answer. So I trouble you to know what you think I should do. If to answer what I had better day--I really feel quite ashamed of troubling you.[23]

After Nightingale's physical collapse in 1857 some correspondence is missing. Nightingale's invalid lifestyle for most of the rest of her life circumscribed contact with others. Her correspondence helped her maintain contact with people. From 1858 to 1863 letters from Nightingale to Moore have not been found. The few available from Moore to Nightingale were from May through December of 1862. The letters are all very loving in tone. Reverend Mother thanked Nightingale for gifts and for a visit to Nightingale's home. One dated 28 October 1862 Moore stated, "You are almost the only one, dearest Miss Nightingale to whom I can speak freely on religious subjects. I mean my very own feelings on them."[24] Reverend Mother also expressed a wish that she and Nightingale could meditate as they ought. Moore referred to some controversy she had with the Bishop over Nightingale but stated, "Still dearest Miss Nightingale you must really give the Catholics credit for loving and revering you very much!"[25] Moore conveyed a sense that the two shared feelings of religious love and commitment "our faith is the same."[26]

A letter from Nightingale dated 21 October 1863 evidently written in response to one from Moore is often quoted to convey Nightingale's regard for her:

> I began a letter to you some days ago to tell you that one of the bright jewels in your crown will be your conduct in the Crimean War, to use St. Gertrude's phraseology. But I don't remember what you allude to about the key and don't see any harm in it if it were so. That I always thought you ought to have been the superior and I the inferior and it was not my fault that it was not so. That I always thought how magnanimous and spiritual your obedience in accepting such a position and how utter my incapacity in making it tenable for you, and how I should have failed without your help. That I always wondered at your unfailing patience, forbearance and sweetness, courage under many trials peculiar to ourselves or yourselves, decide what was common to all. If I did not express this more which I always felt it was because I wanted so much that you

could put up with me that I felt it was no use to say to your face either then or since how I admired your ways. As for your having shown temper to me I don't like to write the word. I can't conceive what you were thinking of. I marveled how you could bear with us, I would gladly have avoided some difficulties which you must have keenly felt but I could not. And I said less about my inability than I otherwise should because I always felt our Lord alone can reward her, it is not for me to speak. All this and much more I said in my letter but then when I wrote last to you I could not leave my bed to find it and afterwards it did not seem worthwhile to send it. I am so very sorry for Sister Gonzaga. It is so very uncomfortable to live in that scramble. I have to thank you for a dear kind comfort just received but I write in such haste, every loving Florence Nightingale.[27]

Additional excerpts describe what Moore's letters meant to Nightingale. December 15, 1863 she wrote, "but I have your dear letters, and you cannot think how much they have encouraged me. They are almost the only earthly encouragement I have."[28] And 21 June 1864 Nightingale penned:

No dearest Rev'd Mother, you can't think that your letter would ever 'trouble' me. I know how little time you have to write which makes me all the more grateful. On the contrary, they are the greatest refreshment I have. But answering is often beyond me.[29]

FLORENCE NIGHTINGALE AND REV'D MOTHER: SHARED RELIGION AND THE MYSTICS

Victorian women commonly exchanged letters about religious and spiritual concerns. Nightingale and Rev'd Mother were no exceptions as is already evident. Nightingale frequently discussed the saints

and mystical writers, and found mutuality with
Rev'd Mother in reading of the mystics. The letters
allude to books frequently exchanged as gifts or
loans.

December 15, 1863 Nightingale in a long
letter to Rev'd Mother discussed the mystics thus:

> I have felt so horribly ungrateful for never
> having thanked you for your books. S. Jean
> de la Croix's life I keep thankfully. I am
> never tired of reading that part where he
> prays for the return of all his service, ...
> I return the life of S. Catherine of Genoa. I
> like it so much. It is a very singular and
> suggestive life. I am so glad she accepted the
> being Directress of the Hospital. For I think
> it was much better for her to make the
> Hospital servants do right then to receive
> their 'injuries'-- much better for the poor
> patients, I mean. I am quite ashamed to keep
> Ste. Therese so long. But there is a good deal
> of reading in her--and I am only able to read
> at night . . . But St. Catherine of Sienna says:
> {'And + other times I allow that to happen to
> him, in order that he take more care to flee
> from himself and come have a recourse in
> me++ and that he consider that by love I am
> giving him the means to extract the key to
> true humility judging himself unworthy of
> peace and respite from thought, like my other
> followers--+ on the other hand judging
> himself deserving of the ills that he suffers'
> ++}---I send you back St. Frances de Sales,
> with many thanks--I like him in his old
> dress--I like that story where the man loses
> his crown of martyrdom, because he will not
> be reconciled with his enemy. It is a sound
> lesson. I am going to send you back S.
> Francis Xavier. His is a life I always like to
> study as well as those of all the early Jesuit
> fathers.[30]

In a Christmas Eve, 1863 letter Nightingale
began:

> I send my poor little Christmas gift for your

children, and my great Christmas wishes . . .
As S. Catherine of Genoa says, when she
thinks that {'God became man in order to
make man into God'} I like those words so
much--that belief in perfection . . . I often
say that prayer of St. Catherine of Sienna.
{I offer and recommend to you my very
beloved children, for they are my soul. XXX
to you external father, I, unworthy, offer
again may own life for them--XXX that
when and ever it shall please your goodness,
you take me from my body and return me to
the body with ever greater pain [. . .]
provided that I see the reformation of the
Holy church XX & c& c&c . . .}
St. Catherine did not see the reformation she
desired and I shall not see the reformation of
the Army. But I can truly say that, whatever
I have known our Lord to desire of me. I
have never refused Him (knowingly)
anything--and I can feel the same now. Pray
for us then, dearest Rev'd Mother that we
may know God's goodwill toward us.[31]

Nightingale was fond of St. John of the Cross
as she reveals in one of the letters:

I am quite ashamed of keeping St. John of
the Cross so long. But I kept St. Teresa much
longer. I feel like a child who excuses itself
for being naughty by telling how much
naughtier it is sometimes. I hope to send back
the 2nd Vol. soon. I am often afraid that I
have not so much as entered into the first
Obscure Night. Yet that Obscure Night does
seem so applicable to me. I have never found
St. John of the Cross mystical or fanciful--
On the contrary, he seems to have had the
most wonderful practical knowledge of the
ways of God in the heart of man.[32]

The next letter, 23 January 1865, Nightingale
sent tender wishes to Moore on the anniversary of
first taking the habit. She credited Rev'd Mother
with experiencing "the blessing it is to know and feel
one is doing His will--tho I am never in full

possession of that feeling."[33] Nightingale always longed for the sense of God's presence in her life, a presence she felt Moore had. Nightingale also admired the absolute purity of the mystics in their commitment to service and willingness to sacrifice, other qualities she attributed to Rev'd Mother. In a religous essay written during the 1860's Nightingale said "St Teresa's strength and that of the whole school of Mystic Ascetics was not in their doctrine of a God . . . but in their absolute purity of intention--their absolute linking of themselves in the idea of service . . ."[34] Nightingale called it mankind creating mankind.

The longing for a deep spiritual life sounded throughout Nightingale's letters to Rev'd Mother. In the last letter to Rev'd Mother available, Nightingale stated:

> Alas _____ I feel as if I was only quite in the infancy of serving God--I am so careful & troubled and have such a want of calmness about His work & His poor--as if they were my work & my poor instead of His. I have not learnt yet the first lesson of His service . . . But I am sure I don't succeed in being filled with His righteousness--And so I suppose that I regard too little Himself and too much myself.[35]

Years later Nightingale summed up her thoughts on the mystical life and service:

> But the two thoughts which God has given me all my life have been. First to infuse the mystical religion into the forms of others (always thinking they [nurses] would shew it forth much better than I . . .) . . . Secondly to give them an organization for their activity in which they could be trained to be the "handmaids of the Lord."[36]

The relationship of mystical life and service in nursing history needs further study by nursing scholars.

CONCLUSION

Letters to Reverend Mother ended in 1868 with this sentiment:

Your dear Reverence, is very good to me. I was so thankful to see your handwriting again. --I know so well how you can never take the least rest, but must lead all the Exercise, and everything else, your own dear self.--But it does me good, I assure you it does, (tho' I can't bear myself,) if I think that your dear Reverence is offering me to God, that whatever He wills may be carried out in me. I have so little of the only true patience.[37]

The reason for the cessation remains unclear. It was possible that the two had an unrecorded disagreement, but this seems unlikely given other correspondence regarding the Sisters. Nightingale at this time was occupied with Indian Sanitary conditions, writing articles and essays, and other activities. Her health was poor and she was experiencing great weakness. Lost letters account for other gaps in correspondence and are probably the most likely explanation for the end of the correspondence. Perhaps poor health of both Nightingale and Rev'd Mother contributed to fewer letters. Moore died in December, 1874. In a letter dated 12 December 1874 to Sister Mary Gonzaga Nightingale said, "I know not what to write, Perhaps she is at this moment with God."[38]

F.B. Smith characterized Nightingale as using people to meet her need for power. In this reading of Nightingale's difficulty in relationships, they resulted not from her need for power but from her idealized need for perfection and mutuality, i.e., sympathy, a quality of fellow feeling, with others before she was able to sustain a relationship. Without sympathy her relationships were disappointing even when she experienced power.

Moore never disappointed Nightingale. Her unfailing love and respect for Nightingale provided the sympathy she required:

> You see I always count upon your sympathy
> and tell you our doings--tho' I think you are
> the only Rev'd Mother in the world who
> would or could hear them with indulgence,
> they must all seem so futile and imperfect.[39]

Sympathy was the fellow-feeling Nightingale needed
to serve God and mankind. There was mutuality
between these two women. What was done, said and
felt by each toward the other was given and received
openly. Nightingale does not appear guarded in her
letters. And Moore spoke of her own feelings of
religion.

Nightingale found friendship with Rev'd
Mother. In a religious essay titled "What is
Friendship?" Nightingale writes "There must be a
third among them--A third in all these 'twos' to
make them real or 'ideal' friends. And that third
must be God."[40] Moore and Nightingale shared this
third.

One hundred years later in the 1970's Irene
Claremont de Castillejo wrote in her book *Knowing
Woman: A Feminine Psychology* a very similar
description:

> For there is to be a meeting, it seems as
> though a third, a something else, is always
> present. You may call it Love, or the Holy
> Spirit. Jungians would say that it is the
> presence of the Self. If this 'Other' is present,
> there cannot have failed to be a meeting.[41]

Florence Nightingale has this relationship with Rev'd
Mother Mary Clare Moore during her active years in
the Crimean War and beyond. She also had this kind
of relationship during her troubled teen years with
Aunt Hannah Nicholson and in her later years with
Benjamin Jowett. Nightingale's concept of friendship
needs further exploration.

Elizabeth Gaskell, an astute observer of
Victorian women, described Nightingale as one who
loved mankind but had difficulty with loving
individuals:

> --but then this want of love for individuals
> becomes a gift and a very rare one, if one
> takes it in conjunction with her intense love

for the race: her utter unselfishness in serving
and ministering. I think I have told you all-
-even to impressions--but she is really so
extraordinary a creature that impressions may
be erroneous--[42]

The paper illustrates a gentle aspect of
Florence Nightingale's complex personality. She had
problems with relationships within and without her
family because of her internal struggles to work out
a vocation to serve mankind and satisfy an inner
desire for a deep spiritual experience. In Rev'd
Mother Nightingale found a spiritual friend who
helped her with the struggle to integrate practical
work with spiritual goals. Florence Nightingale was
not driven by the desire for power but by her lofty
spiritual ideal of perfecting herself and mankind.

NOTES

1. F.B. Smith, *Florence Nightingale Reputation and Power*. (New York, St. Martin's Press, 1982), p. 23.
2. Walter Principe, "Toward Defining Spirituality," *Sr: Studies in Religion/Science Religieuses*, XII (Spring, 1983), p. 136.
3. Florence Nightingale, *Suggestions for Thought to the Seekers after Truth Among the Artizens of England*. (3 volumes) George E. Eyre and William Spottiswoode. (London: by author, 1860). Vol II, p. 186.
4. JoAnn Widerquist, *Spirituality of Florence Nightingale*, unpublished paper presented at American Association for History of Nursing, September 25, 1988.
5. Smith, op. cit., p. 12.
6. Nightingale Religious Essays, British Library, 45,843 f. 97, n.d.
7. Ibid. f. 174.
8. Sir Edward T. Cook, *The Life of Florence Nightingale*. 2 volumes, Macmillian and Co. (London, 1913), p. 148.

9.   Sr. Mary McAuley Gillgannon, "The Sisters of Mercy as Crimean War Nurses." (Unpublished doctoral dissertation, Dept. of History, University of Notre Dame, 1962).

10.   Sir Shane Leslie, *The Oxford Movement: 1833-1933* (London Burn, Oates and Washburn, Ltd, 1933). p. xi.

11.   Smith, op. cit. p. 27.

12.   The different arrangement, the unannounced arrival, the chaos of the situation as well as Nightingale's inexperience in administration created a situation that produced conflict between Nightingale and the leaders of the second group for the remainder of the war. Nightingale considered nursing to be a secular vocation done out of an individual commitment to God and from a personal calling. Other nurses, especially members of the second group of Sisters, considered nursing to be part of their religious vocation and approached the care of people from a different frame of reference. The overarching context of Anglo-Irish politics at the time also complicated the already tense relationship between Nightingale and these nuns, called the "Irish Sisters," who came to provide nursing in the Crimean War with all the inherent prejudices of their political situation. *"I Have Done by Duty": Florence Nightingale in the Crimean War 1854-56*, Edited by Sue M. Goldie (Iowa City, University of Iowa Press, 1988), Chpt. 5.

13.   Sister Mary McAuley Gillgannon, "The Sisters of Mercy as Crimean War Nurses." (Unpublished doctoral dissertation, Dept. of History, University of Notre Dame, 1962), op. cit. p. 45-46.

14.   Evelyn Bolster, *The Sisters of Mercy in the Crimean War* (Cork Ireland: The Mercier Press, 1964). Sister Helena Concannon, "The Irish Sisters of Mercy in the Crimean War," *Irish Messenger*. 5 Gt. Denmark St., Denmark St., Dublin, (no date), p. 1-27. Gillganon, op.

cit.

15. Sister Teresa Green, Archivist Bermondsey Convent, personal communication. (March 28, 1989; *A Calender of Letters of Florence Nightingale*, (Ed.) Sue M. Goldie, (London: Wellcome Institute for the History of Medicine, 1977).

16. Sir Shane Leslie, "Forgotten Passages in Florence Nightingale's Life," *Dublin Review*, 161, October, 1917, p. 197 and Cook Vol. I, op. cit. p. 487.

17. Florence Nightingale to Rev'd Mother Nightingale Letters, Wellcome Institute, November 19, 1855.

18. Florence Nightingale to Rev'd Mother, Wellcome Institute, April 29, 1856.

19. Florence Nightingale to Rev'd Mother, BL Add. Mss 45,789 f. 13, July 7, 1956.

20. Frank A. King, "Miss Nightingale and Her Ladies in the Crimea," *Nursing Mirror*, XXII, October 1954, p. XII.

21. Florence Nightingale to Sr. M. Gonzaga *Nightingale Letters*, Wellcome Institute, July 23, 1856.

22. Florence Nightingale to Rev'd Mother, BL Add. Mss 45,789 f. 55, September 8, 1868.

23. Florence Nightingale to Rev'd Motehr, Wellcome Institute, May 12, 1864.

24. Rev'd Mother to F.N. GLRO: The Nightingale Collection. HI/ST/NC2/V16/62, HI/ST/NC2/V23/62-V28/62, HI/ST/NC2/V32/62, October 28, 1862.

25. Ibid.

26. Ibid.

27. Florence Nightingale to Rev'd Mother, BL Add, Mss 45,789 f. 11-12, October 21, 1863.

28. Florence Nightingale to Rev'd Mother, BL Add. Mss 45,789 f. 13, December 15, 1863.

29. Florence Nightingale to Rev'd Mother, BL Add. Mss 45,789 f. 25-26, June 21, 1864.

30. Florence Nightingale to Rev'd Mother, BL Add. Mss 45,789 f. 13-16, December 15, 1863.

31. Florence Nightingale to Rev'd Mother, BL Add. Mss 45,789 f. 13-16, December 5, 1863. (Brackets English translation).

32. Florence Nightingale to Rev'd Mother, BL Add. Mss 45,789 f. 34, January 9, 1865.

33. Florence Nightingale to Rev'd Mother, BL Add. Mss 45, 789 f. 37, January 23, 1865.

34. Florence Nightingale Religious Essays,BL Add. Mss 45,843 f.f. 63 n.d.

35. Florence Nightingale to Rev'd Mother, BL Add. Mss 45,789 f. 65, September 8, 1868.

36. Florence Nightingale to Benjamin Jowett, BL Add. Mss 45,785 f. 109, ? 1889.

37. Florence Nightingale to Rev'd Mother, BL Add. Mss 45,789 f. 55, September 8, 1868.

38. Florence Nightingale to Sr. M. Gonzaga, Convent Sisters of Mercy, December 12, 1874.

39. Florence Nightingale to Rev'd Mother, BL Add. Mss 45,789, f. 29, September 3, 1864.

40. Florence Nightingale Religious Essays, BL Add. Mss 45,843 f. 158 n.d.

41. Irene Claremont de Castillejo, *Knowing Women: A Feminine Psychology*, (New York: Harper & Row, 1973) p. 12.

42. *The Letters of Mrs. Gaskell*, J.A.V. Chapple and Arthur Pollard, (Ed.), (Cambridge: Harvard University Press, 1967) p. 320 Letter #217 E. Gaskill to Emily Sheen from Lea Hurst, October 27, 1854.

WOMEN FOUNDERS, NURSES AND THE CARE OF CHILDREN AT THE HOSPITAL FOR SICK CHILDREN IN TORONTO 1875 TO 1899

Judith Young

Nineteenth century medical science had little specialized treatment to offer sick children. A comfortable home was the best place to care for a sick child; therefore, hospitals for children were founded for the poor. They provided food, a clean environment, and "spiritual nurture"; the latter was an attempt to impart socially acceptable values to less fortunate members of society.[1] The Hospital for Sick Children in Toronto was no exception and reflected the concern of philanthropic members of the middle class towards those raised in "homes of wretchedness and sin."[2]

In founding H.S.C., Elizabeth McMaster and her group of upper middle class women were no doubt influenced by developments in Britain and the United States. Between 1865 and 1875, a new children's hospital was founded in Britain every six months.[3] In the U.S.A., the first children's hospital dates from 1855. The Toronto of the 1870s was a rapidly expanding, predominantly Protestant, British city. Successful Anglican and Nonconformist merchants and landowners provided leadership in the city.[4] Elizabeth McMaster, born in Toronto in 1847,

309

had married, at 17, into a prominent family that was staunchly Baptist and philanthropic. H.S.C. owed its beginnings and continuation to the zeal and dedication of this remarkable woman.

The founding committee consisted of 22 women, mainly the wives of prominent businessmen. Mrs. McMaster became President and Hospital Secretary. All aspects of H.S.C. management were, until 1891, controlled by the Committee. This included finance, fund raising, hiring, supervision of nurses and servants, purchasing, and approval of admissions and discharges. Physicians applied for appointments. Committee members rotated for a week at a time as daily visitors in order to supervise the household. Business meetings were held monthly and members who failed to attend for three consecutive months ceased to be on the committee. Weekly prayer meetings were held and all members urged to attend. Mrs. McMaster felt she led a divine mission and hoped that the spirit of Christian charity would influence people to donate to the hospital. Prayers were fervently offered particularly when funds were low. Little active fundraising was done--a philosophy which proved a major cause of friction when businessmen became involved with financial affairs.

Up to 1891, patients were cared for in a series of modestly renovated houses. The initial 6 iron cots expanded to 40 beds by 1886, when H.S.C. moved to its fourth location. This building was

> "old and dingy but the wards bright and cheerful. Pretty pictures, mottoes and bible texts cover(ed) the walls . . . an aquarium provided much interest . . . there is a 'silent chamber' where our very sick children can be kept quiet . . . much time and thought [was spent] furnishing this ward."[5]

H.S.C. admitted "sick children destitute and friendless" and those "whose parents owing to poverty were unable to attend them."[6] Accident cases such as burns and fractures were treated, but the majority of

Women Founders, Nurses and the Care of 311
Children at the Hospital for Sick
Children in Toronto 1875-1899

children had orthopedic disorders related to tuberculosis or congenital deformities. For over two decades hip joint disease was the leading cause of admission. Many children were confined to bed for long periods with splints and weights, some staying months and years. In 1889, the average stay was sixty four days. A day on the girls' ward is described as follows:

> After breakfast and prayers each little maiden if able is expected to knit or sew, as playing all day long would make play tiresome. At 10 a.m. when the ward maid has the beds in order and while one little one after another is tenderly carried by our nurse to the bathroom to have their wounds dressed, the toys are distributed and play begins in earnest. Children play at "doctor," "nurse" and at being "lady visitors"-dolls have a leg bandaged, a splint put on or a weight added. One doll has whooping cough, one hip disease, another club foot.[7]

Children able to be up had lunch at ward tables. In the afternoon the Lady Visitors arrived and children "pounce on their favourites and beg a story."[8] Visitors left at 5 p.m. and a tea of milk, bread and butter, currant loaf, apple sauce and biscuits was served. The evening routine included prayers at bedtime. The boys played with soldiers and Noah's arks but also had duties assigned. These included rolling bandages, distributing bibs and doing errands for those in bed. There were also outings to nearby Queen's Park, magic lantern shows, and Sunday services. Religious instruction was an important aspect of care. Committee members, nurses, and students of a nearby theological college all assisted with religious teaching. Some secular teaching was provided by visiting Committee members.

Discipline of the children appeared strict but kind. Boys gave the most problems and perhaps this is why a small workroom was set aside so that "when not in the open air and if well enough boys could occupy their time."[9] The making of paper pillows was the first task and ladies read and talked to the boys as they worked. Disruptions on the wards were discussed at committee meetings. On one occasion, a boy, "whose companionship was believed to be hurtful to the others," was isolated. This was done "as delicately as possible" and the "isolated little boy continued the subject of kind and watchful care."[10]

Dying children received special attention. The death of Mary Cross, in 1879, happened suddenly with the Matron beside her and ended a "short and suffering life." Her mother was sent for "as soon as possible."[11] In 1884, a "silent chamber" was provided as a peaceful place where "little ones passing away may be taken and where their mothers may remain with them till the spirit shall return unto God who gave it."[12] Committee members were undoubtedly compassionate towards families, though, in keeping with the times, placed severe restrictions on visiting. Unless children were very ill, parents were only allowed to visit for an hour on Wednesdays. Until 1883, family visiting had been allowed twice weekly on Wednesday evening and on Sunday, and there is some evidence that the Sunday time was eliminated to enable religious services and teaching to proceed undisturbed.[13] Committee members and genteel young ladies, however, visited daily to read and sing to the patients.

A recurring problem was finding suitable placement for patients who were incurably ill, severely retarded, or orphaned. Josephine Kane, admitted at 2 years of age with hip disease, remained at H.S.C. throughout her childhood and was educated at a city school. She was, however, an exception. Transfers took much time and correspondence. In desperation over the placement of the "idiot boy" Harry Hienson, too young for an asylum, the Committee even considered the Toronto jail.[14]

Limited early management was delegated to nurses, though the Matron, at first responsible for

Women Founders, Nurses and the Care of 313
Children at the Hospital for Sick
Children in Toronto 1875-1899

marketing and meals, had her role expanded to include hiring and supervision of nurses. The first Matrons were not altogether satisfactory. Problems included poorly cooked food, inadequate supervision of children's meals and impertinent remarks to committee members. Perhaps Mrs. McMaster's standards were exacting. The fifth Matron, a Miss Fowler, was appointed in 1880 and remained for 6 years. She was highly regarded and in 1883, "as a vote of confidence," was presented with "a valuable silver locket and chain."[15]

The caliber of early nurses varied. Though in March of 1878, nurses were not proving entirely satisfactory, the previous year the Committee regretted the departure of a nurse who had left to be with her children in the Orphan's Home. Several early nurses had dependent children. In 1883, Nurse Carpenter requested that her adopted daughter live with her at H.S.C. and a night nurse was engaged who agreed to accept $6 per month instead of the usual $9, if she might have her only child with her. Early nurses were often referred to by Christian names, and we hear of Nurse Barbara in the boys ward and Nurse Nell who has a "nice motherly face, such as inspires confidence and affection."[16] Character was important as nurses were expected to impart moral training as part of their care. The 1886 Annual Report described H.S.C. nurses as spiritually minded, devoted Christians. In 1887, nurses, in their off duty time, organized Gospel meetings at a nearby lodging house, until the proprietor intervened.[17] Miss Fowler was obviously concerned about the status of the nurses and in 1883, suggested separate dining from the servants and the provision of a uniform.

The Committee demonstrated fairness and concern for the well-being of staff. An hour a day was allotted to each nurse for rest. Volunteer help was accepted to allow for vacations and in times of staff illness. In 1883 a nurses' home next to the hospital was provided. This secured "perfect quiet at night besides the advantage of rest in an atmosphere

314 *Women Founders, Nurses and the Care of*
Children at the Hospital for Sick
Children in Toronto 1875-1899

free from the taint of sickness."[18] The same year
Mrs. McMaster increased money for housekeeping
because she felt staff were denying themselves in
order to make ends meet.

The first formally trained nurse was hired in
1886. Miss Hannah Cody, a graduate of Toronto
General Hospital, replaced the Matron as Lady
Superintendent, starting a new era of nursing
supervision. The same year one pupil nurse was
accepted for training. She graduated in 1888. Growth
of the H.S.C. school was very modest because, by
1891, only 8 students had completed the informal
course. The Annual Report of 1890, however, does
describe Monday and Friday evening lectures by
doctors and the Lady Superintendent and the
provision of textbooks on nursing and physiology.

The provision of a modern hospital building
was a constant problem for the Ladies Committee
and led to the 1878 appointment of the first male
trustees. The role of the trustees, at this time, was
limited to the holding of property for H.S.C. In
1883, a wealthy Toronto businessman, John Ross
Robertson, donated a house on Toronto Island for
use as a summer hospital. He became increasingly
involved in H.S.C. affairs and a major financial
contributor. Robertson enjoyed his role as benefactor.
He was a jovial Santa Claus at Christmas and
arranged diversions such as sleigh rides for the
children. Although Robertson initially had no role in
management of the hospital, his wealth and local
influence made him a powerful force. In 1886, he
became Chairman of the Building Committee and
steered this work to successful completion. The new
hospital was to open in 1891 and in 1889 Mrs.
McMaster resigned as President of the Ladies
Committee in order to train as a nurse at the Illinois
Training School, Chicago. The Ladies Committee was
preparing to hand over management of H.S.C. to a
Board of Trustees, although it was agreed that after
completion of her training, Mrs. McMaster would
return as Lady Superintendent. In this capacity she

Women Founders, Nurses and the Care of 315
Children at the Hospital for Sick
Children in Toronto 1875-1899

would be responsible to the Trustees for day-to-day management of the hospital and supervision of nurses.

NEW HOSPITAL AND NEW MANAGEMENT: 1891 TO 1899

The new hospital in downtown Toronto was described as "Romanesque," "with a suggestion of the French Chateau." Called "an architectural monument for the city," it had "handsome red brick front, peaked towers, terra cotta ornaments, massive arched entrance and grand stone carvings."[19] Obviously the building was a far cry from the modest houses utilized up to this time and impoverished families must have been awed by the impressive facade and imposing interior. There was accommodation for at least 100 patients with large public wards 21 by 54 feet. It also had a few private rooms and 6 bed private wards which were designed to appeal to middle class, paying patients who might be newly attracted to the hospital by recent modest advances in medicine. It was also evident that hospitals themselves would become more respectable by encouraging a better class of clientele.[20] The small private units provided a marked contrast to the large impersonal public wards where the majority of children were cared for.

The move in September 1891 marked a major change in management when the Ladies Committee authorized transfer of all financial responsibility to a Board of Trustees. The Committee was to retain "charge of the household [and could] confer and make recommendations to the Trustees." The Annual Report described

"This happy arrangement whereby a large part of the burden of care . . . was transfered from the shoulders of a few weak women to those of strong and capable businessmen, [and] is regarded as a most remarkable answer to prayer."[21]

Robertson was elected Chairman of the Board.

Although the transfer seemed amicable, hard feelings quickly arose between Robertson and Mrs. McMaster and between Robertson and the Committee. In retrospect, clashes between the former seem inevitable, though they had worked together harmoniously in the past. Elizabeth McMaster, however, was not a weak woman. She had shown amazing strength in founding and managing H.S.C., but perhaps more remarkably had, as a recent widow with 4 children, undertaken a nurse's training at the age of 42. H.S.C. was her divine mission and she had dominated decision making for 16 years. Perhaps she did not realize the extent of the power which had been handed to Robertson and the Trustees.

The Ladies Committee found they no longer had much influence. Charge of the household was limited, because all expenditure, even such items as a meat chopper and apple corer, had to be approved. Robertson discounted prior claims by Committee members to the naming of wards, as he wished to reserve this privilege for major financial contributors. He planned more active fundraising, but his methods were contrary to Committee beliefs. They felt that if prayer was sufficiently fervent and consistent, God would provide; this philosophy was abhorrent to Robertson, who was determined to make H.S.C. fiscally sound. Instead of praying for funds, the Ladies found themselves praying for "kindly feelings between Trustees, the Committee and hospital staff, that all jealousies and hard feelings be done away."[22]

McMaster's leadership of nursing at H.S.C. was shortlived. In November 1891 there was serious disagreement with the Board when she sent out two nurses to a city hospital to assist with an outbreak of diphtheria. There were also differences of opinion with regard to the small H.S.C. training school. The Board felt H.S.C. was unable to provide an adequate training for a valid certificate, though they quickly

Women Founders, Nurses and the Care of   317
Children at the Hospital for Sick
Children in Toronto 1875-1899

reversed this decision as soon as McMaster left. Further controversy arose when McMaster nursed her sick daughter on the isolation ward at H.S.C. Robertson wished isolation staff to be totally separate in order to reduce the spread of infection, and in carrying out her duties the Lady Superintendent needed to move throughout the main wards. When McMaster herself became ill, the Ladies Committee prayed that their former President would have wisdom and patience when she met with opposition to her views. After a period recuperating, McMaster returned, but soon tendered her resignation. This was accepted with alacrity by the Board despite pleadings from the Committee. The Trustees denied a request that she be made honorary President of the Ladies Committee. The official reason for her departure was ill health and family obligations. Kesiah Underhill, housekeeper under McMaster, was appointed Acting Superintendent and remained for nearly 4 years. It is not known whether Underhill had trained as a nurse, though evidence points to the fact that she had not.

With more children, larger units, and a nurse training program, rules governing ward management and the discipline of staff proliferated. The regulations in 1897 stated,

> "Convalescent patients to rise at 6 am - nurse
> in charge will see toilets are properly made.
> Bed patients given water to wash. Helpless
> patients in charge of the day nurse."[23]

Day time diversion was still provided by visiting members of the Ladies Committee who brought dolls, books, sewing and woolwork. From 1892, a teacher from the Toronto Board of Education taught convalescent patients and those admitted for surgery.

In keeping with Victorian ideas of behavior, children were expected to tolerate discomfort and separation from family with equanimity. A five-year-old boy is described as "marvellous through intense suffering," never fretting "when his mother left," although "one of his strange little ways was to cover his head for hours together and only remove (the cover) for meals and medication."[24] A ten-year-old "tried to suppress tears when in pain so as not to give trouble."[25] Both had hip disease. Hip disease, attributed at the time to malnourishment, accidents or carrying younger children, remained the leading cause of admission through the 1890s, along with other orthopedic conditions. In the new hospital, the spread of infectious diseases, particularly diphtheria, is recorded with increasing frequency. Prayers were continually offered for those stricken with this much feared disease.

The majority of patients continued to come from poor homes and many required "drastic methods of purification" before entering the wards.[26] In 1897, 200 indigent patient families were investigated to make sure they were unable to contribute. The investigator found the homes "destitute of comfort" and reported that he had no idea poverty existed to such a degree.[27]

Nursing meanwhile was becoming a more respected profession, and the H.S.C. School slowly expanded. At the first formal graduation ceremony, in 1983, eight graduates received medals. Out of 15 graduates between 1886 and 1893, seven had supervisory jobs. There were 20 nurses in training and it was soon hoped to send out nurses for private duty.

Underhill, however, was proving less than satisfactory. In March 1894 the Committee was praying that Underhill be "considerate, sympathetic and kind and true to the interests of the children."[28] She was sent to a convention of nurses in New York City to gain useful knowledge. By 1896, Robertson cited the training school as weak. His report noted that the

> "Lady Superintendent was not agreeable or pleasant in manner and was inclined to be repellent. She had neither the general or technical education requisite for the job. [Her] choice of nurses was not advantageous . . . she was not capable of inspiring respect

Women Founders, Nurses and the Care of   319
Children at the Hospital for Sick
Children in Toronto 1875-1899

. . . [and was] capricious in her regulations."[29]
As a result Underhill was relieved of her responsibilities, given two months salary, and left precipitously.

Louise Brent, Superintendent of the Toronto Grace Hospital who had trained at the Brooklyn City Hospital, New York, was appointed. Brent proved to be a person of some stature who developed the school and became a noted nursing leader. When the *American Journal of Nursing* commenced publication in 1900, she was placed in charge of the children's section. There is little information on the relationship of the new Superintendent to the Ladies Committee. Brent did attend some of the weekly Committee meetings to discuss matters such as improvement in the laundry and graduating ceremonies. There is no direct evidence that nursing had a role in the decision of the Ladies Committee to leave H.S.C. However, the increasing role and prestige of the Lady Superintendent no doubt negated some of the contribution the Ladies Committee felt they could make.

Throughout the 1890s, the Committee continued with assigned housekeeping duties and visiting the children. Members remained as hospital Treasurer and Corresponding Secretary. There was communication with Robertson who sometimes came into devotional meetings. The Committee did appreciate his work but also prayed frequently for greater understanding of their role. The dream of a special ward for incurably ill children became more distant when the Board tightened admission criteria. The philosophy of Committee and Trustees appeared increasingly at odds and the "happy arrangement" increasingly unhappy as the decade passed.

The final departure of the Committee came as a direct result of further erosion of their responsibilities by a new male hospital Secretary. The Treasurer and Corresponding Secretary reported that their work had been taken away from them. A formal letter was written to Robertson regarding this slight. Robertson professed astonishment at the charges and was "much hurt."[30] He visited both ladies to apologize. However, differences appeared irreconcilable. Although Robertson indicated that he felt H.S.C. would be hurt by the Committee's departure, he gave them "little encouragement as to (their) work."[31] The Committee felt the hospital was "now efficiently run by employees" and found "their usefulness in it gone."[32]

When the Ladies Committee resigned from H.S.C. in 1899, to continue its work elsewhere,[33] a void was left in both the material and psychosocial care of the children. The ladies had organized physical necessities such as clothing and nutritious food, but most important, had provided for developmental needs such as play, attention and instruction. There is evidence that as H.S.C. expanded in the 1890s, the environment for the children became more institutionalized. Although professional nurses brought order and nursing expertise, it is unlikely that student nurses, controlled by strict routines and even stricter supervisors, could create a happy environment for the children.

H.S.C. was founded in an era when children's hospitals were primarily charity institutions providing food and shelter in a morally uplifting environment. Medical treatment was severely limited and there were no trained nurses in Canada. The Ladies Committee managed the small hospital as a Christian household and children benefited from a home-like atmosphere with childhood activities an essential part of daily routines. By the 1890s, advances in science, medicine and nursing were strongly influencing hospital planning and the H.S.C. quickly expanded. Scientific advance, with its promise of cure, became the paramount consideration, not a nurturing child-centered environment. The Ladies Committee left H.S.C. because they felt their usefulness had gone. Trained nurses, controlled by the Board of Trustees, had taken over the duties of day-to-day

Women Founders, Nurses and the Care of 321
Children at the Hospital for Sick
Children in Toronto 1875-1899

management. The nurses implemented the strict, militaristic regulations set by the Board. They did not, however, provide play and activities for the children, and in this way fill the void left by the departing Committee. Patients were now mainly confined to bed in large impersonal wards. The new pattern of care, with its militaristic rules and dehumanized, institutional environment set the stage for care in subsequent decades.

NOTES

1. Vogel, M.J. *The Invention of the Modern Hospital*. Chicago: University of Chicago Press, 1980, p. 24.
2. Hospital for Sick Children. *Annual Report 1882*. Deposited in the H.S.C. archives.
3. Graham, S. "Little Victims: Sick Children in Victorian Society." *Nursing Times*, 73 (1977), 1246-1248.
4. Goheen, P.G. *Victorian Toronto 1850-1900*. Chicago: University of Chicago Press, 1970, p. 57.
5. Annual Report 1887.
6. Annual Report 1876.
7. Annual Report 1882.
8. Annual Report 1882.
9. Ladies Committee of the Hospital for Sick Children. Minutes of Meetings. November 9, 1876. Deposited in the H.S.C. archives.
10. Committee Minutes February 4, 1879.
11. Committee Minutes March 5, 1879.
12. Annual Report 1884.
13. Committee Minutes May 4, 1883.
14. Committee Minutes November 5, 1880.
15. Committee Minutes January 26, 1883.
16. Annual Report 1883.
17. Annual Report 1887.
18. *The Hospital for Sick Children College Street Toronto*. Author and publisher unknown.

1891. p. 26.
19. *The Hospital for Sick Children*, p. 4.
20. Vogel, M. *The Invention of the Modern Hospital*. p. 77.
21. Annual Report 1892.
22. Committee Minutes, November 6, 1891.
23. Board of Trustees of the Hospital for Sick Children. Minutes of Meetings. February 10, 1897. Deposited in the H.S.C. archives.
24. Annual Report 1892.
25. Annual Report 1897.
26. Annual Report 1897.
27. Trustee Minutes, March 1897.
28. Committee Minutes, March 9, 1894.
29. Trustee Minutes, October 3, 1896.
30. Committee Minutes April 28, 1899.
31. Committee Minutes April 28, 1899.
32. Committee Minutes May 4, 1899.
33. The Ladies Committee subsequently founded Bloorview Hospital in Toronto for physically disabled children.

SECTION VI

BIBLIOGRAPHY

NIGHTINGALE BIBLIOGRAPHY

by

Bonnie Bullough

Vern Bullough

Lilli Sentz

Abbot, M.E. "Portraits of Florence Nightingale,"*Bost. Med. Surg. J.*, 175 (September 14, 1916): 413-422; (September 28, 1916): 453-457.

"Address by the Archbishop of York (Florence Nightingale Memorial Service)," *Nurs. Times* 66 (May 21, 1970): 670.

The Adelaide Nutting Historical Collection. Teachers College, Columbia University, New York, NY at Department of Nursing, School of Medicine, Columbia University and at School of Nursing, University of Kansas, Kansas City, KS. A collection of anecdotes, tributes, and letters relating to Miss Nightingale's life and career.

Agnew, L.R.C. "Florence Nightingale--Statistician," *Am. J. Nurs.* 58 (May 1958): 664-665.

Aikens, C.A. *Lessons From the Life of Florence Nightingale.* New York: Lakeside, 1915 (48 pp.).

Andrews, C.T. "Miss Nightingale at Scutari," *Nurs. Times*, 56 (December 30, 1960): 1624-1626.

Andrews, M.R.S. *A Lost Commander: Florence Nightingale.* Garden City, NY: Doubleday, Doran & Co., 1929 (299 pp.).

_____. "Soldier's Angel". *Great Lives, Great Deeds. Read. Digest*, (1964): 551-556.

"Angel in War: Miss Nightingale and Her Nurses," *Contemp.* 106 (September, 1914): 42-44.

Arango, L. "Florence Nightingale: Heroine of Hospitals," *Epheta*, 8 (October/December 1969): 13-26 (Spa.).

Arnstein, M.G. "Florence Nightingale's Influence on Nursing," *Bull. NY Acad. Med.*, 32 (1956): 540-546.

"At Embley Park and East Wellow," *Nurs. Times*, 33 (July 24, 1937): 730-731.

"At the Crimean Exhibition. The Florence Nightingale Relics,"*Nurs. Mirror*, 62 (January 18, 1936): 299.

Austin, R.F. "Health Contributions of Dr. Joseph Lister and Florence Nightingale," *J. Med. Assoc. Ala.*, 3 (October 1943): 149-151.

Ball, O.T. "Florence Nightingale," *Mod. Hosp.*, 78 (May 1952): 88-90, 144.

Baly, M.E. *Florence Nightingale and the Nursing Legacy.* Dover, NH: Croom Helm, 1986.

_____. "Florence Nightingale On Nursing Today," *Nurs. Times*, 65(1), (January 2, 1969): 1-4.

_____. "A New History of Nursing. Three. The Nurse: Elite (Florence Nightingale)," *Nurs. Times*, 80(42) (October 17-23, 1984): 55-57.

_____. "The Nightingale Nurses, 1860-1870," *Bull. Hist. Nurs. Group R. Coll. Nurs.*, 8 (Autumn 1985): 8-25.

_____. "The Nightingale Reforms and Hospital Architecture," *Bull. Hist. Nurs. Group R. Coll. Nurs.*, 11 (Autumn 1986): 1-7.

_____. "Shattering the Nightingale Myth," *Nursing Times*, 82(24) (June 11-18, 1986): 16-18.

Alldridge, L. *Florence Nightingale, Frances Ridley Havergal, Catherine Marsh and Mrs. Ranyard* (London: Cassell, 1885).

Bano, R. "Florence Nightingale: Pioneer of Nursing Profession," *Nurs. J. India*, 75(5) (May 1984): 99, 118.

Barnsley, R.E. "Miss Nightingale and the College (Royal Army Medical College)," *J. Roy. Army Med. Cps.*, 111(1), (1965): 66-73.

Barritt, E.R. "Florence Nightingale's Values and Modern Nursing Education," *Nurs. Forum* (Chic.) 12 (1973): 7-47.

Barth, R.S. *Fiery Angel: The Story of Florence Nightingale.* Coral Gables, FL: Glade House, 1945 (95 pp.). Fictionalized biographical sketch.

Baylen, J.O. "The Florence Nightingale-Mary Stanley Controversy: Some Unpublished Letters," *Med. Hist.*, 18(2), (April, 1974): 186-193.

Bellis, H. *Florence Nightingale. Women of Renown Series.* London: Newones, 1953 (43 pp.)

Bennett, B.A. "Florence Nightingale as an Educator," *Nurs. Mirror*, 91 (May 19, 1950): 147-148.

Benson, A.C. and Esher, V. (Eds.). *The Letters of Queen Victoria. A Selection from Her Majesty's Correspondence Between the Years 1837 and 1861*, 3 Vols. London: Murray, 1907.

Berges, F. and Berges, C. "A Visit to Scutari (Florence Nightingale)," *American Journal of Nursing* 86(7) (July 1986): 811-813.

Berkeley, R. *The Lady with the Lamp*. London: Gollancz, 1929 (136 pp.).

Berman, J.F. "Forentia and the Clarabellas--A Tribute to Nurses" (Nightingale, F., Barton, C., Maas, C.), *J. Ind. Med. Assoc.*, 67 (August 1974): 717-719.

Bishop, W.J. *Bio-bibliography of Florence Nightingale*. Completed by Sue Goldie. London: Dawsons of Pall Mall, 1962 (160 pp.).

_____. "Florence Nightingale's Letters," *Am. J. Nurs.*, 57 (May 1957): 607-609.

Blanc, E. "Nightingale Remembered - Reflections on Times Past," *California Nurse*, 75(10) (May 1980): 7.

Blanchard, J.R. "Florence Nightingale--A Study in Vocation," *New Zeal. Nurs.*, 32 (June 1939): 193-197.

Blanchard, R. "Life of Florence Nightingale," *Hosp. Prog.*, 11 (November 1930): 490-492.

Blomquist, R. "Elisabet Dillner and the Uppsala Museum of Medicine and Nursing," *News Lett. Florence N. Int. Nurs. Assoc.* (1973): 4-7.

Boissier, P. "Florence Nightingale und Henry Dunant. Zwei verwandte Schicksale. *Jahrb. Univ. Duesseld.* (1970/71): 273-282.

Boisvert, D.J. "Florence Nightingale's Cap," *N. Engl. Galaxy* 20 (2) (1978): 42-51.

Bower, C.R. "Another Portrait of Miss Nightingale," *Am. J. Nurs.*, 28 (November 1928): 1099-1100.

Boyd, N. *Josephine Butler, Octavia Hill, Florence Nightingale: Three Victorian Women Who Changed Their World.* London, Macmillan, 1982.

Bridges, D.C. "Florence Nightingale Centenary" (Editorial), *Int. Nurs. Rev. News*, 1 (April 1954): 3.

Broe, E.J. "Florence Nightingale and Her International Influence," *Int. Nurs. Rev. News*, 1 (April 1954): 17-19.

_____. "Florence Nightingale--International Pioneer," *New Zeal. Nurs. J.* 47 (April 1954): 44-47.

"The Carriage Used by Miss Florence Nightingale in the Crimean War," *Nurs. Notes & Mid Chron.*, 46 (July 1933): 97.

Bullough, B., Bullough, V., Eleano, B. *Nursing: A Historical Bibliography.* New York: Garland, 1981.

Cartwright, F.F. Miss Nightingale's Dearest Friend," *Proc. R. Soc. Med.* 69(3) (March 1976): 169-175.

Charles, W. *Florence Nightingale: The Lady From Scutari.* Rev. Ed. London: Blackie, 1969.

Chavez, N. "Florence Nightingale: Her Life and the Projection of Her Work in Modern Nursing," *Enfermeras*, 14 (January-June 1967): 28-36 (Sp.).

Church of St. John the Evangelist. *The Love Story of Florence Nightingale and John Smithurst.* Elora, Ont.: 1963.

Clayton, R.E. "How Men May Live and Not Die in India (Florence Nightingale)," *Australasian Nurses Journal* 2(33) (April 1974): 10-11 passim.

_____. "Florence Nightingale's Work in India," *Nurs. J. India*, 65 (October 1974): 261ff.

Cohen, B. "Florence Nightingale," *Pour. Sci.* (79) (1984): 66-75.

Cohen, I.B. "Florence Nightingale," *Scientific American* 250(3) (March 1984): 128-137.

Colby-Monteith, M. "The Angel of the Crimea and More," *Pac. Cst. J. Nurs.* 33 (May 1937): 284-286.

Collins, W.J. "Florence Nightingale and District Nursing," *Nurs. Mirror* 81 (May 12, 1945): 74.

Columbia University. *Catalog of the Florence Nightingale Collection.* New York: Department of Nursing Alumnae Association, 1956 (79 pp.).

Cook, E. "Florence Nightingale," *Nurs. Times,* 50 (January 2, 1954): 4-6 through (December 24, 1954): 1438-1439.

_____. *The Life of Florence Nightingale,* 2 Vols. London: Macmillan & Co., 1913-1914, and subsequent editions.

Cook, E. and Nash, R. *A Short Life of Florence Nightingale.* New York: Macmillan, 1931.

Cooper, L.U. *The Young Florence Nightingale.* New York: Roy, 1960.

Cope, Z. "Florence Nightingale and District Nursing," *Dist. Nurs.,* 1 (November 1958): 179-180.

_____. "Florence Nightingale and Nurses' Duties," *Dist. Nurs.,* 1 (December 1958): 213-214.

_____. "Florence Nightingale and Her Nurses," *Nurs. Times,* 56 (May 13, 1960): 597-598.

_____. *Florence Nightingale and the Doctors.* Philadelphia: J.B. Lippincott, 1958 (163 pp.).

_____. "John Shaw Billings, Florence Nightingale and the Johns Hopkins Hospital," *Med. Hist.,* 1 (1957): 367-368.

_____. *Six Disciples of Florence Nightingale*. London: Pitman Medical, 1961 (74 pp.).

Coxhead, E. "Miss Nightingale's Country Hospital," *Country Life*, 152 (November 23, 1972): 1362-1364.

"A Criticism of Miss Florence Nightingale" (Editorial), *Nurs. Times*, 3 (February 2, 1907): 89.

Cruse, P. "Florence Nightingale", *Surgery* 88(3) (September 1980): 394-399.

Davey, C. *Lady With A Lamp*. New York: Roy, 1956.

"The Death of Florence Nightingale," *Am. J. Nurs.*, 10 (September 1910): 919-920; see also *Bost. Med. Surg. J.*, 163 (August 25, 1910): 335.

Dean, E. (Alderman). *Great Women of the Christian Faith*. New York: Harper and Row, 1959 (pp. 214-217).

Deniz, E. "Florence Nightingale," *Turk. Hemire Derg.*, 20 (April-June 1970): 5-8 (Turk.).

Dennis, K.E. "Florence Nightingale: Yesterday, Today and Tomorrow," *Advances in Nursing Science* 7(2) (January 1985): 66-81.

Diebolt, B. and Malterre-Barthes, A. "The Centennial of a School. Historical Wealth and Transmission of Values. The Florence Nightingale School at Bagatelle," *Soins* 454 (May 1985): 45-47.

Dilworth, A.W. (Ed.). "Florence Nightingale Bibliography," *Nurs. Res.* 5 (October 1956): 85-88.

Dock, L.L. "English Letter," *Am. J. Nurs.*, 14 (June 1914): 728-730.

Dodd, E.F. *Florence Nightingale*. Madras: Macmillan, 1957.

Draper, J.M. "A Brief Sketch of the Life of Florence Nightingale," *Tr. Nurs.*, 38 (January 1907): 1-4.

Dunbar, V.M. "Florence Nightingale's Influence on Nursing Education," *Int. Nurs. Rev.*, 1 (October 1954): 17-23.

Dwyer, B.A. "The Mother of Our Modern Nursing System," *Filipino Nurs.*, 12 (January 1937): 8-10.

Dyhre, B. "You Can Speak Realistically About Nightingale," *Sygeplejersken* 77(6) (February 9, 1977): 15.

Ellett, E.C. "Florence Nightingale," *Tr. Nurs.*, 32 (May 1904): 305-310.

Elton, L. "Florence Nightingale," *Nurs. Times*, 35 (December 2, 1939): 1442-1443.

Emerson, H. "Miss Nightingale: R.N., U.S.A.," *Survey*, 50 (May 1, 1923): 184-185.

"An Evening with Florence Nightingale," *Hosp. Prog.*, 1 (May 1920): 41-53; 3 (April 1923): 202-204; 4 (March 1924): 163-165.

Fernandez, C., Gusine, F., Pardo, A. and Sales, D. "The Model of Florence Nightingale," *Revista De Enfermeria* 9(1) (January 1986): 35-39.

Fink, L.G. "Catholic Influences in the Life of Florence Nightingale," *Hosp. Prog.*, 15 (December 1934): 482-489.

Fleming, T.J. "Beauties Who Changed the Course of History," *Cosmopolitan*, 140 (June 1956): 24.

"F.N.," *Am. J. Nurs.*, 36 (November 1937): 1198-1200.

"Florence Nightingale," *Am. J. Nurs.*, 35 (May 1935): 402; see also *Aust. Nurs. J.*, 6 (February 1908): 48; *Hosp.* (London), 31 (February 1935): 50; Editorial *Med. Dial.* 5 (July 1903): 122-124; *Nurs. J. India* 1 (September 1910): 162-166; *Nurs. Mirror* 99 (May 7, 1954): viii; 103 (May 11, 1956): i; *Nurs. Times* 30 (November 3, 1934): 997; *Pac. Cst. J. Nurs.* 19 (May 1923): 281-287.

"Florence Nightingale, May 12, 1980--August 13, 1910," *Pub. Hlth. Nurs.*, 23 (May 1931): 232; see also 24 (May 1932): 252; 25 (May 1933): 25.

"Florence Nightingale as a Leader in the Religious and Civic Thought of Her Time," *Hosp.*, 10 (July 1936): 78-84.

"Florence Nightingale as a Young Woman--Born May 12, 1820," *Nurs. Mirror*, 95 (May 9, 1953): i.

"Florence Nightingale at 73" (Editorial), *Nurs. Times*, 24 (November 3, 1928): 1330.

"The Florence Nightingale Bibliography," *So. Afr. Nurs. J.*, 22 (April 1956): 16.

"Florence Nightingale Bibliography is Compiled" (News), *Mod. Hosp.*, 36 (May 1931): 126.

"Florence Nightingale Celebration in New York," *Johns Hop. Nurs. Alum. Mag.*, 9 (June 1910): 66-68.

"Florence Nightingale Commemorative Plaque in British Cemetery, Istanbul, (Turkey)," *Nurs. Mirror*, 99 (June 11, 1954): 698.

"The Florence Nightingale Lamp" (Editorial), *Prac. Nurs. Dig.*, 1 (July 1954): 26.

"Florence Nightingale Medal," *Rev. Int. Croix Rge*, 37 (November 1955): 730-736.

"Florence Nightingale, O.M.," *Brit. J. Nurs.*, 45 (August 20, 1910): 141-147.

"Florence Nightingale Pledge for Nurses," *Nurs. Mirror*, 99 (May 7, 1954): 40.

"Florence Nightingale--Supposed Portrait," *Nurs. Mirror*, 59 (April 28, 1954): 63.

"Florence Nightingale's Letter of Advice to Bellevue (Hospital School of Nursing, New York, NY)," *Am. J. Nurs.*, 11 (February 1911): 361-364.

"Florence Nightingale's Voice," *Am. J. Nurs.*, 35 (October 1935): 958.

"Florence Nightingale's War Cart," *Nurs. Mirror*, 52 (November 22, 1930): 155.

"Florence Nightingale's Work for Public Health" (Editorial), *Am. J. Pub. Hlth.*, 4 (June 1914): 510-511.

Folendorf, G.R. "Florence Nightingale, Her Service to Mankind," *Pac. Cst. J. Nurs.*, 35 (July 1939): 406-407.

Foley, E.L. "A Pilgrimage to the Shrine," *Am. J. Nurs.*, 20 (December 1919): 232-234

Fox, E. "Florence Nightingale Revisited: Or Scenes From Village Life," *Bull. Hist. Nurs. Group R. Coll. Nurs.* 10 (Spring 1986): 1-8.

Fraga, M. and Tenebaum, L. "Florence Nightingale--Model for Today's Nurse," *Florida Nurse* 29(5) (May 1981): 11.

Frankenstein, L. "The Lady With a Lamp," *Red. Cr. Courier*, 16 (December 1936): 15-17.

French, Y. *Florence Nightingale, 1820-1910.* London: Hamish Hamilton, 1954.

"From the Journal 50 Years Ago," *Am. J. Nurs.*, 54 (May 1954): 591.

"Fynes-Clinton Memorial Lecture. Florence Nightingale," *Nurs. Notes & Mid. Chron.*, 46 (July 1933): 97.

Garnett, E. *Florence Nightingale's Nuns.* New York: Farrar, Straus & Cudahy, 1961.

Gilgannon, Sr. Mary McAuley. *The Sisters of Mercy as Crimean War Nurses.* Notre Dame, IN: University of Notre Dame Unpublished Dissertation, 1962.

Gill, F.C. "Glorious Company," *Epworth*, 1 (1958): 132.

Goldie, S.M. (Ed.) *I have Done My Duty: Florence Nightingale in the Crimean War, 1954-56.* Iowa City: University of Iowa Press, 1987. 326 pp.

Goldie, S. and Bishop, W.J. *A Calendar of the Letters of Florence Nightingale.* Oxford: Oxford Microform Publications for the Wellcome Institute for the History of Medicine, 1983.

Goldsmith, M. *Florence Nightingale. The Woman and the Legend.* London: Hodder & Stoughton, 1937 (320 pp.).

Goldwater, S.S. "Seeing Hospitals with Florence Nightingale," *Mod. Hosp.*, 35 (September 1930): 57-59.

Gonzalez, M.R. "Florence Nightingale," *Salub y assist.*, 5 (January-February 1946): 103-109 (Sp.).

Gordon, J.E. "A 17th Century Florence Nightingale," *Ctry. Life (Lond.)* 150 (1871): 155-156.

_____. "Nurses and Nursing in Britain. 21. The Work of Florence Nightingale. I. For the Health of the Army," *Midwife & Health Visitor* 8(10) (October 1972): 351-359.

_____. "Nurses and Nursing in Britain. 22. The Work of Florence Nightingale. II. The Establishment of Nurse Training in Britain," *Midwife & Health Visitor* 8(11) (November 1972): 391-396.

_____. "Nurses and Nursing in Britain. 23. The Work of Florence Nightingale. 3. Her Influence Throughout the World." *Midwife & Health Visitor* 9(1) (January 1973): 17-22.

_____. "Distinguished British Nurses of the Past. 5. Mrs. Sarah Wardroper--Florence Nightingale's Collaborator," *Midwife Health Visit Community Nurse* 11(9) (September 1975): 203-301.

Gordon, R. *The Private Life of Florence Nightingale.* London: William Heinemann, 1978.

Gould, M. "A Woman of Parts. F. Nightingale," *News Lett. Florence N. Int. Nurs. Assoc.,* 21 (Autumn 1970): 4.

_____, and Gamlen, C. "A Woman of Parts (F. Nightingale)," *Nurs. Times,* 66 (May 7, 1970): 606-607.

_____. "A Woman of Parts. Florence Nightingale," (Japan) *Sogo Kango Comprehensive Nursing Quarterly* 15(1) (1980): 95-99.

Grant, D. "British Nurse in Turkey--1954," *Nurs. Mirror,* 99 (May 7, 1954): 367.

"Greatness in Little Things. Some Unpublished Letters of Florence Nightingale with Comments by David Cleghorn Thomson," *Nurs. Times,* 50 (May 8, 1954): 508-510.

Greenleaf, W.H. "Biography and the Amateur Historian: Mrs. Woodham-Smith's Florence Nightingale," *Victorian Stud.,* 3 (1959): 190-202.

Greenwood, M. *Some British Pioneers of Social Medicine.* London: Oxford University Press, 1948, pp. 98-106.

Grier, B. and Grier, M. "Contributions of the Passionate Statistician (Florence Nightingale)," *Res. Nurs. Health* 1(3) (October 1978): 103-109.

Grier, M.R. "Florence Nightingale: Saint or Scientist?," *Res. Nurs. Health* 1(3) (October 1978): 91.

Grigson, G., and Gibbs-Smith, C.H. *People.* New York: Hawthorn, 1956, p. 306.

Grunnston, D. "Pioneers in the Art of Healing. 1. Florence Nightingale . . .," *Brit. J. Nurs.*, 100 (October 1952): 103-104; 100 (December 1952): 123; 101 (January 1953): 101-108.

Guzman, G. de. "Florence Nightingale," *Filipino Nurs.*, 10 (July 1935): 10-14.

Haldane, E. *Mrs. Gaskell and her Friends.* New York: Appleton, 1931 (318 pp.).

Hall, E.F. *Florence Nightingale.* New York: Macmillan Co., 1920 (84 pp.).

Hallock, G.T., and Turner, C.E. *Florence Nightingale.* New York: Metropolitan Life Insurance Co., 1928 (24 pp.).

_____. *Florence Nightingale and the Founding of Professional Nursing.* New York: Metropolitan Life Insurance Co., 1959 (24 pp.).

Hallowes, R. "Distinguished British Nurses--14. Florence Nightingale." *Nurs. Mirror*, 105 (September 27, 1957): viii-x.

Hamesh, D.D.M. "Florence Nightingale's Writings," *Nurs. J. India*, 63 (May 1972): 149 passim.

Harding, W.G. "Florence Nightingale's Lamp," *Ohio St. Med. J.*, 56 (1960): 176.

Harmelink, B. *Florence Nightingale.* New York: Watts, 1969.

Haydon, A.L. *Florence Nightingale: A Heroine of Mercy.* London: Andrew Melrose, 1908 (107 pp.).

Hearn, M.J. "Florence Nightingale," *Quart. J. Chin. Nurs.*, 1 (April 1920): 12-14.

Hebert, R.G. *Florence Nightingale--Saint, Reformer, or Rebel?* Malabar, FL: Krieger, 1981.

"Her Letters (Florence Nightingale)," *Nurs. J. India*, 46 (June 1955): 210; 46 (July 1955): 236; 46 (August 1955): 268; (October 1955): 326.

Hill, A.J. "Nightingale, Sainte ou Diablesse?" *Infirm. Can.* 10 (November 1980): 34-36.

"Historic Carriage," *So. Afr. Nurs. J.*, 20 (May 1954): 23.

Holmes, M. *Florence Nightingale: A Cameo Life-Sketch*. London: Women's Freedom League, 1912 (20 pp.).

Hosono, K. "The Logical Structure in the 'Notes on Nursing' (Florence Nightingale)," *Sogo Kango - Comprehensive Nursing Quarterly* 15(4) (1982): 51-60. (Jap.)

"House Party at Embley Park," *Nurs. Mirror*, 103 (August 31, 1956): viii-x.

Houstoun, J.F. *Names of Renown*. Glasgow: Gibson, 1954, pp. 166-177.

Hubble, A. "William Ogle of Derby and Florence Nightingale," *Med. Hist.*, 3 (July 1959): 201-211.

Hurd, H.M. "Florence Nightingale--A Force in Medicine," *Johns Hop. Nurs. Alum. Mag.*, 9 (June 1910): 68-81.

Huxley, E. *Florence Nightingale*. New York: G.P. Putnam's Sons, Inc., London: Weidenfeld & Nicolson, 1975 (354 pp.).

Inoue, N. "Life of Florence Nightingale and Effects of Her Teachings," *Kango, Kyoshitsu* 16 (May 1972): 14-20 (Jap.).

Isler, C.N. "Florence Nightingale. The Call To War," *RN*, 33 (May 1970): 42, 45, 74; "The Early Years," 33, (May 1970): 39, 41; "The Final Years," 33 (May 1970): 50, 52; "The Great Experiment," 33 (May 1970): 46, 49; "Rebel with a Cause," 33 (May 1970): 35, 37.

Isphording, B. *Florence Nightingale en de Verpleging Van Toen Tot Nu.* (Lochem, Stichting) *Tijdschrift voor Ziekenverpleging.*, 1970, 96 pp. (Dutch)

_____. "Florence Nightingale: enn Merkwaardiga Vrouw en Haar Geschiedenis," *Tijdschr. Ziekenverpl.* 23 (April 28, 1970): 447–452. (Dutch)

Iveson-Iveson, J. "Nurses in Society: A Legend in the Breaking (Florence Nightingale)," *Nursing Mirror* 156(19) (May 11, 1983): 26–27.

Jake, D.G. "Florence Nightingale . . . Mission Impossible," *Arz. Med.*, 32(11), (November 1975): 894–895.

James, A.C. "Florence Nightingale. The Great Teacher of Nurses," *Pac. Cst. J. Nurs.*, 16 (May 1920): 282–285.

_____. *Is That Lamp Going Out? To the Heroic Memory of Florence Nightingale.* New York: Hodder & Stoughton, 1911 (48 pp.).

Jaro, H.J.A. "Florence Nightingale. A Life of Wisdom and Courage at the Service of Justice and Mercy," *J. Int. Coll. Surg.*, 34(6), (1960): Sect. 2, 13–15.

Johansson, B. *"God Bless You, My Dear Miss Nightingale": Letters from Emmy Caroline Rappe to Florence Nightingale 1867-1870.* Stockholm: Almqvist & Wiksell International, 1977, 57 pp. (Stockholm Studies in English, 38.)

Jones, A.H. "The White Angel: Hollywood's Image of Florence Nightingale," in *Images of Nurses*, ed. A.H. Jones. Philadelphia: U of Penn Press, 1978.

Jones, H.W. "Some Unpublished Letters of Florence Nightingale," *Bull. Hist. Med.* 8 (November 1940): 1389–1396.

Kalisch, B.J. and Kalisch, P.A. "Heroine Out of Focus: Media Images of Florence Nightingale. Part I. Popular Biographies and Stage Productions. *Nursing & Health Care* 4(4) (April 1983): 181-187.

_____. "Heroine Out of Focus: Media Images of Florence Nightingale. Part II. Film, Radio, and Television Dramatizations," *Nursing & Health Care* 4(5) (May 1983): 270-278.

Kanai, K. "Florence Nightingale and the World of Modern Nursing Philosophy--A Study of the Religious and Non-religious Aspects," (II) (Japan) *Sogo Kango - Comprehensive Nursing Quarterly* 11(4) (1976): 76-98.

_____. "Literature on Nightingale and Related Matters - My Search of the Literature on Florence Nightingale," *Sogo Kango - Comrpehensive Nursing Quarterly* 14(1) (January 1979): 67-90. (Jap.)

Kaneko, M. "An Encounter with Nightingale," *Sogo Kango - Comprehensive Nursing Quarterly* 14(4) (1980): 22-28. (Jap.)

_____. "The Nature of Observation Expressed in the Observation of the Sick: (Florence Nightingale)," *Sogo Kango - Comprehensive Nursing Quarterly* 16(4) (1982): 40-50. (Jap.)

Karll, A. "Florence Nightingale," *Nurs. J. India* 74(5) (May 1983): 110.

Karman, T. "Florence Nightingale, Pioneer of Public Health Statistics," *Orv. Hetil.*, 112 (April 4, 1971): 813-815 (Hun.).

Kawakita, Y. "Nightingale in the History of Medical Philosophy--On the Meaning of Health," *Kango* 34(2) (February 1982): 39-53. (Jap.)

Kerling, N.J. "Letters from Florence Nightingale," *Nurs. Mirror*, 143(1) (July 1, 1976): 68.

Kiereini, E.M. "The Way Ahead: On the Occasion of Florence Nightingale Oration at the Perth Concert Hall-Australia, 24th October, 1979. "The Way Ahead," *Kenya Nursing Journal* 10(1) (June 1981): 5-8.

Kim, Y.M. "Florence Nightingale," *Korean Nurse*, 6 (1967): 174-176 (Kor.).

King, F.A. "Miss Nightingale and Her Ladies in the Crimea," *Nurs. Mirror*, 100 (October 22, 1954): 11-12; 100 (October 29, 1954): 8-9; 100 (November 5, 1954): 5-6; 100 (November 12, 1954): 10-11.

Kodama, K. "From the Old Notes on Florence Nightingale," *Songo Kango Comprehensive Nursing Quarterly* 15(4) (1980): 12-17. (Jap.)

_____. "Care and Cure Defined in the 'Notes on Nursing: (Florence Nightingale)'," *Sogo Kango - Comprehensive Nursing Quarterly* 16(4) (1982): 29-39. (Jap.)

Koike, A. "Hitherto Unknown Profile of Florence Nightingale," *Sogo Kango - Comprehensive Nursing Quarterly* 15(1) (1980): 100-108. (Jap.)

Kominami, Y. "Literature on Florence Nightingale," *Compr. Nurs. Q.*, 7 (Summer 1972): 25-54. (Jap.)

Konami, Y. "Studies on Nightingale: The Role of the Matron," *Sogo Kango - Comprehensive Nursing Quarterly* 15(4) (1980): 29-36. (Jap.)

Konderska, Z. "The Birthday of Nursing (Florence Nightingale)," *Pieleg. Polozna.*, 8 (October 1971): 12-13 (Pol.)

Konstantinova, M. "Student Nurses' Page. In the Cradle of Nursing," *Am. J. Nurs.*, 24 (October 1923): 47-49.

Kopf, E.W. "Florence Nightingale as Statistician," *Res. Nurs. Health* 1(3) (October 1978): 93-102.

Kovacs, A.R. "The Personality of Florence Nightingale," *Int. Nurs. Rev.*, 20 (May-June 1973): 78-86. Reprint *Sogo Kango: Comprehensive Nursing Quarterly* (1976): 66-74.

Kroksnes, I. "Florence Nightingale--Fearless, Well-informed Nursing Administrator," *Kroksnes I Sykepleien*, 62(9), (May 5, 1975): 378-379 (Nor.).

Kurumada, M. "Introductory Notes on Lying-in Institutions and Problems of Management--Hospital Management and Florence Nightingale," *Sogo Kango - Comprehensive Nursing Quarterly* 18(1) (1983): 107-119. (Jap.)

Kyogoku, T. and Kanai, K. "On Florence Nightingale's 'Notes on Saving of the Poor': A Discussion," *Sogo Kango - Comprehensive Nursing Quarterly* 20(2) (May 1985): 83-102. (Jap.)

"The Lady with a Lamp," *Nurs. Times*, 25 (February 9, 1929): 154; *Pub. Hlth. Nurs.*, 21 (May 1929): 227-229.

"The Lady with a Lamp. A Noble Tribute to a Noble Woman," *Mid. Chron. & Nurs. Notes*, 64 (October 1951): 304-305.

Lammond, D. *Florence Nightingale*. London: Duckworth, 1935 (144 pp.).

Large, J.T. "Florence Nightingale, 1830-1910: A Nurse For All Times," *PA. Nurse* 40(4) (April 1985): 5, 12.

Lear, E. "Nightingale, Florence--Drawings Made at Scutari," *Med. Press*, 241 (1959): 89.

Lee, C.A. "Discussion/Life of Florence Nightingale," *Kansas Nurse* 62(5) (May 1987): 12-13.

_____. "Thrusts of Florence Nightingale in the Social Context of the 19th Century," *Kansas Nurse* 62(2) (February 1987): 3-4.

Lee, E. "A Florence Nightingale Collection," *Am. J. Nurs.*, 38 (May 1938): 555-561.

Leighton, M. *The Story of Florence Nightingale.* New York: Grosset & Dunlap, 1964.

Leslie, S. "Forgotten Passages in the Life of Florence Nightingale," *Dublin Review*, Oct. 22, 1954, 90-98.

Leslie, S. *Henry Edward Manning, His Life and Labours*, 2nd Ed. London: Burns, Oates & Washbourne, 1921 (520 pp.).

Letters From Florence Nightingale to Rev'd Mother Mary Care Moore (Co-Workers on the Crimean War) London: 14 Sisters of Bermondsey, 1982.

"The Letters of Florence Nightingale," *Dist. Nurs.*, 1 (May 1958): 37-38; (June 1958): 61-63.

Levine, M.E. "Florence Nightingale. The Legend That Lives," *Sogo Kango - Comprehensive Nursing Quarterly* 6 (Fall 1971): 38-46.

Levy, G. *Arthur Hugh Clough, (1819-1961).* London: Sidgwick, 1938 (236 pp.).

Linden, K. "Florence Nightingale is Placed Among Mankind's Benefactors," *Am. J. Nurs.*, 50 (May 1950): 265.

Litchfield, H. (Ed.). *Emma Darwin. A Century of Family Letters, 1792-1896.* London: Murray, 1915.

"Literature on Florence Nightingale," *Hosp. Prog.*, 12 (April 1931): 188.

Longford, E. *Emminent Victorian Women.* London: Weiden and Nicolson, 1981.

Lyons, B. "Nursing Revisited: What Florence Nightingale Would Say," *Prarie Rose* 53(4) (October-December 1984): 16.

MacDonnell, F. *Miss Nightingale's Young Ladies: The Story of Lucy Osburn and Sydney Hospital.* Sydney: Angus & Robertson, 1970.

Mackie, T.T. "Florence Nightingale and Tropical and Military Medicine," *Am. J. Trop. Med.*, 22 (January 1942): 1-8.

Makabe, G. "Foundation of Nursing. Letter Collection of Florence Nightingale," *Sogo Kango - Comprehensive Nursing Quarterly* 17(4) (1982): 8-34. (Jap.)

_____. "Nightingale's Expectation on Women--An Impression of Her Writings," *Sogo-Kango - Comprehensive Nursing Quarterly* 15(4) (1980) 70-72. (Jap.)

Marks, G., and Beatty, W.K. *Women in White.* New York: Charles Scribner, 1971 pp. 161-174.

Maruoka, R. "Description of Florence Nightingale and Her Ideals," *Kangogaku Zasshi - Japanese Journal of Nursing* 52 (3) (March 1988): 268-276. (Jap.)

"Mary Baker Eddy Mentioned Them," *Christian Science Sentinel.* Boston: Christian Science Pub., 1961, pp. 160-161.

Masson, F. *Victorians All.* London: Chambers, 1931 (128 pp.).

Matensen, R. "Nightingale--No Rebel Behind the Myth," *Sykepleien*, 64 (1977): 1022-1024 (Nor.).

"Materials for the Study of Florence Nightingale," *Tr. Nurs.*, 86 (May 1931): 656-657.

Matheson, A. *Florence Nightingale. A Biography.* London: Nelson, 1913 (374 pp.).

Maxwell, J.P. "Florence Nightingale," *Quart. J. Chin. Nurs.*, 11 (January 1930): 16-25.

McFee, I.N. *The Story of Florence Nightingale.* Dansville, NY: F.A. Owen, MD.

McInnes, E.M. "Florence Nightingale and the Goddess (Letters from Florence Nightingale to Rachel Williams Recently Presented to St. Thomas's)," *St. Thom. Hosp. Gaz.*, 61 (1963): 73-74.

McKee, E.S. "Florence Nightingale and Her Followers," *Washville J. Med. Surg.*, 103 (September 1909): 385-392.

"Memories of Florence Nightingale," *Nurs. Times*, 35 (August 12, 1939): 1008.

Menon, M. "The Lamp She Lit (Florence Nightingale)," *Nursing Journal of India* 71(8) (August 1980): 214-215.

"Military Nursing. Florence Nightingale--Military Nurse," *J. Am. Med. Assoc.*, 187 (1964): 672-673.

Miller, B.W. *Florence Nightingale, The Lady and the Lamp.* Grand Rapids Zondervan Pub. House, 1950.

"Miscellany. Florence Nightingale's Medals," *Bos. Med. & Surg. J.*, 165 (September 7, 1911): 391.

"Miss Florence Nightingale: Signatures of 650 St. Thomas Nurses," *Nurs. Mirror*, 28 (May 19, 1900): 95.

"Miss Goodrich's Nightingale Tribute," *Tr. Nurs. Hosp. Rev.*, 97 (August 1936): 130.

"Miss Nightingale, Minister of Health," *Nurs. Times*, 27 (May 9, 1931): 529-530.

Monteiro, L. "Letters to a Friend (Florence Nightingale, Catherine Marsh)," *Nurs. Times*, 69 (November 8, 1973): 1474-1476.

_____. "Response in Anger: Florence Nightingale on the Importance of Training for Nurses," *Journal of Nursing History* 1(1) (November 1985): 11-18.

_____. "Forum on Historical Research. Response in Anger--An Unsent Letter to the Editor: Investigation of a Letter Written by Florence Nightingale," *Nurs. Res. Conf.* (9) (1973): 283-293.

Moore, M.F. *Florence Nightingale, Pioneer of Nursing.* London: Macmillan, 1960.

Moriyama, Y. "Health and Various Historical Eras: The Concepts of Health Held by Hippocrates, Thomas Moore, Francis Bacon, and Nightingale and Their Historical Backgrounds," *Kango Kyoiku - Japanese Journal of Nurses Education* 26(9) (September 1985): 555-569.

Morney, P. de. *Best Years of Our Lives.* New York: Century Press, 1955 pp. 88-100.

Mosby, C.V. *A Little Journey to the Home of Florence Nightingale.* St. Louis: C.V. Mosby, 1938 (38 pp.).

Muir, C.S. *Women, The Makers of History.* New York: Vantage Press, 1956, pp. 162-166.

Mukano, N. and Kanai, H. "Notes on Pauperism by Florence Nightingale, *Sogo Kango - Comprehensive Nursing Quarterly* 20(1) (February 1985): 53-79. (Jap.)

Muraki, K. "Florence Nightingale," *Kango Gijutsu - Japanese Journal of Nursing Art* 31(6) (April 1985): 749-750. (Jap.)

Murrow, E.R. *This I Believe: 2.* New York: Simon & Schuster, 1954, pp. 204-206.

Murthi, A.N.S. *Names You Should Know.* Ambala, Cant., India: Army Educ. Stores, 1954, pp. 65-73.

Nagasawa, Y. "Encounter with Nightingale - A Discovery of Nightingale in the Field of Hospital Designs," *Sogo Kango - Comprehensive Nursing Quarterly* 15(4) (1980): 59-69. (Jap.)

Nagatoya, Y. "Publication on History of Nursing and Florence Nightingale. Additional Notes," *Jap. J. Nurs. Educ.*, 11 (March 1970): 60-63 (Jap.).

_____. "Florence Nightingale's Influence on the Science of Nursing in Japan." In *Proceedings of the XXIII International Congress of the History of Medicine.* London, 1974, pp. 467-469.

Naree-Rochanapuranada (nfn). "Florence Nightingale and Modern Nursing," *Thai Nurs. Assoc. J.*, 3 (July 1965) L: 185-180 (Thai).

Nash, R. (Ed.). *Florence Nightingale to her Nurses.* London: Macmillan & Co., 1914 (147 pp.).

_____. *A Short Life of Florence Nightingale: Abridged from the Life by Sir Edward Cook.* New York: Macmillan, 1925 (404 pp.).

_____. *A Sketch of the Life of Florence Nightingale.* London: Soc. for Promoting Christian Knowledge, 1937 (32 pp.).

_____. "Florence Nightingale According to Mr. Strachey," *Nineteenth Century* 103 (Feb. 1928), 258-65.

National League for Nursing Education. *Early Leaders of Nursing Education (Calendar 1921).* New York: The League, 1920.

_____. *Early Leaders of Nursing Education (Calendar 1931).* New York: The League, 1930.

Nauright, L. "Politics and Power: A New Look at Florence Nightingale," *Nursing Forum* 21(1) (1984): 5-7.

Neagle, A. "Portraying Florence Nightingale," *Nurs. Mirror,* 93 (May 18, 1951): 121-122.

Nelson, J. "Florence, The Legend," *Nurs. Mirror,* 142(20) (May 13, 1976): 40-41.

Newman, G. *The Commemoration of Florence Nightingale*. London: International Council of Nurses, 1937 (16 pp.).

_____. "The Commemoration of Florence Nightingale" (reprint), *Int. Nurs. Rev.*, 1 (October 1954): 4-10.

_____. "Florence Nightingale and Hospital Services," *Nurs. Mirror*, 58 (May 17, 1934): 476; (March 24, 1934): 491; (May 31); (April 7): 10.

Newman, T.R. "Florence Nightingale (1820-1910)," *Nurs. Times*, 45 (February 4, 1950): 121-123.

Newton, M.E. "The Power of Statistics," *Pub. Hlth. Nurs.*, 43 (September 1951): 502-505.

"The Nightingale Bibliography" (Editorial), *Am. J. Nurs.*, 57 (May 1957): 585.

Nightingale, F. *How People May Live and Not Die In India*. London: Longman, Green, Longman, Roberts and Green, 1864.

_____. *Introductory Notes On Lying-in Institutions*. London: Longmans, Green and Co., 1871.

_____. *Organization of Nursing*. Liverpool: Holden, 1865.

_____. *Notes on Hospitals*. London: Parker, 1859.

_____. *Notes on Nursing*. New York: D. Appleton and Co., 1860 and subsequent editions; London: Harrison, 1859 and subsequent editions.

_____. *Notes on Nursing for the Labouring Class*. London: Harrison, 1876.

_____. "'Remarks on a Register for Nurses' by Florence Nightingale (1892)," *Sogo Kango - Comprehensive Nursing Quarterly* 22(1) (1987): 29-49.

_____. *Subsidiary Notes as to the Introduction of Female Nursing Into Military Hospitals in Peace and in War.* London: Harrison, 1858.

_____. *Suggestions for Thought to the Seekers After Truth Among the Artizans of England.* London: Privately printed for Eyre & Spottiswoode, 1860.

_____. *Reproduction of a Printed Report Originally Submitted to the Bucks County Council in the Year 1892.* London: King, 1911.

_____. *Notes on Matters Affecting the Health, Efficiency, and Hospital Administration of the British Army.* London: Harrison, 1858.

_____. "Introductory Notes on Lying-in Institutions by Florence Nightingale," *Sogo Kango - Comprehensive Quarterly* 18(1) (1983): 59-73.

_____. *Cassandra.* New York: Feminist Press at the City University of New York, 1979.

_____. "Letter to the Nurses of the Nightingale Fund School," *Caridad, Ciencia Y Arte* 8(25) (January-March 1971): 3-4.

_____. *Florence Nightingale on Hospital Reform.* New York: Garland Publishing, 1988.

Nightingale (Florence) at Harley Street; Her Reports to the Governors of Her Nursing Home. London: Dent, 1970 (197 pp.).

"A Nightingale Letter," *Acad. Bookman* 22(2) (1969): 11.

"Nightingale Letter to Alice Fisher in Philadelphia," *Am. Nurs.*, 8(2) (January 31, 1976): 2.

"Nightingaliana," *J. Roy. Brit. Nurs.*, 2 (September 1950): 145.

Nishida, A. "Understanding of Man in the 'Notes on Nursing', (Florence Nightingale)," *Sogo Kango - Comprehensive Nursing Quarterly* 16(4) (1982): 9-22. (Jap.)

Nolan, J.C. *Florence Nightingale.* New York: Junior Literary Guild & Messner, 1946 (209 pp.).

"No Other Earth," *Today's Hlth*, 40 (November 1962): 63.

Noyes, C.D. "Florence Nightingale--Sanitarian and Hygienist," *Red Cr. Courier*, 10 (January 1931): 41-42.

"Nurse's Service," *Brit. J. Nurs.*, 100 (April 1952): 36.

"Nursing Echoes," *Brit. J. Nurs.*, 100 (April 1952): 36.

"Nursing News and Announcements. Florence Nightingale Exhibit," *Am. J. Nurs.*, 10 (July 1910): 766-770. Exhibit was forerunner of Adelaide Nutting Historical Collection.

Nuttall, P. "Miss Florence Nightingale: 'The Passionate Statistician'," *Nurs. J. India* 75(6) (June 1984): 128-129.

_____. "The Passionate Statistician (Florence Nightingale)," *Nursing Times* 79(39) (September 28 - October 4, 1983): 25-27.

Nutting, M.A. *Adelaide Nutting Historical Collection.* Teachers College and the School of Nursing, Columbia University, New York, NY; School of Nursing, University of Kansas, Lawrence, KS.

_____. "Florence Nightingale as a Statistician," *Pub. Hlth. Nurs.*, 19 (May 1927): 207.

Okada, M. "Notes on 'Cassandra': 1 (Florence Nightingale)," *Sogo Kango - Comprehensive Nursing Quarterly* 19(3) (August 15, 1984): 63-78. (Jap.)

_____. "Florence Nightingale and I," *Kango Kyoiku - Japanese Journal of Nurses Education* 28(5) (May 1987): 258-261. (Jap.)

Oliver, H. "The Shore Smith Family Library: Arthur High Clough and Florence Nightingale," *Book Collect* 28 (1979): 521-529.

O'Malley, I.B. *Florence Nightingale, 1820-1856.* London: Thornton Butterworth, 1931 (416 pp.).

_____. "Florence Nightingale After the Crimean War (1856-1861)," *Tr. Nurs.* 94 (May 1935): 401-407.

Oman, C. "Florence Nightingale as Seen by Two Biographers," *Nurs. Mirror*, 92 (November 17, 1950): 30-31.

Osborne, J.I. *Arthur Hugh Clough.* Boston: Houghton Mifflin, 1920 (191 pp.).

Osvath, Z. "Florence Nightingale (1820-1910)," *Orv. Hetil.*, 111 (February 22, 1970): 455-457 (Hun.).

Pace, D.A. *Valiant Women.* New York: Vantage Press, 1972, pp. 61-62.

Palmer, I.S.: *Florence Nightingale and the First Organized Delivery of Nursing Services.* Washington, D.C., American Association of Colleges of Nursing, 1985.

_____. *Through a Glass Darkly: Nightingale to Now.* Washington, D.C., American Association of Colleges of Nursing, 1983.

_____. *Florence Nightingale, Founder of Modern Nursing.* Boston University Libraries, Nursing Archive, Division of Special Collection, 1976.

_____. "Introduction," *Letters of Florence Nightingale.* Boston, MA, Boston University Nursing Archive, 1974.

_____. "From Whence We Came," an historical analysis of the development of American Nursing, *The Nursing Professional: A Time to Speak.* N.L. Chaska, Ed. New York: McGraw-Hill, 1982.

_____. "Florence Nightingale and International Origins of Modern Nursing," *Image* 13(2) (June 1981): 28-31.

_____. "Florence Nightingale: The Myth and the Reality," *Nurs. Times* 79(31) (August 3-9, 1979): 40-42.

_____. "Florence Nightingale: Myth and Reality," *Nurs. Times* (August 3, 1983).

_____. "Florence Nightingale: Reformer, Reactionary, Researcher," *Nurs. Res.* 26(2) (March-April 1977): 84-89.

_____. "Through a Glass Darkly: Nightingale Revisted," *Nursing Outlook* 31(4) (July-August 1983): 229-233.

_____. "Nightingale Revisted," *Kango* 35(12) (November 1983): 112-122.

_____. "Florence Nightingale, Reactionary, Researcher," *Sogo Kango - Comprehensive Nursing Quarterly* 12(4) (November 1977): 20-44. (Jap.)

_____. "Florence Nightingale and the Salisbury Incident," *Nurs. Res.* 25(5) (September-October 1976): 370-377.

_____. "Origins of the Education of Nurses," *Nursing Forum* 22(3) (1985).

Parker, E.C. "The Contributions of the Writings of Florence Nightingale," *Am. J. Nurs.*, 31 (May 1931): 619-622.

Parker, P. "Florence Nightingale: First Lady of Administrative Nursing," *Supervisor Nurse* 8(3) (March 1977): 24-25.

"The Passing of Florence Nightingale," *Nurs. J. Pac. Cst.*, 6 (November 1910): 481-519.

Paterson, E.H. "Florence Nightingale, and Nursing in Hong Kong," *Hsiang-kang Hu Li Tsa Chih* (37) (November 1984): 6-9.

Paull, E. "Florence Nightingale. A Brief Sketch of Her Life and Work," *Nurs. J. India*, 44 (May 1953): 113-114.

Pearce, E.C. "The Influence of Florence Nightingale on the Spirit of Nursing," *Int. Nurs. Rev.*, 1 (April 1954): 20-22.

Penner, S.J. "The Remarkable Miss Nightingale," *Kansas Nurse* 62(5) (May 1987): 11.

Peter, M. "A Personal Interview with Florence Nightingale," *Pac. Cst. J. Nurs.*, 12 (May 1935): 270-271.

Petroni, A. "Florence Nightingale," *Munca Sanit.*, 15 (July 1967): 434-438 (Rum.).

Phillips, E.C. "Florence Nightingale--A Study," *Pac. Cst. J. Nurs.*, 16 (May 1920): 272-274.

Pickering, G. "Letter: Florence Nightingale's Illness," *Brit. Med. J.*, 4 (5945), (December 14, 1974): 656

Pickering, G.W. *Creative Malady: Illness in the Lives and Minds of Charles Darwin, Florence Nightingale, Mary Baker Eddy, Sigmund Freud, Marcel Proust, Elizabeth Barret Browning.* New York: Oxford University Press, 1974, p. 327.

Pollard, E.F. *Florence Nightingale, The Wounded Soldiers' Friend.* London: Partridge, 1902 (160 pp.).

Presbyterian Hospital School of Nursing (New York City). *Catalogue of the Florence Nightingale Collection.* New York: School of Nursing, Presbyterian Hospital, 1937 (63 pp.).

Prince, J. "Education for a Profession: Some Lessons from History (Florence Nightingale)," *Int. J. Nurs. Stud.* 21(3) (1984): 153-163.

"Public Health Nursing (Florence Nightingale as a Consultant)," *Pac. Cst. J. Nurs.*, 16 (May 1920): 299-300.

Quinn, E.V., and Prest, J.M. (Eds.). *Dear Miss Nightingale - A Selection of Benjamin Jowett's Letters 1860-1893.* New York: Oxford University Press, 1987.

Rao, G.A. "Florence Nightingale," *Nurs. J. India,* 62 (June 1971): 179.

Rappe, E.C. *God Bless You, My Dear Miss Nightingale.* Stockholm: Almqvist & Wiksell International, 1977.

Rasmussen, I.F. *Nightingale (Royal United Services Institution, London).* Copenhagen: T. Sygepler, 1960. No. 24 in Kopenhagen University Med. Hist. Mus. Ars. (1959-1961).

Rees, R. "Two Women Mystics," *20th Cent.,* 164 (August 1958): 101-102.

Reid, E.G. *Florence Nightingale: A Drama.* New York: Macmillan Co., 1922 (118 pp.).

Rhynas, M. "Intimate Sketch of Life of Florence Nightingale," *Canad. Nurs.,* 27 (May 1931): 229-231; see also *Canad. Hosp.,* 14 (May 1937): 13-16.

Richards, L.E. *Florence Nightingale: Angel of the Crimea.* New York: Appleton, 1909 (167 pp.).

_____. (Ed.) "Letters of Florence Nightingale," *Yale Rev.* 24 (1934): 326-347.

Richards, L. "Foreign Department. Recollections of Florence Nightingale," *Am. J. Nurs.* 20 (May 1920): 404-410.

Roberts, I. "Reminiscences (Florence Nightingale)," *Nursing Times,* 77(38) (September 16-22, 1981): 1018.

Robinson, G.B. "Centenary of Florence Nightingale, Forerunner of the Trained Nurse," *Tr. Nurs.,* 64 (May 1920): 404-410.

Rogers, P. "Florence Nightingale: The Myth and the Reality," *Nursing Focus*, 3(11) (July 1982): 10.

"The Romantic Florence Nightingale," *Canad. Nurs.*, 64 (May 1968): 57-59.

Rosenberg, C.E. "Florence Nightingale on Contagion: The Hospital as Moral Universe." In Rosenberg, C.E. (Ed.) *Healing and History: Essays for George Rosen.* Folkestone, Eng.: Dawson; New York: Science History Publications, 1979, pp. 116-136.

Ross, M. "Miss Nightingale's Letters," *Am. J. Nurs.*, 53 (May 1953): 593-594.

Ross, T. "A Visit to Florence Nightingale House," *Nursing Mirror & Midwives Journal*, 140(15) (April 10, 1975): 39-41.

Roxburgh, R. "Miss Clough, Miss Nightingale and the Highland Brigade," *Victorian Stud.*, 15 (1971): 75-79.

_____. "Miss Nightingale and Miss Clough: Letters from Crimea," *Victorian Stud.*, 13 (September 1969): 71-89.

Ruebner, B. "Florence Nightingale, Pioneer of Public Health and Medical Statistics," *N. S. Med. Bull.*, 36 (1957): 375-376.

Rundall, F.B.A. "Florence Nightingale's Place in British History," *Bull. of New York Acad. Med.*, 32 (1956): 536-539.

Sabatini, R. *Heroic Lives--Richard I; Saint Francis of Assissi; Joan of Arc; Sir Walter Raleigh; Lord Nelson; Florence Nightingale.* Boston: Houghton Mifflin, 1934, pp. 363-416 (416 pp.).

"St. Paul's--May 12, 1954," *Nurs. Times*, 50 (May 22, 1954): 545.

Schmidt, V. "What Was Wrong with Florence Nightingale?," *Sykeplein* 67(17) (October 5, 1980): 16-21.

_____. "What Was the Matter with Florence Nightingale?," *Sygeplejersken* 80(31) (August 6, 1980): 4-10.

Schuyler, C.B. "Molders of Modern Nursing: Florence Nightingale and Louisa Schuyler." Ed.D. dissertation, Columbia University Teachers College, 1975 (351 pp.).

Scovil, E.R. "Florence Nightingale and Her Nurses," *Am. J. Nurs.*, 15 (October 1914): 13-18.

_____. "Florence Nightingale's Notes on Nursing," *Am. J. Nurs.*, 27 (May 1927): 355-357.

_____. "The Later Activities of Florence Nightingale," *Am. J. Nurs.*, 20 (May 1920): 609-612.

_____. "Florence Nightingale," *Am. J. Nurs.*, 14 (October 1913): 28-32.

_____. "The Life Story of Florence Nightingale," *Am. J. Nurs.*, 17 (December 1916): 209-212.

_____. "Personal Recollections of Florence Nightingale," *Am. J. Nurs.*, 11 (February 1911): 365-368.

Sedan, F. "Florence Nightingale and Turkish Education," *Pub. Hlth. Nurs.*, 39 (June 1947): 349.

"A Service of Rededication to Nursing--Suitable for Florence Nightingale's Birth, May 12," *Nurs. Mirror*, 95 (April 25, 1952): 75-76.

"Seven Hundred Nurses in Colorful Ceremony (Florence Nightingale Memorial)," *Irish Nurs. News*, 4 (August-September 1954): 6-7.

Seymer, L.R. (Buckler). *Florence Nightingale*. New York: Macmillan Co., 1950 (154 pp.).

_____. "Florence Nightingale," *Nurs. Mirror*, 99 (April 2, 1954): 34-36.

_____. *Florence Nightingale.* London: Faber and Faber, 1950 (154 pp.).

_____. "Florence Nightingale at Kaiserswerth," *Am. J. Nurs.*, 51 (July 1951): 424-426.

_____. *Florence Nightingale's Nurses.* London: Pitman, 1960.

_____. "Florence Nightingale Oration," *Int. Nurs. Bull.*, 3 September 1947): 12-17.

_____. "The Nightingale Jewel," *Am. J. Nurs.*, 55 (May 955): 549-550.

_____. "A Nursing Centenary for July, 1951," *Nurs. Mirror*, 93 (July 20, 1951): 277-278.

_____. *Selected Writings of Florence Nightingale.* New York: Macmillan Co., 1954 (396 pp.).

_____. "The Writings of Florence Nightingale: An Oration Delivered by Mrs. Lucy Seymer," *Sogo Kango - Comprehensive Nursing Quarterly*, 20(3) (August 1985): 22-46. (Jap.)

Seymer, S. "The Writings of Florence Nightingale," *Nurs. J. India*, 70(5) (May 1979): 121-128.

Shalders, G.M. "A Few Memories of Miss Nightingale," *Queens Nurs. Mag.*, 27 (March 1934): 38-39.

Shannon, R. "Re-evaluation of Florence Nightingale: A Review of 'Florence Nightingale: Reputation and Power' by F.B. Smith," *Kango Kyoiku*, 23(11) (November 1982): 677-685. (Jap.)

Shibata, T. "Introduction and a Study of Reference Materials Concerning the Life of Florence Nightingale. 3. A Section of the Diary of Miss Umeko Tsuda on Her Visit to Miss Nightingale," *Kango Kyoiku - Jap. J. Nurs. Educ.*, 15(4) (April 1974): 272-279 (Jap.).

_____. "Introduction and A Study of Reference Materials Concerning the Life of Florence Nightingale. 2. Nightingale and the Nightingale Training School," *Kango Kyoiku - Jap. J. Nurs. Educ.*, 15 (February 1974): 116-121 (Jap.).

_____. "The Literature on Nightingale: Introduction and Comments. 1. The First Edition of the Notes on Nursing and Its Japanese Translation," *Kango Kyoiku - Jap. J. Nurs. Educ.*, 15(1) (January 1974): 49-56 (Jap.).

_____. "On a Visit to Sites Associated with Florence Nightingale," *Jap. J. Nurs. Educ.*, 37 (May 1973): 588-594 (Jap.).

_____. "On Visiting Places Associated with Florence Nightingale," *Jap. J. Nurs. Educ.*, 37 (August 1973): 1006-1010; (September 1973): 1180-1184 (Jap.).

Shonan, Y. "Trip to Embley. A Visit to Nightingale's Tomb," *Compr. Nurs. Q.*, 8 (Spring 1973): 94-99 (Jap.).

Siekmeier, M. "Florence Nightingale--A Remarkable Woman Followed Her Calling," *Krankenpflege*, 40(5) (May 1986): 184-186.

Simpson, C.E. "International Hospital Day," *Quart. J. Chin. Nurs.*, 9 (February 1928): 13-14.

Skeet, M. *Notes on Nursing*. Edinburgh; New York: Churchill, Livingstone, 1980.

Skvortso, K.A. "Florence Nightingale, Nurse," *Klin. Med.* (Mosk), 54(2), (February 1976): 147-149 (Rus.).

Smith, F.B. *Florence Nightingale: Reputation and Power*. London: Croom Helm, 1982.

Smith, F.T. "Florence Nightingale: Early Feminist," *American Journal of Nursing* 81(5) (May 1981): 1021-1024.

_____. "Florence Nightingale: Early Feminist," *Kango Kyoiku - Japanese Journal of Nurses Education* 23(11) (November 1982): 671-676.

"Some Letters from Florence Nightingale," *Hosp.* (London), 30 (December 1934): 335-336.

"Some Nursing Treasures," *Am. J. Nurs.*, 37 (May 1937): 476-479.

Sotejo, J.V. "Florence Nightingale--Nurse for All Seasons," *ANPHI Pap.*, 5 (April-June 1970): 4.

"South Africa Has a Florence Nightingale Festival," *Nurs. Mirror*, 100 (December 10, 1954): i.

Spring, E. and Spring, D. "The Real Florence Nightingale? Essay Review," *Bulletin of the History of Medicine* 57 (2) (Summer 1983): 285-290.

Stark, M. and MacDonald, C. (Eds.). *Cassandra: An Essay by Florence Nightingale.* Old Westbury, NY: Feminist Press, 1979, 60 pp.

Stedman, A. *The Story of Florence Nightingale.* New York: Frederick A. Stokes Co., 1926 (63 pp.).

Stephen, B. "Florence Nightingale's Home," *Int. Nurs. Rev.*, 11 (July 1937): 331-334.

Stewart, I.M. "Florence Nightingale--Educator," *Teach. Coll. Rec.*, 41 (December 1939): 208-223.

Sticker, A. "Florence Nightingale and Kaiserswerth School," *Sogo Kango - Comprehensive Nursing Quarterly* 13(3) (1978): 65-75. (Jap.)

Strachey, L. "Florence Nightingale." In *Adventures in Modern Literature*, 3rd Ed. Edited by R.M. Stauffer and others. New York: Harcourt, Brace & World, 1951, pp. 332-361.

_____. "Strongest Will Be Wanted at the Washtub." In *Turning Point*. Edited by P. Dunaway and G. DeKay. New York: Random House, 1958, pp. 55-68.

_____. *Eminent Victorians: Cardinal Manning, Florence Nightingale, Dr. Arnold, General Gordon*. New York: G.P. Putnam's Sons, 1918 (310 pp.), many editions.

Sullivan, H.A. *Florence Nightingale Collection at Wayne State University: An Annotated Bibliography*. Detroit: Wayne State University Library, 1963 (20 pp.).

Summers, A. *Angels & Citizens*. 1988.

Svaboe, H.M. "Florence Nightingale--Angel or Determined Old Maid," *Sykepleien* 74(8) (May 8, 1987): 18-21.

Takahashi, M. "A Tour of the Areas Related to Florence Nightingale," *Kango Kyoiku Japanese Journal of Nurses Education* 22(1) (January 1981): 54-60. (Jap.)

Takeyama, M. "Conclusion of the Translation of the 'Life of Florence Nightingale'," *Sogo Kango - Comprehensive Nursing Quarterly* 16(3) (August 1981): 76-83. (Jap.)

Talbott, J.H. *Biographical History of Medicine*. New York: Grune & Stratton, 1970, pp. 806-808.

Tamura, M. "On Research on Florence Nightingale--A Future Overview," *Sogo Kango - Comprehensive Nursing Quarterly* 15(4) (1980): 18-21. (Jap.)

Tappe, E.D. "Florence Nightingale and Rumanian Nursing," *Slav. East Eur. Rev.* 49 (1971): 125-127.

Tarrant, W.G. *Florence Nightingale as a Religious Thinker*. London: British & Foreign Unitarian Assn., 1920 (32 pp.).

Tatton-Brown, W. "Owed to the Nightingale," *Sogo Kango - Comprehensive Nursing Quarterly* 14(4) (1979): 32-46. (Jap.)

Teramoto, M. "Me and the Florence Nightingale Letter Collection," *Sogo Kango - Comprehensive Nursing Quarterly* 17(4) (1982): 35-38. (Jap.)

Thomas, H., and Thomas, D.L. *50 Great Modern Lives.* New York: Hanover House, 1956, pp. 210-218.

Thompson, J.D. "The Passionate Humanist: From Nightingale to the New Nurse," *Nurs. Outlook* 28(5) (May 1980): 290-295.

_____. "The Passionate Humanist: From Nightingale to the New Nurse," *Sogo Kango - Comprehensive Nursing Quarterly* 16(1) (1981): 60-73. (Jap.)

Tooley, S.A. *The Life of Florence Nightingale,* 5th Ed. London: S.H. Bousfield, 1904 (344 pp.); 6th Ed. New York: Macmillan Co., 1905 (347 pp.).

Tracy, M.A. "Florence Nightingale and Her Influence on Hospitals," *Pac. Cst. J. Nurs.* 36 (July 1940): 406-407.

"Trois Anniversaires (The Deaths of Florence Nightingale, Gustave Moynier and Henry Dunant)," *Rev. Int. Croix R.,* 42 (1960): 656-672 (Fr.).

Tsuboi, Y., Haga, S., Matsuda, M., Takahashi, Y. "Relationship Between the Nightingale Nursing School and Tokyo Hospital Nursing School," *Sogo Kango - Comprehensive Nursing Quarterly* 16(1) (1981): 36-46. (Jap.)

Tuulio, T. "Florence Nightingale . . ., *League Red Cr. Soc. Mth. Bull.,* 20 (February 1939): 27-28.

Usui, H. "Notes on Notes on Nursing," *Compr. Nurs. Q.,* 9(2), (Summer 1974): 68-76 (Jap.).

_____. "Notes on Notes on Nursing by Nightingale," *Compr. Nurs. Q.,* 8 (Winter 1973): 39-50 (Jap.).

_____. "Observations on Notes on Nursing by Florence Nightingale," *Compr. Nurs. Q.*, 11(T), (1976): 55-66 (Jap.).

_____. "Remarks on Notes on Nursing by Nightingale," *Compr. Nurs. Q.*, 8 (Summer 1973): 15-26 (Jap.).

_____. "Development of the Concept of Nursing by Florence Nightingale," *Sago Kango - Comprehensive Nursing Quarterly* 37(1) (January 1985): 142-161. (Jap.)

Urkmen, S. "Florence Nightingale and Nursing," *Turk. Hemsireler Dergisi - The Turkish Journal of Nursing* 36(1) (1986): 31-32.

Van der Peet, R. "Florence Nightingale and Her Viewpoint of Nursing in Relation to the Life and Work of Charles Darwin," *Tijdschrift Voor Ziekenverpleging* 36(17) (August 23, 1983): 530-536. (Dutch)

Van Doren, C. (Ed.). *Letters to Mother*. Great Neck, NY: Channel, 1959, pp. 252-254.

Varney, R. and Simpson, D. "Nightingale," *Nursing Times* 73(5) (February 3, 1977): 50-51.

Verney, H. "The Complete Aunt (Florence Nightingale)", *Osterr Schwesternztg*, 24 (May 1971): 130-133 (Ger.).

_____. *Florence Nightingale at Harley Street: Her Reports to the Governors of Her Nursing Home, 1853-1854.* London: J.M. Dent & Sons, 1970.

_____. "The Perfect Aunt--FN 1820-1910," *News Lett. Florence N. Int. Nurs. Assoc.*, 70 (Spring 1970): 13-16.

Verney, P. "A Crimean Bed Time Story," *Nurs. Mirror*, 90 (May 7, 1954): 7-13.

Verney, R. "Florence Nightingale: By Her God-daughter," *Nurs. J. India*, 68 (1977): 123-125.

Vicinus, M. and Nergaard, B.　*Ever Yours, Florence Nightingale: Selected Letters.* Cambridge, Ma.: Harvard University Press, 1990.

Wakeford, C. *The Wounded Soldiers' Friends.* London: Headley Bros., Ltd., 1917.

Walton, P. "The Lady with the Lamp (Florence Nightingale)," *Phlp. J. Nurs.*, 41 (January-March 1972): 11-12.

_____. "The Lady with the Lamp (Florence Nightingale," *Nurs. J. India* 77(5) (May 1986): 115-116.

Watkin, B. "Notes on Nightingale," *Nurs. Mirror*, 142(19), (May 6, 1976): 42.

Webb, R.N., and Blackwood, P.E. *The How and Why Wonder Book of Florence Nightingale.* New York: Grosset & Dunlap, 1962.

Welch, M. "Nineteenth-century Philosophic Influences on Nightingale's Concept of the Person," *J. Nurs. Hist.* 1(2) (1986): 3-11.

West, R.M. "Florence Nightingale Memorial Service," *Am. J. Nurs.*, 31 (June 1931): 710-712.

"Westminster Abbey, Florence Nightingale Commemoration Service Tuesday, May 12th, 1970 at 6:30 p.m. the 150th Anniversary of Her Birth," *News Lett. Florence N. Int. Nurs. Assoc.*, (Autumn 1970): 19-20.

Wheeler, C.E. "Viewpoint: Essay in Response to Republication of a Biography (Florence Nightingale)," *Advances in Nursing Science* 6(4) (July 1984): 74-79.

"White Angel," *Am. J. Nurs.*, 36 (June 1936): 574-575.

White, F.S. "At the Gate of the Temple," *Pub. Hlth. Nurs.* 15 (June 1923): 279-283.

"Who Is Mrs. Nightingale?," *London Times*, (October 30, 1854).

Widmer, C.L. "Grandfather and Florence Nightingale," *Am. J. Nurs.*, 55 (May 1955): 569-571.

Wilkins, F. *Six Great Nurses*. London: Hamilton, 1962.

Williams, J.H.H. *Healing Touch*. Springfield, Il.: Charles C. Thomas, 1951, pp. 157-217.

Willis, I.C. *Florence Nightingale*. New York: Coward-McCann; London: Allen, 1931 (275 pp.).

Winchester, J.H. "Tough Angel of the Battlefield: The Real Florence Nightingale," *Today's Hlth.*, 45 (May 1967): 30ff.

Winslow, C.-E.A. "Florence Nightingale and Public Health Nursing," *Pub. Hlth. Nurs.*, 39 (July 1946): 330-332.

Wintle, W.J.F. *Florence Nightingale and Frances E. Willard. The Study of Their Lives*. London: Sunday School Union, 1912.

Wolstenholme, G.E. "Florence Nightingale: New Lamps for Old," *Proc. R. Soc. Med.*, 63 (December 1970): 1282-1288; see also *Sogo Kango*, 12 (1977): 59-78 (Jap.).

Woodall, M.E. "Role and Identity of the Nurse: Notes and Thoughts of Florence Nightingale," *Professioni Infermieristiche* 33(4) (October-December 1980): 166-169.

Woodham-Smith, C.B. *Florence Nightingale, 1820-1910*. London: Constable, 1950 (615 pp.); New York: McGraw-Hill, 1951; New York: Atheneum, 1983, 382 pp.

_____. "Florence Nightingale 1820-1910," (abridged) *Read. Digest*, 59 (August 1951): 145-168.

_____. *Loney Crusader: The Life of Florence Nightingale, 1820-1910*. New York: Whittlesey House, 1951.

_____. *Florence Nightingale 1820-1910*. New Ed. Abr. London: Collins, 1964 (445 pp.).

_____. "Florence Nightingale as a Child," *Nurs. Mirror*, 85 (May 10, 1947): 91-92.

_____. "Florence Nightingale's Pet Owl," In *Saturday Book*. New York: Macmillan Co., 1949, pp. 171-179.

_____. "Florence Nightingale Revealed," *Am. J. Nurs.*, 52 (May 1952): 570-572.

_____. "The Greatest Victorian," *Nurs. Times*, 50 (July 10, 1954): 738-741.

_____. *Lady-in-Chief*. London: Methuen, 1956 (210 pp.).

_____. "They Stayed in Bed," *Harper's*, 212 (June 1956): 41.

Worchester, A. "Florence Nightingale, May 12, 1820-1920," *Bost. Med. Surg. J.*, 183 (August 12, 1920): 193-201.

Wren, D. *They Enriched Humanity*. London: Skilton, Ltd., 1948, pp. 106-130.

Wyndham, L. *Florence Nightingale, Nurse to the World*. New York: World Pub. Co., 1969.

Yen, V.P. "Florence Nightingale," *Nurs. J. China*, 15 (July 1933): 98-100, 118-120.

Yoshikawa, R. "Biography of Nightingale Published in the Early Meiji Era - On 'Self-Help for Women'," *Sogo Kango - Comprehensive Nursing Quarterly* 17(1) (1982): 91-102. (Jap.)

Yoshioka, S. "Florence Nightingale Biography," *Jap. J. Nurs. Educ.*, 30 (February 1966): 86-87 (Jap.).

Yumaki, M. "Discussion: Nursing Described by Nightingale and Modern Nursing--Thoughts on Nursing After Completion of Translation of Nightingale's Writings," *Compr. Nurs. Q.* 9(2), (Summer 1974): 77-84. (Jap.)

_____. "Notes from the Editor of the Collection of Florence Nightingale's Writings," *Compr. Nurs. Q.* 10(2), (May 15, 1975): 64-65 (Jap.).

_____. "50 Years of the Studies of Florence Nightingale," *Sogo Kango - Comprehensive Nursing Quarterly* 15(4) (1980): 7-11. (Jap.)

_____. "Nightingale's Concept of God," *Sogo Kango - Comprehensive Nursing Quarterly* 16(4) (1982): 23-28. (Jap.)

Zhukova, L.A. "Woman with the Lamp (Florence Nightingale)," *Meditsinskaia Sestra* 45(2) (February 1986): 51-53.